Siegel's

CRIMINAL LAW

*Essay and Multiple-Choice Questions
and Answers*

Fifth Edition

BRIAN N. SIEGEL
J.D., Columbia Law School

LAZAR EMANUEL
J.D., Harvard Law School

JASON TANNENBAUM
J.D., University of Pennsylvania Law School

Revised by

Sam Kamin
*Professor and Director, Constitutional Rights &
Remedies Program*
University of Denver
Sturm College of Law

 Wolters Kluwer
Law & Business

The authors gratefully acknowledge the assistance of the California Committee of Bar Examiners, which provided access to questions on which many of the essay questions in this book are based.

About Wolters Kluwer Law & Business

Wolters Kluwer Law & Business is a leading global provider of intelligent information and digital solutions for legal and business professionals in key specialty areas, and respected educational resources for professors and law students. Wolters Kluwer Law & Business connects legal and business professionals as well as those in the education market with timely, specialized authoritative content and information-enabled solutions to support success through productivity, accuracy and mobility.

Serving customers worldwide, Wolters Kluwer Law & Business products include those under the Aspen Publishers, CCH, Kluwer Law International, Loislaw, Best Case, ftwilliam.com and MediRegs family of products.

CCH products have been a trusted resource since 1913, and are highly regarded resources for legal, securities, antitrust and trade regulation, government contracting, banking, pension, payroll, employment and labor, and healthcare reimbursement and compliance professionals.

Aspen Publishers products provide essential information to attorneys, business professionals and law students. Written by preeminent authorities, the product line offers analytical and practical information in a range of specialty practice areas from securities law and intellectual property to mergers and acquisitions and pension/benefits. Aspen's trusted legal education resources provide professors and students with high-quality, up-to-date and effective resources for successful instruction and study in all areas of the law.

Kluwer Law International products provide the global business community with reliable international legal information in English. Legal practitioners, corporate counsel and business executives around the world rely on Kluwer Law journals, looseleafs, books, and electronic products for comprehensive information in many areas of international legal practice.

Loislaw is a comprehensive online legal research product providing legal content to law firm practitioners of various specializations. Loislaw provides attorneys with the ability to quickly and efficiently find the necessary legal information they need, when and where they need it, by facilitating access to primary law as well as state-specific law, records, forms and treatises.

Best Case Solutions is the leading bankruptcy software product to the bankruptcy industry. It provides software and workflow tools to flawlessly streamline petition preparation and the electronic filing process, while timely incorporating ever-changing court requirements.

ftwilliam.com offers employee benefits professionals the highest quality plan documents (retirement, welfare and non-qualified) and government forms (5500/PBGC, 1099 and IRS) software at highly competitive prices.

MediRegs products provide integrated health care compliance content and software solutions for professionals in healthcare, higher education and life sciences, including professionals in accounting, law and consulting.

Wolters Kluwer Law & Business, a division of Wolters Kluwer, is headquartered in New York. Wolters Kluwer is a market-leading global information services company focused on professionals.

Introduction

Although law school grades are a significant factor in obtaining post-law school employment, no formalized preparation for finals is provided at most law schools; students are generally expected to fend for themselves in learning how to take a law school exam. Ironically, law school exams may bear little correspondence to the teaching methods used by professors during the school year. At least in the first year, professors require you to spend most of your time briefing and discussing individual cases. While a valuable exercise, case briefing is probably not great preparation for writing issue-spotting exams. In briefing cases, you are made to focus on one or two principles of law at a time; you don't get practice in relating one issue to another or in developing a picture of how the various pieces fit together. When exams finally arrive, you're forced to make an abrupt 180-degree turn. Suddenly, you are asked to recognize, define, and discuss a variety of issues buried within a single multi-issue fact pattern. Alternatively, you may be asked to select among a number of possible answers, all of which may look inviting but only one of which is right.

The comprehensive course outline you've created so diligently, and with such pain, means little if you're unable to apply its contents on your final exams. There is a vast difference between reading opinions in which the legal principles and applying those same principles to hypothetical essay exams and multiple-choice questions.

The purpose of this book is to help you bridge the gap between distilling a rule of law from cases and ***understanding how to use that rule*** in an exam. After an initial overview describing the exam-writing process, you see a large number of hypotheticals that test your ability to write analytical essays and to pick the right answers to multiple-choice questions. *Read them—all of them!* Then test your knowledge by attempting to answer these questions on your own. Finally, review the suggested answers that follow. You'll find that the key to superior grades lies in learning to apply your knowledge through questions and answers, not simply in understanding the holding of various cases.

GOOD LUCK!

Table of Contents

Essay Answers

Multiple-Choice Questions

Multiple-Choice Answers

Table and Index

Preparing Effectively for Essay Examinations

To achieve superior scores on essay exams, a law student must (1) learn and understand "blackletter" principles and rules of law for each subject; (2) analyze how those principles of law arise within a test fact pattern; and (3) write clearly and succinctly a short discussion of each principle and how it relates to the facts. One of the most common misconceptions about law school is that you must memorize each word on every page of your casebooks or outlines to do well on exams. The reality is that you can commit an entire casebook to memory and still do poorly on an exam. Our review of hundreds of student answers has shown us that most students can recite the relevant rules correctly. The students who do **best** on exams, however, are those who are able to analyze how the rules relate to the facts in the questions and are able to communicate their analysis to the grader. The following pages cover what you need to know to achieve superior scores on your law school essay exams.

The "ERC" Process

To study effectively for law school exams you must be able to "ERC" (*E*lementize, *R*ecognize, and *C*onceptualize) each legal principle covered in your casebooks and course outlines.

Elementizing means reducing each legal theory and rule you learn to a concise, straightforward statement of its essential elements. Without knowledge of these elements, it's difficult to see all the issues as they arise. For example, if you are asked, "What is self-defense?" it is **not** enough to say, "Self-defense is the idea that if someone is about to hit you, you can prevent him from doing it." This layperson description would leave a grader wondering if you had actually attended law school. An accurate statement of the self-defense principle would go something like this: "When one reasonably believes she is in imminent danger of an offensive touching, she may assert whatever force she reasonably believes necessary under the circumstances to prevent the offensive touching from occurring." This formulation correctly shows that there are four separate, distinct elements that must be satisfied before the defense of self-defense can be successfully asserted: (1) the actor must have a *reasonable belief* that (2) the touching that she seeks to prevent is *offensive* and that (3) the offensive touching is *imminent*, and (4) she must use no greater force than she *reasonably believes necessary under the circumstances* to prevent the offensive touching from occurring.

Recognizing means perceiving or anticipating which words or ideas within a legal principle are likely to be the source of issues and how those issues are likely to arise within a given hypothetical fact pattern. With respect to the self-defense concept, there are four *potential* issues. Did the actor reasonably believe the other person was about to make an offensive contact with her? Was the contact imminent? Would the contact have been offensive? Did she use only such force as she reasonably believed necessary to prevent the imminent, offensive touching?

Conceptualizing means imagining situations in which each of the elements of a rule of law can give rise to factual issues. ***Unless you can imagine or construct an application of each element of a rule, you don't truly understand the legal principles behind the rule!*** In our opinion, the inability to conjure up hypothetical fact patterns or stories involving particular rules of law creates a likelihood that you will miss issues involving those rules on an exam. It's ***crucial*** (1) to ***recognize*** that issues result from the interaction of facts with the words defining a rule of law and (2) to develop the ability to ***conceptualize*** or ***imagine*** fact patterns using the words or concepts within the rule.

For example, a set of facts illustrating the "reasonable belief" element of the self-defense rule might be the following:

> A encounters B in a bar. A is a small, frail man. B, by contrast is a weightlifter, mixed martial artist, and bounty hunter. While the two were watching a football game on the television over the bar, an argument ensued about the relative merits of the two teams. As so often happens, things escalated quickly. B threatened A, saying he would "beat the living daylights out of him." Concerned that B would make good on his threat, A pulled a gun and shot B, killing him instantly. If prosecuted for the killing, A might assert that he reasonably believed it necessary to use deadly force to protect himself. The government might counter that no reasonable person would take an offhand threat made during a football game as a serious one. The defendant might then point out that the relative sizes of the two men made the threat particularly acute and that a reasonable man of his size and shape would reasonably perceive the threat to be a deadly one.

An illustration of how the word "imminent" might generate an issue is the following:

> X and Y had been feuding for some time. One afternoon, X suddenly attacked Y with a hunting knife. However, Y was able to wrest the knife away from X. At that point, X retreated about four feet away from Y and screamed, "You were lucky this time, but next time I'll have a gun and you'll be finished." Y, having good reason to believe that X would subsequently carry out his threats (after all, X had just attempted to kill Y), immediately

thrust the knife into X's chest, killing him. While Y certainly had a reasonable belief that X would attempt to kill him the next time the two met, Y would probably not be able to assert the self-defense privilege because the element of "imminence" was absent.

A fact pattern illustrating the actor's right to use only that force which is reasonably necessary under the circumstances might be the following:

D rolled up a newspaper and was about to strike E on the shoulder with it. As D pulled back his arm for the purpose of delivering the blow, E drew a knife and plunged it into D's chest. While E had every reason to believe that D was about to deliver an offensive impact on him, E probably could not successfully assert the self-defense privilege because the force he utilized in response was greater than reasonably necessary under the circumstances to prevent the impact. E could simply have deflected D's blow or punched D away. The use of a knife constituted a degree of force by E that was not reasonable, given the minor injury he would have suffered from the newspaper's impact.

As you learn rules, you should always be thinking about what elements each rule contains and what kinds of factual scenarios are likely to test each of those elements. As you read factual scenarios, you should think about what issues are raised by those facts. The easier it becomes to match up facts to elements, the better you will be at spotting issues on an exam.

Issue-Spotting

One of the keys to doing well on an essay examination is issue-spotting. In fact, issue-spotting is *the* most important skill you will learn in law school. If you recognize a legal issue, you can find the applicable rule of law (if there is one) by researching the issue. But if you fail to see the issues, you won't learn the steps that lead to success or failure on exams or, for that matter, in the practice of law. It is important to remember that (1) an issue is a question to be decided by the judge or jury and (2) a question is "in issue" when it can be disputed or argued about at trial. The bottom line is that *if you don't spot an issue, you can't raise it or discuss it*.

The key to issue-spotting is to learn to approach a problem in the same way an attorney does. Let's assume you've been admitted to practice and that a client enters your office and tells you that he has been arrested and charged with a crime. He will want to know what happens next, what he can do to defend himself, and what outcomes are possible. To answer your client's questions intelligently, you will have to decide the following: what crimes might the client be charged with, what are the elements of those crimes, and what facts will be necessary to determine whether the elements have been satisfied. *Only by anticipating the answers to these questions can you adequately provide your client with competent legal advice.*

How to Discuss an Issue

Keep in mind that *rules of law determine which issues are raised by a particular set of facts.* That is, an issue only arises when the facts bring into question whether an element of a legal rule is satisfied. Consider, for example, a homicide question. It must generally be shown that the defendant, through a voluntary act or omission causes the death of another person with a culpable mental state. A fact pattern might make it clear that the defendant caused the death of another person and that he did it through his voluntary act. The only issue raised by the fact, then, would be whether the defendant acted with a sufficiently culpable mental state to be guilty of a homicide crime. It is those rules—the ones governing culpable mental states—that should be the focus of the student's answer.

A good way to learn how to discuss an issue is to study the following mini-hypothetical and the two student responses that follow it.

Mini-Hypothetical

B is a security guard at a manufacturing plant. A, who knows of B's position, approaches B and asks for his help in stealing from the plant. A plans to break into the plant after hours and asks B to leave a door unlocked when he leaves work for the night. Although B hopes that A will not carry through, he acts upon A's request and leaves the door open. A enters, takes valuable equipment, and pawns it for cash. Discuss B's liability for aiding and abetting A's theft.

Pertinent Principles of Law:

1. While one is generally under no obligation to act to prevent another from committing a crime, liability for an omission to act is appropriate where the law otherwise imposes a duty to act. Such obligation can come from status (parent to child), from statute (schoolteacher to pupil), or from contract (employee to employer).

2. An accomplice is liable for the acts of another when, acting with the kind of culpability otherwise required for the underlying crime, she both aids and intends to aid the other's criminal conduct. That is, one is liable for another's misdeeds if she facilitates that conduct with the conscious object of helping the other achieve her criminal objectives.

First Student Answer

Is B liable for aiding and abetting A's crime?

A is guilty of theft. He took a thing of value from the possession of another with the intent to permanently deprive its owner of its use. B is guilty of aiding and abetting that theft. A defendant is guilty of aiding and abetting another's when he facilitates that conduct and intends to do so. The facts state that B aided A's theft from the warehouse by leaving a door unlocked for him. Furthermore, there is evidence that B intended to aid A. He may have hoped that A wouldn't commit the crime, but it is clear that he intended to help him. Therefore he satisfies both of the statutory requirements and is guilty as an accomplice.

Second Student Answer

A is guilty of theft. He took property from the owner of the warehouse with the intent to permanently deprive him of its use.

Furthermore, B is liable as his accomplice because he both aided A's offense and intended to do so. B aided the offense by leaving the door open, allowing A to enter. It is possible that A would have committed the offense without B's assistance, but that is irrelevant to B's culpability; aiding and abetting liability does not require causation. Because B's leaving the door open for A facilitated—however slightly—the commission of the offense, B has done enough to qualify him as an accomplice.

It could be argued that B did not *do* anything to facilitate A's conduct, but rather he merely omitted to lock the door when he left. This argument will likely fail, however. As the factory owner's employee, B had a contractual obligation to protect the building from theft and his failure to do so will suffice to satisfy the *actusr eus* of accomplice liability. Thus, whether leaving the door open is seen as an act or an omission, it is sufficient to give rise to culpability.

Furthermore, B had a sufficient *mens rea* to make him liable as an accomplice. Although he might have hoped that A would not steal from the warehouse, that fact alone is insufficient to absolve him. Although there is no direct evidence on this point, a jury could reasonably conclude that B facilitated the theft not merely knowingly but intentionally. Alternatively, in a jurisdiction that allows liability based simply on knowing facilitation, B's guilt is even clearer.

Critique

Let's start by examining the First Student Answer. The answer comes to the correct conclusion—that B is liable as an accomplice to A's crime—but it is otherwise not a very good answer.

The first answer missed entirely the question of whether leaving the door open was an act or an omission. Notice that while this question ends up being irrelevant to the resolution of B's guilt, it likely is not irrelevant to the calculation of the student's grade. If the professor saw the act/omission distinction as important, the first student received no points for it.

Perhaps worse, the first answer contains very little analysis on any point. The rule is stated and facts might be mentioned, but the answer does not *explain* how conclusions are arrived at. This is one of the most common mistakes seen on law school exams; students often assume a conclusion rather than walking the reader through the analysis of why a legal rule is or is not satisfied.

The Second Student Answer is much better than the First Student Answer. First, it spotted the act/omission issue, noted that it was irrelevant to the resolution of the case, and analyzed it appropriately. The student was not merely showing off her knowledge by talking about extraneous issues, though; she showed the examiner that she understood how acts and omissions differ, that she knew how to apply that difference on these facts, and that she saw how that issue fit into the larger picture.

Moreover, the second answer is generally far richer than the first. It engages in more analysis—explaining why B's hope that A would not commit the crime would not absolve A, say—and goes into greater nuance on the rules. It notes that any aid is sufficient, that causation is not necessary. It raises the omission rule and applies it to these facts accurately. While not perfect—it doesn't actually state the full rule, doesn't really explain why B acted with intent here—it is likely an "A" answer.

Structuring Your Answer

Graders will give high marks to a clearly written, well-structured answer. Each issue you discuss should follow a specific and consistent structure that a grader can easily follow.

The Second Student Answer basically utilizes the *I-R-A-A-O format* with respect to each issue. In this format, the *I* stands for *Issue*; the *R* for *Rule of law*; the first *A* for *one side's Argument*; the second *A* for *the other party's rebuttal Argument*; and the *O* for your ***Opinion as to how the issue would be resolved***. The *I-R-A-O* format emphasizes the importance of (1) discussing **both** sides of an issue and (2) communicating to the grader that, where an issue arises, an attorney can only advise his or her client as to the *probable* decision on that issue.

A somewhat different format for analyzing each issue is the more traditional *I-R-A-C format*. Here, the *I* stands for *Issue*; the *R* for ***Rule of law***; the *A* for ***Application of the facts to the rule of law***; and the *C* for ***Conclusion***. *I-R-A-C* is often a legitimate approach to the discussion of a particular issue, within the time constraints imposed by the question. The *I-R-A-C format* must be applied to each issue in the question; it is not the solution to the entire answer. Thus, if there are six issues in a question, you should offer six separate, independent *I-R-A-C* analyses.

We believe that the *I-R-A-C* approach is preferable to the *I-R-A-A-O* formula. However, either can be used to analyze and organize essay exam answers. Whatever format you choose, however, you should be consistent throughout the exam and remember to do the following:

First, you must communicate to the grader the ***precise rule of law*** controlling the facts. In their eagerness to commence their arguments, students sometimes fail to state the applicable rule of law first. Remember, the *R* in either outlining approach stands for ***Rule of law***. Defining the rule of law *before* an analysis of the facts is essential in order to allow the grader to follow your reasoning.

Second, you should ***analyze all of the relevant facts***. Remember that facts have significance in a particular case ***only as they affect the applicable rules of law***. The facts presented must be analyzed and examined to see whether they make any one element of the applicable rules either present or absent. This is the basic process of legal analysis.

Third, it is important to treat ***each side of an issue with equal detail***. If a hypothetical describes how an elderly man was killed when he ventured upon the land of a huge power company to obtain a better view of a nuclear reactor, your sympathies might understandably fall on the side of the old man. The grader will nevertheless expect you to see and make every possible argument for the other side. Don't permit your personal viewpoint to affect your answer; a good lawyer never does! When discussing an issue, always state the arguments for each side.

Finally, don't forget to ***state your opinion or conclusion*** on each issue. One of the most common errors in exam taking is simply stating possibilities without giving some impression of how an issue will ultimately be resolved. Keep in mind, however, that your opinion or conclusion is probably the *least* important part of an exam answer. Why? Because your professor knows that no attorney can tell his or her client exactly how a judge or jury will decide a particular issue. By definition, an issue is a legal dispute that can go either way. An attorney, therefore, can offer the client only his or her best opinion about the likelihood of victory or defeat on an issue. Because the decision on any issue lies with the judge or jury, no attorney can ever be absolutely certain of the resolution.

Discuss All Possible Issues

As we've noted, a student should draw *some* conclusion or opinion for each issue raised. Whatever your conclusion on a particular issue, it is essential to anticipate and discuss *all of the issues* that would arise if the question were actually tried in court.

Let's assume that a homicide question involves issues of *mens rea, actus reus,* causation, and defenses. In a courtroom, if the defendant prevails on any of these issues, he or she will be found not guilty. When taking an exam, however, even if you feel strongly that the defendant did not have the requisite *mens rea* to be convicted of a homicide offense, you *must* go on to discuss all of the other potential issues as well (actus reus, causation, and defenses). Why should you have to discuss every possible issue if you are relatively certain that the outcome of a particular issue would be dispositive of the entire case? Because at the commencement of litigation, neither party can be *absolutely positive* about which issues he or she will prevail upon at trial. We can state with confidence that every attorney with some degree of experience has won issues he or she thought he or she would lose and has lost issues on which victory was assured. Because one can never be absolutely certain how a factual issue will be resolved by the fact finder, a good attorney (and exam writer) will consider *all* possible issues.

To understand the importance of discussing all of the potential issues, you should reflect on what you will do in the actual practice of law. If you represent the defendant, for example, it is your job to raise every possible defense. If there are five potential defenses, and your pleadings only rely on three of them (because you're sure you will win on all three), and the plaintiff is somehow successful on all three issues, your client may well sue you for malpractice. It is an attorney's duty to raise *all* legitimate issues. A similar philosophy should be followed when taking essay exams.

Of course, not all issues should be covered in equal depth. If a question raises difficult questions on one issue but is relatively straightforward on others, your answer should reflect these differences. Thus, for example, in a criminal law question, the central question may be whether the defendant committed burglary—that is, whether he broke and entered a dwelling house at night with the intent to commit a felony therein. It may be obvious based on the facts of a particular question that the defendant entered a dwelling house at night. The crux of the defendant's liability will thus be determined by the last element: whether he had the intent to commit a felony at the time he made entry. A successful answer will demonstrate that the writer is aware of all of the elements, will recognize that many of the elements are not in question, and will focus on those elements that present the closest questions.

What exactly do you say when you've resolved the initial issue in favor of the defendant, and discussion of any additional issues would seem to be moot? The answer is simple. You begin the discussion of the next issue with something like, "Assuming, however, the plaintiff prevailed on the foregoing issue, the next issue would be. . . . " The grader will understand and appreciate what you have done.

The corollary to the importance of raising all potential issues is that you should avoid discussion of obvious nonissues. Raising nonissues is detrimental in three ways: First, you waste a lot of precious time; second, you usually receive absolutely no points for discussing an issue that the grader deems extraneous; and third, it suggests to the grader that you lack the ability to distinguish the significant from the irrelevant. The best guideline for avoiding the discussion of a nonissue is to ask yourself, "Would I, as an attorney, feel comfortable raising that particular issue or objection in front of a judge?"

Delineate the Transition from One Issue to the Next

It's a good idea to make it easy for the grader to see the issues you've found. One way to accomplish this is to cover no more than one issue per paragraph. Another way is to underline each issue statement. Provided that time permits, we recommend that you use both techniques. The essay answers in this book contain numerous illustrations of these suggestions.

One frequent student error is to write two separate paragraphs in which all of the arguments for one side are made in the initial paragraph, and all of the rebuttal arguments by the other side are made in the next paragraph.

This organization is *a bad idea*. It obliges the grader to reconstruct the exam answer in his or her mind several times to determine whether all possible issues have been discussed by both sides. It will also cause you to state the same rule of law more than once. A better-organized answer presents a given argument by one side and follows that immediately in the same paragraph with the other side's rebuttal to that argument.

Understanding the "Call" of a Question

The statement *at the end* of an essay question or of the fact pattern in a multiple-choice question is sometimes referred to as the "call" of the question. It usually asks you to do something specific like "discuss the rights of the parties," "list X's rights," "advise X," "give the best grounds on which to find the statute unconstitutional," "state what D can be convicted of," "recommend how the estate should be distributed," and so forth. The call of the question should be read carefully because it tells you exactly what you're expected to do. If a question asks, "what is X's criminal liability?" or "what crimes can X and Y be charged with?" you should spend almost no time on issues like Z's criminal liability. You will usually receive absolutely no credit for discussing issues or facts that are not required by the call. On the other hand, if the call of an essay question is simply "discuss" or "discuss the rights of the parties," then *all* foreseeable issues must be covered by your answer.

Students are often led astray by an essay question's call. For example, if you are asked for "what is X's criminal liability" or to "advise X," you may think you may limit yourself to X's viewpoint with respect to the issues. This is *not correct*! You cannot resolve one party's rights against another party without considering the issues that would arise (and the arguments the other side would assert) in actual litigation. By contrast, if the question asks, "what is the strongest case for holding X liable on these charges?" you should not be shy about making the case against X. In short, although the call of the question may appear to focus on the rights of one of the parties to the litigation, a superior answer will cover all the issues and arguments that person might *encounter* (not just the arguments he or she would *make*) in attempting to pursue his or her rights against the other side.

The Importance of Analyzing the Question Carefully Before Writing

The overriding *time pressure* of an essay exam is probably a major reason why many students fail to analyze a question carefully before they begin writing. Five minutes into the allocated time for a particular question, you may notice that the person next to you is writing furiously. This thought then flashes through your mind: "Oh my goodness, he's putting down more words on the paper than I am, and therefore he's bound to get a better grade." It can be stated *unequivocally* that there is no necessary correlation between the number of words on your exam paper and the grade you will receive. Students who begin their answer after only five minutes of analysis have probably seen only the most obvious issues and missed many, if not most, of the subtle ones. They are also likely to be less well organized.

Opinions differ as to how much time you should spend analyzing and outlining a question before you actually write the answer. We believe that you should spend at least 12 to 18 minutes analyzing, organizing, and outlining a one-hour question before writing your answer. This will usually provide sufficient time to analyze and organize the question thoroughly *and* enough time to write a relatively complete answer. Remember that each word of the question must be scrutinized to determine if it (1) suggests an issue under the operative rules of law or (2) can be used in making an argument for the resolution of an issue. Because you can't receive points for an issue you don't spot, it is usually wise to read a question *twice* before starting your outline.

When to Make an Assumption

The instructions for a question may tell you to *assume* facts that are necessary to the answer. Even when these instructions are *not* given, you may be obliged to make certain assumptions about missing facts in order to write a thorough answer. Assumptions should be made only when you are told or when you, as the attorney for one of the parties described in the question, would be obliged to solicit additional information from your client. On the other hand, assumptions should *never be used to change or alter the question*. Don't ever write something like "if the facts in the question were . . . , instead of . . . , then . . . would result." If you do this, you are wasting time on facts that are extraneous to the problem before you. Professors want you to deal with *their* fact patterns, not your own.

Students sometimes try to "write around" information they think is missing. They assume that their professor has failed to include every piece of data necessary for a thorough answer. This is generally *wrong*. The professor may have omitted some facts deliberately to see if the student *can figure out what to do* under the circumstances. However, in some instances, the professor may have omitted them inadvertently (even law professors are sometimes human).

The way to deal with the omission of essential information is to describe (1) what fact (or facts) appears to be missing and (2) why that information is important. Take, for example, the aiding and abetting example above. It was not made clear why exactly the security guard, B, agreed to help his friend, A, steal from the factory that B had agreed to protect. This could, of course, be relevant in determining whether B had the requisite *mens rea* to be found guilty as an accomplice. So, for example, if A had been threatening B and had intimidated B into helping with the theft, this might negate the intent that many states require for accomplice liability. By contrast, if A had agreed to give B some of the proceeds from the theft, that would give B a stake in the venture and his culpability would be assured. A good answer will notice these missing facts and explain, as this paragraph has, how those facts could make a difference. Assumptions should be made in a manner that keeps the other issues open (i.e., they lead to a discussion of all other possible issues). Don't assume facts that would virtually dispose of the entire hypothetical in a few sentences. To return again to the security guard case, it would be a mistake to simply presume that A promised B a portion of the proceeds. This assumption would make B's guilt far easier to prove. Such a facile approach would rarely be appreciated by the grader. The proper way to handle this situation would be to state, "If we assume that A did not promise B a portion of the proceeds from the theft, we must find another way to determine whether B had a sufficiently culpable mental state." You've communicated to the grader that you recognize the need to assume an essential fact and that you've assumed it in a way that enables you to proceed to discuss all other issues.

Case Names

A law student is ordinarily **not** expected to recall case names on an exam. The professor knows that you have read several hundred cases for each course and that you would have to be a memory expert to have all of the names at your fingertips. If you confront a fact pattern that seems similar to a case that you have reviewed (but you cannot recall its name), just write something like, "One case we've read held that . . . " or "It has been held that. . . . " In this manner, you have informed the grader that you are relying on a case that contained a fact pattern similar to the question at issue.

The only exception to this rule is in the case of a landmark decision (e.g., *Roe v. Wade*). Landmark opinions are usually those that change or alter established law.[1] These cases are usually easy to identify, because you will probably have spent an entire class period discussing each of them. For example, in the substantive criminal law class, cases like *Regina v. Dudley and Stephens* or *Pinkerton v. U.S.* are likely discussed often enough in class that you should be familiar with their names an holdings. In these special cases, you may be expected to recall the case by name, as well as the proposition of law it stands for. However, this represents a very limited exception to the general rule that counsels against wasting precious time trying to memorize and reproduce case names.

How to Handle Time Pressures

What do you do when there are five minutes left in the exam and you have only written down two-thirds of your answer? One thing *not* to do is write something like, "No time left!" or "Not enough time!" This gets you nothing but the satisfaction of knowing you have communicated your personal frustrations to the grader. Another thing *not* to do is insert in the exam booklet the outline you may have made on a piece of scrap paper. Professors will rarely look at these.

First of all, it is not necessarily a bad thing to be pressed for time. The person who finishes five minutes early has very possibly missed some important issues. The more proficient you become in knowing what is expected of you on an exam, the greater the difficulty you may experience in staying within the time limits. Second, remember that (at least to some extent) you're graded against your classmates' answers and they're under exactly the same time pressure as you. In short, don't panic if you can't write the "perfect" answer in the allotted time. Nobody does!

The best hedge against misuse of time is to *review as many old exams as possible*. These exercises will give you a familiarity with the process of organizing and writing an exam answer, which, in turn, should result in an enhanced ability to stay within the time boundaries. If you nevertheless find that you have about 15 minutes of writing to do and only 5 minutes to do it in, write a paragraph that summarizes the remaining issues or arguments you would discuss if time permitted. As long as you've indicated that you're

---

1.   In Constitutional Law and Criminal Procedure, many cases will qualify as "landmark" cases. Students studying these subjects should try to associate case names with the corresponding holdings and reproduce both in their exam answers.

aware of the remaining legal issues, you'll probably receive some credit for them. Your analytical and argumentative skills will already be apparent to the grader by virtue of the issues that you have previously discussed.

Formatting Your Answer

Make sure that the way you write or type your answer presents your analysis in the best possible light. In other words, if you write, do so legibly. If you type, remember to use many paragraphs instead of just creating a document in which all of your ideas are merged into a single lengthy block of print. Remember that your professor may have a hundred or more exams to grade. If your answer is difficult to read, you will rarely be given the benefit of the doubt. On the other hand, a paper that is easy to read creates a very positive mental impact upon the professor.

The Importance of Reviewing Prior Exams

As we've mentioned, it is ***extremely important to review old exams***. The transition from parsing blackletter law to writing an essay exam can be a difficult experience if the process has not been practiced. Although this book provides a large number of essay and multiple-choice questions, ***don't stop here***! Most law schools have recent tests online or on file in the library, by course. If they are available only in the library, we strongly suggest that you make a copy of every old exam you can obtain (especially those given by your professors) at the beginning of each semester. The demand for these documents usually increases dramatically as "finals time" draws closer.

The exams for each course should be scrutinized ***throughout the semester***. They should be reviewed as you complete each chapter in your casebook. Often the order of exam questions follows the sequence of the materials in your casebook. Thus, the first question on a law school test may involve the initial three chapters of the casebook; the second question may pertain to the fourth and fifth chapters; and so on. In any event, ***don't wait*** until the semester is nearly over to begin reviewing old exams.

Keep in mind that no one is born with the ability to analyze questions and write superior answers to law school exams. Like any other skill, it is developed and perfected only through application. If you don't take the time to analyze numerous examinations from prior years, this evolutionary process just won't occur. Don't just ***think about*** the answers to past exam questions; take the time to ***write the answers down***. It is also wise to look back at an answer a day or two after you've written it. You will invariably see (1) ways to improve your organizational skills and (2) arguments you missed.

As you practice spotting issues on past exams, you will see how rules of law become the sources of issues on finals. As we've already noted, if you don't **understand** how rules of law translate into issues, you won't be able to achieve superior grades on your exams. Reviewing exams from prior years should also reveal that certain issues tend to be lumped together in the same question. Thus, for example, where a fact pattern involves two or more people involved in the commission of a crime, it is a good idea to consider both conspiracy and accomplice liability. Furthermore, if someone dies in the course of that crime, it is important to consider whether felony murder has become relevant as well.

As Always, a Caveat

The suggestions and advice offered in this book represent the product of many years of experience in the field of legal education. We are confident that the techniques and concepts described in these pages will help you prepare for, and succeed at, your exams. Nevertheless, particular professors sometimes have a preference for exam-writing techniques that are not stressed in this book. Some instructors expect at least a nominal reference to the *prima facie* elements of all pertinent legal theories (even though one or more of those principles are **not** placed into issue). Other professors want their students to emphasize public policy considerations in the arguments they make on a particular issue. Because this book is intended for nationwide consumption, these individualized preferences have **not** been stressed. The best way to find out whether your professor has a penchant for a particular writing approach is to ask him or her to provide you with a model answer to a previous exam. If a model answer is not available, speak to second- or third-year students who received a superior grade in that professor's class. Bear in mind that the exam preferences of your professor, however idiosyncratic, are far more important than any of the general provisions of this section. Find out what it is your professor wants and try your best to give that to her.

One final point. While the principles cited in the answers to the questions in this book have been drawn from commonly used sources (casebooks, hornbooks, etc.), it is conceivable that they may be slightly at odds with those taught by your professor. In instances in which a conflict exists between our formulation of a legal principle and the one taught by your professor, *follow the latter*! Because your grades are determined by your professors, their views should always supersede the views contained in this book.

A Few Words from the Revisor

This edition partially revises earlier editions of the book. Some of the new essay questions and new multiple-choice questions involve familiarity with the Model Penal Code, while some questions that have been retained from earlier editions do not. Teaching the Model Penal Code has become part of many law school courses—but perhaps not all. The new mix of questions—some restricted to common law doctrines, some asking you to compare the common law result with that under the Model Penal Code—may better reflect how the course is taught in many law schools around the country.

I am anxious to learn if you find either of these changes helpful—and if you think the next revision should contain even more references to the Model Penal Code, or even case citations, where they might prove helpful. Please send any comments to *skamin@law.du.edu.*

Essay Questions

Question 1

David broke into the home of Arnold. No one was at home. After taking several expensive items, David attempted to escape from Arnold's house. Arnold, however, arrived home from a hunting trip just as David was climbing out a side window. Arnold yelled at David to stop, but David began to run down the street. Arnold grabbed his hunting rifle and attempted to shoot David in the leg. The bullet missed David, but fatally shot Bill, who was driving a car down David's street. Edith, Bill's wife, was also in the car and suffered a stroke after seeing her husband shot. The car rolled into a tree and came to a stop. Fred, a passerby, opened the driver's door with the intention of assisting the occupants. However, when he saw the bullet wound in Bill's chest, Fred decided there was nothing he could do. Fred noticed that Bill wore an expensive watch and began to remove it. Bill opened one eye and faintly motioned Fred away. Fred, however, took the watch off Bill's hand, saying, "You won't need this where you're going, my friend." Moments later, Bill died. Subsequently, Arnold, David, and Fred were apprehended by the police.

What crimes were committed and by whom?

Question 2

Able, a police undercover agent, invited Baker and Charley, whom Able suspected of having committed a series of recent crimes, to her home for a few drinks. Able mentioned to them how impressed she was with the daring and skill of the persons responsible for the recent crimes. Baker then suggested that a nearby drugstore would be a "pushover" to rob. Able decided to join in the robbery, in hopes of obtaining evidence of Baker's and Charley's past crimes.

All three drove to the store, which was operated by Dogge. While Baker waited in the car, Charley mingled with several customers in the part of the store nearest the entrance. Able approached Dogge, drew her gun, and handed Dogge a note that read, "I am a police undercover agent. Pretend to be frightened. Give me the money in the cash register." Dogge complied with Able's direction. Able turned to leave, and, as she neared Charley, Dogge drew a gun from beneath the counter and fired at Able. The shot missed Able, but struck Easey, a customer who was standing in the line of fire. Charley then drew his gun and shot Dogge. Immediately after the shooting, Able replaced the money in the cash register and went to the aid of Dogge. Baker and Charley fled, but were later apprehended.

Dogge recovered from his wounds. Easey initially showed improvement toward recovery of her wounds, but she subsequently contracted a virus while still in the hospital and died.

Discuss the possible criminal culpability of all parties.

Question 3

Bob, age 13, and Hal, age 16, bored by the prospect of another long summer afternoon, set out on their favorite pastime—rummaging through the garages and toolsheds of neighbors. In the past, they had sometimes lingered and used the tools found there, but other times they had taken small items. For the first time, Hal's younger brother, Mike, age 6, tagged along.

The boys entered Smith's garage, which was attached to the rear of her home, through the closed but unlocked garage door. Bob and Hal rummaged through the toolboxes and practiced cutting wood on the table saw. Mike, alone near a corner shelf in the garage, saw a gold watch that had been left there inadvertently by Smith. Mike picked up the watch, put it in his pocket, and without a word left for home.

After about an hour in the garage, Bob and Hal also left and continued to Jones's toolshed for the stated purpose of taking a large screwdriver that had, on a prior occasion, caught Bob's fancy. Jones's shed was detached and sat about 50 yards from his house, but within a 3-foot-high picket fence that surrounded the shed and house. Although the door was always locked, the boys had never had difficulty in prying open the door, and on this occasion they again broke the lock.

As Hal pushed the door open and stepped into the shed, he was shot in the head, suffering a fatal wound. On the prior evening, Jones had mounted a loaded pistol in the shed, aimed at the door and connected so that the pistol would discharge automatically if the door were pushed open. Jones told the police he mounted the gun to protect his property from thieves, but that he intended only to scare them away and never intended to kill anyone. There is no state statute prohibiting the use of spring guns.

1. Bob and Mike are charged with burglary of Smith's garage and larceny of Smith's watch.
2. Bob is charged with burglary of Jones's toolshed.
3. Jones is charged with the murder of Hal.

Discuss the results of each charge.

Question 4

Dan was in despair over the state of his business because of unfair business practices by Joe, who had opened a store in direct competition with Dan, right across the street from Dan's business. It appeared that Dan would soon be forced out of business. Dan confided in his good friend, Sam, about his gloomy future, telling him, in a half-jesting fashion, that if he were a real friend he would "take care" of Joe and save him from bankruptcy.

The next day Sam, having considered the plight of his friend, Dan, decided to help Dan. To do this, he planned to have his court-placed ward, Ace, a 27-year-old, mentally handicapped man, break into Joe's store and pour syrup over Joe's merchandise. He explained to Ace that he must put on a skeleton costume and when it was dark he should go into the store Sam would point out and pour the can of syrup all over everything.

The next day, Sam told Dan about his plan. Dan replied, "Sounds great, but don't ask me to do anything to help." Sam replied, "All you have to do is sit back and let it happen."

Late the next evening, Sam took Ace to the block where Joe's store was located. Sam pointed out Joe's store, and Ace proceeded toward it. Before getting to Joe's, however, he heard a loud scream that frightened him. Disoriented, Ace broke into a business place adjoining Joe's, whereupon he simply hurled the unopened can of syrup toward the rear of the store. Unfortunately, the can of syrup hit a gas line causing an explosion that killed Joe, who was in his own store taking his end-of-month inventory. The blast also knocked out Ace.

The police arrested Ace. After the police read Ace his *Miranda* rights, Ace told the police why and what he was doing there.

Discuss fully with what crimes Sam and Dan could be charged and with what results.

Question 5

Helen had been dating Dick for several months. So far, however, the relationship had been purely Platonic. Helen, frustrated by the slow progress of the relationship, sought to change that. She approached Bill, a known drug dealer, and asked him for some ecstasy. Bill went to his wholesaler, Grace, and told her that Helen wanted some "real action" tonight. Grace sold Bill four plastic bags of a white powder, which she asserted was ecstasy. "Be careful with this; it's really potent," said Grace. However, Grace knew that the bags contained only a mixture of sea salt and flour. That night, Bill sold the bags to Helen proclaiming, "This is the strongest ecstasy we've made yet — you're sure to score."

Dick met Helen that night and asked Helen for some liquor. She gave him a shot of scotch, which she had laced with two packets of the white powder she had obtained from Bill. Within minutes, Dick became sick and went outside. Once outside, he screamed at Helen (who had followed him), "You are the devil incarnate! I am going to kill you on the spot!" He pulled out a small pistol and began shooting at Helen, who ducked. The bullets hit Al, an innocent passerby, killing him instantly.

It turns out that, unknown to anyone, Dick was allergic to sea salt and that the combination of sea salt, scotch, and flour dramatically affected his ability to perceive reality. A psychiatrist would testify (if allowed to do so) that Dick was, at that moment, essentially "intoxicated" by the mixture and unable to perceive the true facts. (For purposes of this question, you should assume this is true, even if, in reality, it is problematic.)

In addition to any common law crimes that any of the actors may have committed, consider their liability under the following state statutes:

> 101. Whoever possesses or distributes, or attempts to possess or distribute, any controlled dangerous substance (including ecstasy) is guilty of a felony, punishable by five years' imprisonment.

> 102. Whoever, while on the grounds of a public building, knowingly discharges, or recklessly causes the discharge of, a firearm, is guilty of a crime punishable by two years' imprisonment. If the discharge is done purposely, the punishment is five years' imprisonment.

Question 6

In early November, A, an author, met her friend, B, an employee of a publishing company that was located in a nearby office building. Their discussion focused on the company's soon-to-be published biographical manuscript about an eccentric billionaire, and on the amount of money magazines would probably pay to print excerpts of the manuscript. B gave A a drawing of the publishing company's office, showing exactly where a copy of the manuscript was probably being kept. After carefully reviewing the sketch, A left for the company's building, agreeing to meet B later that night at the home of C (a mutual friend) with the manuscript. A entered the office through a side door marked on the sketch, took the manuscript, and went to C's apartment (where B was waiting). A, unknowingly, had tripped a silent alarm in the publishing office, and the police were able to follow her to the building in which C lived.

Not knowing which apartment the suspect had entered, the police began knocking on every door. Hearing the police search, A and B told C what had happened, and A and B hid in the closet. When the police came to C's apartment, C told the officers that he was alone, and the police left.

A and B then drove to a local tavern for a few drinks. B went to a table while A walked to the bar and struck up a conversation with the bartender. Sometime later, D, a tavern patron, accidentally brushed against the table, spilling B's drink. A loud argument erupted, and soon B and D were fighting. D was quickly joined by some friends. A entered the fight as well, drew a knife, and fatally stabbed D. Panicked, A left the tavern and sped away in her car.

A few blocks away, P, a police officer, observed A's vehicle going through a stop sign and began to chase her. Mistakenly believing she was being apprehended for the tavern incident, A increased her speed until it reached 80 mph. P felt she had to take more drastic action to stop the vehicle and began to fire at A's tires. When P finally succeeded in shooting a tire, A lost control of her car. The car jumped the curb and struck W, a woman who was waiting for a bus. W died later at the hospital as a result of injuries sustained in the accident.

1. What is the criminal responsibility, if any, of A, B, and C for the office building incident?

2. What is the criminal responsibility, if any, of A and B for D's death?

3. What is the criminal responsibility, if any, of A and P for W's death?

Question 7

In the early afternoon, after several hours of drinking, Ames, Brody, and Cole drove to a local market to purchase more liquor. Ames, the driver, waited in the car while Brody and Cole went into the store.

Just before entering, Brody and Cole realized they had no money. When the clerk placed the requested bottle of whiskey on the counter, Cole picked it up. As the clerk waited for payment, Brody drew a revolver and pointed it at the clerk, who gasped and stepped back. The two men ran from the market, Cole waving the bottle and Brody still holding the gun. As they jumped into the waiting car, Brody said to Ames, "Step on it, before the cops get here." Ames drove off at high speed.

Alerted by radio, officers in a patrol car pursued the fleeing trio and pulled alongside their car when it halted at a stop sign. Brody jumped out and fired at police officers Smith and Jones, killing Smith. A gun battle followed, and Cole, who was also armed, joined in the shooting. Brody was then shot and killed by Officer Jones. Officer Jones then apprehended Cole. Ames fled the scene when the gun battle began and was not apprehended until several days later. The jurisdiction has the following murder statute:

1. *Murder.* Murder is the unlawful killing of a human being with malice aforethought.

2. *Express and implied malice.* Such malice may be express or implied. It is express when there is manifested a deliberate unlawful intent to take the life of a fellow human being. It is implied when no reasonable provocation appears or when the circumstances attending the killing show an abandoned and malignant heart.

3. *Murder of first or second degree.* All murder that is perpetrated by any kind of willful, deliberate, and premeditated killing or that is committed in the perpetration of, or in an attempt to perpetrate, a robbery or burglary, is murder of the first degree; all other kinds of murder are of the second degree.

Discuss whether Cole and Ames committed (1) burglary or robbery and (2) murder and, if so, the degree of murder. Include in your discussion all defenses that each may have.

Question 8

Daniel, an amateur geologist, visits Zion National Park, where he finds a stone that he particularly likes. Remembering that he has heard that federal law prohibits taking any item from a national park, he shows the stone to Hermione, a park ranger. Hermione tells him, "the prohibition only applies to items weighing more than three pounds. You're okay. Enjoy." Dan puts the stone in his pocket and goes back to his hotel, which is just outside the park, and puts the stone in his suitcase. That night, while the full moon is bright, Dan wanders around the woods near his hotel. He unknowingly crosses the border between the park and nonfederal land. As he strolls in the moonlight, he is accosted by a person in a mask, who shouts, "your money or your life." The assailant is not carrying a weapon. Daniel picks up a nearby rock and throws it at the masked person, who ducks. The rock plummets over a 500-foot cliff and kills Ansel, who is just setting up his camera to take pictures of the park and moon. The rock is destroyed.

In addition to discussing any criminal liability under the common law assume the following federal statutes:

> 101. Any person who, while on federal land, knowingly removes any item has committed a felony.

> 102. Any person who, while on federal land, knowingly transports, possesses, or destroys, or causes to be transported, possessed, or destroyed, any archeological artifact is guilty of a felony, punishable by two years in prison.

It turns out that:

1. Hermione was wrong—you can't remove **any** item, of any size, from a national park.
2. The rock that Dan threw is an "archeological artifact" within the meaning of Section 102.
3. The masked assailant was only joking—he's Fred, Dan's best friend, who only intended to scare Dan.

Indicate if there would be any changes to your answer if Congress had adopted the Model Penal Code.

Question 9

Dr. Erasmus Jones is one of the world's foremost heart surgeons. On April 10, the State Department called him at his home in Connecticut and requested that he perform a heart operation on "a very important figure in world affairs" (they did not tell him the patient's identity). They did tell him that the operation was to be performed on April 12 at Walter Reed Hospital, in Washington, D.C. Jones was further informed that, while the operation was a delicate one and that the patient would die without it, it would be a routine job for Jones, who had invented and perfected the technique required. Jones explained to the caller that he had just received news that his son had been killed in a traffic accident and he was entirely too nervous and upset to perform the operation. The State Department official pressed on, however, and Dr. Jones reluctantly agreed to meet a special Air Force plane at the Hartford airport the morning of April 11 and perform the operation on April 12.

After the call on the evening of April 10, several friends visited the doctor to comfort him in his grief. He told them about the call as they began drinking. As the evening progressed and the group became intoxicated, one of the visitors said he had heard that an ill Russian general had just defected to the United States. The group concluded that this was probably the important person in question and urged Jones not to help him. One friend suggested that Jones call the State Department and tell them to go to hell, but Jones said, "I don't owe them anything. Let 'em find another man if they can. Frankly, I hope the bastard dies." Jones and his friends then drove up to a remote part of Vermont for a three-day fishing trip.

When Jones did not show up at the airport on the 11th, the State Department tried to locate him, to no avail. The patient, the 75-year-old wife of the prime minister of Canada, died of heart failure late in the evening on April 12.

Discuss what crime(s) Jones and his friends could be charged with, and the defenses, if any, they could raise against those charges.

Question 10

Adam dialed Bob's number on the telephone. Bob's phone was answered by Cal, Bob's brother, who sounds very much like Bob. Adam said, "Hey, Bob, this is Adam. Your pal, Tom, is going to break into Xavier's jewelry store tonight. Let's wait outside the store and grab what he steals. I'll be over at ten o'clock." Cal hung up the telephone without replying.

Adam arrived at Bob's apartment at ten o'clock. Cal had left earlier without telling Bob of Adam's phone call. A explained the reason for his presence to Bob, and the two hurriedly drove toward the jewelry store. As they neared it, Bob said, "I've changed my mind. You go ahead if you want, but stop the car and let me out." Adam did so and then continued on to the store. Bob paused at a phone booth intending to report Adam to the police, but changed his mind and walked directly home without calling.

When Adam arrived at the store, he discovered Cal already there, watching the front door. In a few minutes, as Adam also watched, Tom cautiously approached the store, entered with a master key, and emerged shortly carrying a bag of stolen jewelry. Cal ran toward Tom, snatched at the bag, but missed it. However, Adam leaped on Tom from behind and held his arms while Cal took the bag from him. Adam and Cal then ran toward Adam's car to escape. The police arrived at this moment, responding to a burglar alarm that Tom had set off in the store. Tom surrendered without resistance, but Adam and Cal continued to flee. Cal pulled a pistol and attempted to fire at a pursuing police officer. The gun was defective, however, and exploded when Cal pulled the trigger, killing him instantly.

Discuss the crimes, if any, of which Adam, Bob, and Tom are guilty.

Question 11

Joe is building his $1.3 million dream house. He wants to install a new air-conditioning unit in his house. Aware that the township has rules about such items, he calls the local zoning board one day and asks what restrictions the township has. He is told, over the phone, that the air conditioner cannot turn out more than 500 BTUs per hour. He purchases a unit that turns out only 425 BTUs and tells Hilda, his construction engineer, to pick up the unit and install it the next day. When Hilda discovers that the unit uses 425 BTUs, she phones Joe and tells him that the township will not allow more than 400 BTUs. "That's not what they told me," says Joe. "And if you don't put that air conditioner in today, you can forget the rest of the contract." Hilda, who expected to have a profit of more than $40,000 on the job, installs the air conditioner. That night, the air conditioner causes a fire that destroys four surrounding homes. Two persons in those homes are killed. Hilda was correct—a state statute provides that "Anyone who installs, or causes to be installed, in a private home any appliance using more than 400 BTUs per hour shall be fined $1,000 or be imprisoned for not more than 30 days."

Discuss the liability of Joe and Hilda under the statute, the common law, and the Model Penal Code for any crimes.

Question 12

Don, in need of funds, approached his friend, Oscar, who sold stereo equipment. Oscar told Don he had no cash to give him, but that he owned thousands of dollars' worth of readily saleable and fully insured stereo equipment stored in his own warehouse nearby. Don replied that, under the circumstances, Oscar would not lose any money if some of the equipment "disappeared" and Don sold it. Oscar then said he would give Don a duplicate key to the warehouse so that Don, with Don's brother, Allen, could remove the equipment, on condition that Don reimburse him for any loss that he could not recover from his insurance company. Don said, "That's great"and left with the key.

Don told Allen about the plan, and Allen agreed to help him. Don and Allen entered the warehouse with the key, and the two men loaded Don's truck with $50,000 worth of equipment. After the items were removed and the warehouse locked, it was agreed that Allen would immediately drive the truck and equipment to Mexico, to be joined later by Don. It was also agreed that Don should go home by means of an automobile the two had seen in an enclosed parking area to the rear of the warehouse.

Allen drove away, and Don re-entered the warehouse to reach the parking area. He took the automobile, drove it through the closed and locked gate of the fence that enclosed the parking area, and went to his apartment.

Allen was driving in excess of the speed limit when a highway patrol car attempted to stop him. Allen, believing the theft had been discovered, attempted to escape by driving over 100 mph. In the ensuing chase, the highway patrol officer lost control of her patrol car and was killed when the car overturned.

1. Discuss whether Don committed burglary (a) in the removal of the stereo equipment and (b) in the theft of the vehicle.

2. Discuss whether Don is guilty of either murder or manslaughter in the death of the highway patrol officer.

3. Discuss whether Oscar is criminally liable for any crime(s) for which Don is culpable.

Question 13

Dave had arranged with the Fine Arts Gallery to inspect, after its nighttime closing, the display of Old Masters paintings that he had loaned the gallery. While en route to the gallery for such purpose, Dave saw Amos, a rival art collector. Dave suspected that Amos had in some way obtained from Dave's office his only memorandum of the address of an obscure art dealer who possessed a painting both Dave and Amos coveted. Dave stepped up behind Amos, stuck his pipe in Amos's back, and said, "Don't move or I'll shoot." As Amos raised his arms, Dave took Amos's billfold from his pocket and ran off. The memorandum was indeed in the billfold, and Dave removed and then threw the billfold, with the rest of the contents intact, under a streetlight where he expected Amos to find it.

Dave proceeded to the Fine Arts Gallery, where he found the door broken open and the guard, who resided there, bleeding and unconscious from a head wound. Dave grabbed a lance from an exhibit of ancient weapons and dashed into the room where his paintings were hanging. There he saw Bob slashing the paintings. Dave was too stunned to react for a moment, but he recovered quickly and threw the lance just as Bob slashed another painting. The lance killed Bob.

Discuss with what crimes Dave can reasonably be charged, and what defenses he may reasonably raise.

Question 14

Dan proposed to his friend, Paul, that the two rob the First National Bank (Bank). Paul, thinking that Dan was joking, replied, "Sure, why not?" Dan then produced three pistols and three stocking masks and said, "Okay, let's go." Paul thought that it would be dangerous to back out at that point. He therefore took a pistol, but he secretly resolved to try to thwart the robbery.

On the way to Bank, Dan announced, "We need someone else." Dan then approached a passerby, Mike, pointed a pistol at Mike, and said, "We are going to rob Bank, and you are going to help us or we will kill you." Mike gulped, accepted a mask and an unloaded pistol, and proceeded with Dan and Paul to Bank, doing so only because he reasonably believed the threat was real.

When the three arrived at Bank, Dan assigned Paul to act as lookout. Dan instructed Mike to approach the teller with the pistol and to demand all of the teller's cash. Dan then stood back to cover everyone in Bank, including Mike. Dan whispered to Paul, "We will kill anybody who gives us trouble." Paul said nothing.

Immediately thereafter, Fred, a stranger to Dan, Paul, and Mike, entered Bank. Dan shot and severely wounded Fred, who was a federal bank examiner conducting an audit of Bank's accounts.

Based on properly admitted evidence that established the above facts, Dan and Paul were convicted in a federal court of violation of, and conspiracy to violate, a federal statute providing: "Whoever assaults with a deadly weapon any federal officer engaged in the performance of his duties is guilty of a felony." Dan and Paul have appealed, arguing that the evidence does not support convictions either for violation of the federal assault statute or for conspiracy to violate that statute.

Eight months after the robbery attempt, Fred died of his wounds. Dan, Paul, and Mike were tried in a state court on charges of assault with a deadly weapon on, and murder of, Fred.

Evidence identical to that admitted in the federal court was then received in the state court trial. Mike filed a timely motion for a directed verdict of acquittal on the ground that the evidence established duress as a matter of law.

1. Discuss how the federal appeals court should rule on Dan and Paul's appeal.

2. Discuss how the state trial court should rule on Mike's motion for a directed verdict.

Question 15

ABC Corporation was engaged in buying and selling used cars. Adams, Black, and Cooper held all of the stock and, except for an office assistant, were its only officers and employees.

One day, Adams, while demonstrating a used Oldsmobile in a grossly negligent manner to Riley, a prospective customer, struck and killed Stanley, a pedestrian. Despite the accident, Adams sold the auto to Riley for $1,500 with terms of $100 down and the balance due at the end of the month, at which time delivery would be made. When Riley tendered the balance of the purchase price at the end of the month, he discovered that Adams had knowingly resold the car to Williams. Riley forcibly repossessed the vehicle from Williams.

Black sold a used Chevrolet to Hand for $1,000, whereupon Hand gave Black a certified check payable to Black. Somehow, Hand had procured the check beforehand and had forged the name "U.R. Stuck" as the bank officer who certified the check. Black gave Hand a certificate of title to the automobile.

Cooper, without the knowledge and consent of either Adams or Black, borrowed $500 as a personal loan from a local finance company and, as security, delivered a certificate of title on a used Ford, owned by ABC. Cooper intended to repay the loan within three days.

Discuss all possible bases of criminal liability involved.

Question 16

Alex had received, as a gift from his father, a solid-gold wristwatch engraved with Alex's initials. One day, beset by hard times, Alex pawned the watch at Ben's pawnshop. A month later, Alex returned from work to find that his father had paid him a surprise visit. When Alex's father asked to see the watch, Alex told him it was being cleaned. Fearing that his father might disinherit him if his father learned that he had pawned the watch, Alex rushed down to Ben's after work the next day to redeem it. As a result of rush-hour traffic, however, Alex got there at 10 p.m. to find the pawnshop was closed. Looking inside, Alex could see his watch lying on a counter next to a window. Alex decided to try to get his watch out of the pawnshop so that his father would not become suspicious about its absence. He intended to return the watch once his father had departed.

The window of the pawnshop was slightly ajar, enabling Alex to push it up and extend a pole, which he used to pull the watch toward the window. Alex had just begun to pull the watch out through the window when a grating noise startled Ben, who was eating dinner upstairs with his family. Ben grabbed his gun and rushed downstairs, where he saw the figure of a man crouching just outside the open window. Thinking Alex's pole might be a rifle, Ben fired a shot toward Alex. The bullet ricocheted, just missing Alex. Startled, Alex dropped the pole and ran home, not realizing that his watch had fallen to the ground just beneath the pawnshop window.

Later that evening, Cliff was walking by the pawnshop when he noticed Alex's watch lying on the ground. Cliff decided to take the watch home in an effort to locate the owner. But once Cliff got home, he realized the watch was quite valuable, so he decided to keep it. However, Cliff soon became nervous and gave the watch to his friend, Don, telling him, "Here, you can have this watch, but be careful, it's hot." Don kept the watch.

1. Alex is charged with:
   a. burglary,
   b. larceny,
   c. attempted burglary, and
   d. attempted larceny.
2. Ben is charged with assault with a deadly weapon.
3. Cliff is charged with larceny.

4. Don is charged with:

    a. receiving stolen property, and

    b. attempting to receive stolen property.

Discuss the issues raised by these charges.

Question 17

Carlo operated a gambling casino in a state where gambling is a misdemeanor. One night, Tom, Mac, Fred, and Sam went to the casino shortly before closing time. The four hid in the men's room until the casino closed; then they emerged brandishing guns.

While Tom, Mac, and Sam held the employees at gunpoint, Fred prepared to blow open the safe with nitroglycerin. The safe was in Carlo's office, just off the main gambling floor. It was eight feet tall and four feet square and was large enough to walk into. It sat on the floor in the corner and was not attached to the building, although it was too heavy to move without special equipment. The nitroglycerin went off prematurely and blew the safe open, killing Fred. Tom, Mac, and Sam grabbed three sacks of money from the safe, each containing $10,000, all of which came from the gambling tables.

As the trio was leaving the casino with the money, they encountered Eb on the front steps. Eb shouted, "Death to gamblers!" and shot and killed Mac, and then turned the gun on Sam. Sam shot and wounded Eb, who survived. Tom and Sam jumped into their car with the loot and fled. As they were fleeing, Carlo came out of the casino with a rifle and fired a shot at the departing car. The shot killed Tom.

Eb later told police that he had thought Mac was one of the casino operators; Eb was trying to destroy the casino because he had lost all his money there, wrecking his life. Eb was unaware that anything unusual was going on at the casino.

Discuss the criminal liabilities, if any, of Sam, Eb, and Carlo.

Question 18

Quinn collects vintage cars. One might say that he is obsessed with them. His particular favorite is a 1928 Reo. Phillip, who despises Quinn, is also especially envious of Quinn's Reo. Phillip knows that Regnis, Quinn's friend, will be driving the Reo tonight. Regnis is the conductor of the International Symphony and is one of the great collectors of musical treasures.

Phillip waits for Regnis on a dark, curvy road and forces Regnis off the road. When Phillip approaches the car he finds on the front seat the original composition of the six Brandenburg Concerti, signed by Bach himself. Quinn and Phillip both know that there are no other existing copies. Phillip grabs the music and says to Regnis, "if you don't push this car off the cliff right now, I will destroy these manuscripts. And I hope that Quinn kills you when he finds out what you did to his car." Regnis exits the car and pushes the car off the cliff. Just as the car tumbles over the side, Quinn comes upon the scene. "My baby!" he screams, running at Regnis and battering him with a tire iron. Regnis lives.

Discuss the liability of each actor. You should also discuss what would happen if Regnis had died.

Question 19

Richard Chain, president of Black and Root, a company that cleans up oil spills, is called by George Walker, chairman of Slam Dunk Oil, who tells him that there has been a spill by his company in Colorado. Walker asks Chain to clean up the mess. Chain tells Walker that he will charge Slam Dunk $2,000,000, which includes $500,000 for properly disposing of the oil under state and federal environmental regulations. "Look," says Walker. "We don't have to really dispose of the oil properly. Why don't you charge the company $500,000 and just get rid of the oil somewhere cheap, and we'll split the profits." Chain agrees.

Chain hires Harry to dispose of the oil. They agree to put the oil in 55-gallon drums, fly the drums to Alaska, and put them in a landfill near a national park. Harry has his henchman, Donald Ginfield, put the oil in the drums and mark the drums "Water Matter — Disposable." Harry then hires Colon Comma to fly the plane over the Rockies to Canada. Colon is wary. "Those drums look like the kind of thing you'd use to get rid of bad stuff," he says. "I've seen that kind of drum before. Are you sure this is okay?" Harry shows him a (false) invoice, invokes the names of Chain and Walker (who until that time had spotless reputations), and offers Colon another $10,000. Colon agrees.

On the day the trip is scheduled, the weather is stormy. "We should wait," says Colon. "We might not make it to Vancouver in this weather." Harry offers another $10,000, and Colon takes off, with Ginfield and Harry. There are 5,000 drums in the plane. As they near the Rockies, however, the altimeter shows that the plane is unable to climb above 10,000 feet; the Rockies are nearly 13,000 feet. Colon shouts, "We're too low. The weather is too severe. Those drums are too heavy. We'll never make it over Pike's Peak. We've got to drop some of those drums." Harry and Ginfield throw out 500 drums, the plane makes it over the mountains, and everyone is elated.

Well, almost everyone. It turns out that, beneath the cloud cover created by the storm, a troop of Boy Scouts, on a hike, were directly under the plane when the drums were cast off. Two Boy Scouts were killed by the drums. The scouts were not visible from the air.

When the plane lands in Vancouver, it is discovered that the altimeter was incorrect—the plane was actually at 15,000 feet when the drums were jettisoned.

Colorado has a detailed environmental regulatory statute that specifies the steps by which oil should be disposed of. Needless to say, throwing oil from a plane is not an authorized procedure. The state statute also provides:

> 101. Whoever disposes of oil in violation of these regulations, or causes such a disposal, has committed a misdemeanor, punishable by a fine of $10,000 or 30 days in jail or both. If the disposal is done willfully or knowingly, it is a felony, for which the punishment is no less than 5 or more than 20 years in prison, and a fine of no less than $50,000 and no more than $1,000,000.

Discuss the liability of all the actors for any crimes under the common law and the statute above. If there would be differences if the Colorado regulation had adopted the Model Penal Code, include those differences in your discussion.

Question 20

Beatrice, in need of money, suggests to Conrad that they rob the corner pawnbroker's shop. Conrad agrees, but, knowing of Beatrice's temper, says, "No violence. No weapons. We simply go in, take a few things, and leave." Beatrice acquiesces.

Inside the store, George is attempting to persuade Rod, the owner, to give him "a few dollars" for an outmoded record player. "I can't take it," replies Rod. "I'd never be able to resell it." George takes a revolver from his coat. "I just want its market value. Please." Rod remains adamant. "I can't do it." George puts down the gun and says, "My child has kidney failure. He needs a transplant. I need the money." Rod goes into the register and gives George market value for the player, which George attempts to put on the counter. Unhappily, George is so nervous that he drops the player, and it hits Rod, who was bending down, on the head, knocking him unconscious. George runs out of the door, as Beatrice and Conrad come in.

Beatrice and Conrad notice that the owner is on the floor. Before they can take any items, Rod awakens and struggles to stand up. Conrad screams, "It's you! I've been waiting 20 years for this." Conrad takes a nearby golf club and hits Rod. "Stop!" yells Beatrice. "You agreed no violence." "This guy killed my daughter 20 years ago. Now he'll pay for it," says Conrad. Beatrice, with no materials from the store, runs out of the shop. Conrad pushes Rod back to the floor and hits him 30 more times, killing him. Conrad then removes the record player and several watches from the store and leaves.

Later investigations reveal the following facts. (1) George has no child. He and his wife, Martha, have long fantasized about a child, and to them, at least on some occasions, he is very real. George honestly believed his child was in kidney failure. (2) Twenty years earlier, Rod had been (nonnegligently) driving a car when Conrad's daughter ran directly into its path. An investigation found that Rod had not committed any crime or tort. Conrad had always thought Rod criminally responsible, but had moved away soon thereafter and did not know that Rod was running the pawnshop.

Discuss the criminal liability of George, Conrad, and Beatrice under the common law and the Model Penal Code.

Question 21

Samson, 23 years old, is a first-year teacher at Piedmont High, teaching history to seniors. He soon becomes besotted with Delilah, one of his students, and begins offering special tutoring. One evening at his apartment, one thing, as they say, leads to another, and soon the two are naked. Delilah says, "Maybe this isn't a good idea. This would be my first time. I think I'll go home." But Samson replies, "Don't worry, this is the right thing. I love you, and I want to marry you."

After intercourse, Delilah sobs silently and gets dressed, but Samson remains in bed. Five minutes later, Sally, Samson's fiancée, comes into the apartment, sees Samson in bed, and shouts, "I knew I couldn't trust you." She grabs a bowling ball and throws it at Samson, who ducks. The missile hits Delilah, killing her instantly. Samson meanwhile grabs his nearby pistol, which he fires at Sally. He misses, and the bullet goes through the wall, killing Samson's neighbor, Moab. It turns out that, while most seniors at Piedmont are at least 17 years old, Delilah is only 15 years old. The age for "statutory rape" is 16.

Discuss the possible liability of all the actors under both the common law and the Model Penal Code.

Question 22

On Mischief Night, Mike decided to go to St. Ignatius's Retreat, a large, private, gated community near his house, and soap all the cars and wrap the trees with tissue. He loaded the trunk of his car with the necessary paraphernalia. He picked up his friend, Ike, and once Ike was in the car, told him where they were bound. Ike, who had had a long day, immediately fell asleep. Mike next picked up Louis, but didn't tell him what was planned. Nor did he inform the next passenger, Jules. Mike did, however, give Jules a bottle of beer, spiked with a small amount of sleeping pills, enough to put Jules out for about half an hour. As Mike approached the gate of St. Ignatius's Retreat, Louis looked up and said, "Where are we going? I've heard these guys are really hostile to strangers." "Don't worry," said Mike, "I've got it covered." "Let me out!" cried Louis. "Not a chance," said Mike, gunning the car as he ran through the entryway. There was no guard on duty. Mike sped through the grounds until he came to a cul-de-sac on which there were several large houses. The car came to a screeching halt. At this point, Ike and Jules woke up. When Mike told them where they were, and what he planned for each to do, Ike protested, "I didn't know this was what you meant by a great night out." Just as Ike and Jules opened the car door to leave, however, two police officers arrested the quartet. The four are charged with the following crimes:

> 101. Trespass on private property, defined as "entering, without consent, the private property of another." Trespass is punishable by 30 days in the county jail.

> 102. Attempted malicious mischief, a felony.

Discuss their liability under the common law and the Model Penal Code.

Question 23

Daphne and Velma were playing a game together. The game consisted of shooting at one and other with bb guns. They each took bb guns to a heavily wooded area near their homes. They established a field and declared that if either player left the fields he would be declared the "loser." As both players knew, the edge of the field abutted a steep cliff that dropped precipitously to a public beach below.

As the game progressed, Daphne was dominating play. She was getting off many more shots than Velma and was connecting on more of them as well. Velma, her arms and legs welted with bb scars, sought to surrender by leaving the field of play in the direction of the cliff. Unfortunately, in doing so she fell from the cliff and plunged to the beach below. Perhaps even more unfortunately, she fell on Youngster, a child playing on the beach, killing both herself and Youngster instantly.

Discuss the homicide liability of Daphne in a common law jurisdiction and in a MPC jurisdiction. You may presume that it is a felony in both jurisdictions to engage in mutual combat and that the conduct of these defendants violated that statute.

Question 24

A and his girlfriend C wish to have sex with the other, but because both live at home, neither has the privacy both would like. B, A's good friend, wants to help out and offers his place for the tryst, saying that A and C are welcome to go there anytime. That night, A and C visit B's apartment, and as they are entering with the key B gave them, they are espied by D, C's father who has followed them there. D began shouting obscenities at A, upon which C dropped dead of fright. D then calmed down, called the police, and had A arrested. A told his story to the police, and B was subsequently arrested as well.

The following facts can be proven at trial:

A knew that C was only 17, but believed that one ceased to be a minor at the age of 16.

B reasonably believed that C was 18, as he had seen her convincing fake driver's license only the day before.

D had previously threatened A that if he saw A around his daughter again, D would kill them both.

The statutory rape provision in this jurisdiction makes it a felony to have sex with a minor. Minor is defined in the alcohol, tobacco, and firearms section of the jurisdiction's code as any person under the age of 18.

A and B are charged with attempted statutory rape, involuntary manslaughter, felony murder, and conspiracy to commit statutory rape. Discuss their liability as follows:

1. For statutory rape, consider this jurisdiction's statute as interpreted under both the common law and the Model Penal Code (that is, do NOT apply the Model Penal Code statutory rape provision).

2. For the other crimes (involuntary manslaughter, felony murder, and conspiracy), apply the relevant provisions of the common law and the Model Penal Code.

(D was found incompetent to stand trial. You need not worry about his criminal liability.)

Question 25

D and his friend V agreed to drag race late Friday night on an access road near the local airport. They chose this location because it was often deserted late at night and the two thought it would be the safest time and place for their race. Their cars were evenly matched and both knew that the race would come down to a test of driving skill. D believed that he was a better driver than his friend and was quite confident that he would prevail.

On the appointed night the two set out a course on the access road and raced as planned. As he expected, D opened up an early lead on his opponent. However, as he neared the finish line, D noticed V gaining quickly in his rear-view mirror. D moved his car abruptly to the left in order to cut off V's advance. V thought that he could get past D's attempt to block him but lost control in his attempt to do so. His car careened into a light pole, killing V instantly.

Drag racing is a felony in this jurisdiction. It is defined as "an unlicensed automobile race between two or more people involving speeds above the posted maximums." At the time of the crash, both cars were more than 40 mph above posted limits.

Discuss D's criminal liability under both the common law and the Model Penal Code.

Question 26

D was browsing at the Apple store at the Cherry Creek mall when he noticed V, another customer, surreptitiously slipping several iPods into his pocket. V noticed D watching him and scowled. At this point D, seeing a security guard about to turn down the aisle toward himself and V, walked quickly over and asked the guard an inane question. In the meantime V left the store with the iPods.

D hurried from the store shortly thereafter and caught up with V in the parking lot connected to the mall and called to him:" "Hey, I really helped you out in there, how about a little something for me?" V pushed him away and got into his car, stating, "You didn't do a damn thing. Get away from me." D, angered, attempted to open the door to the car. V gunned the engine, pulling out of the space and into the car of C, a customer. C's car skidded into A, another customer, who was killed instantly.

Grand theft is a felony in this jurisdiction defined as "knowingly taking the property of another in a value exceeding $500 with the intent to permanently deprive the owner of its use." The value of the iPods taken from the Apple store by D was $600. This felony is considered in progress until the perpetrator has "reached a place of temporary safety."

Discuss the criminal liability of D, V, and C under both the common law and the Model Penal Code. (You need not discuss self-defense.)

Essay
Answers

Answer to Question 1

CRIMES OF ARNOLD (A)

Murder

The State (State) could charge Arnold with murder for Bill's (B) death.

A murder occurs when the defendant has committed a homicide (the killing of one human being by another) with malice aforethought (the intent to kill, the intent to cause serious bodily harm, or extreme recklessness). Although A would argue he was attempting only to shoot David (D) in the leg, an intent to cause serious bodily harm could be inferred from A's use of a hunting rifle. Even though A may not have been aware of B, under the transferred intent doctrine (when a person intends to commit a particular crime against one individual, but inadvertently commits the same or a similar crime against another person, that person's intent is deemed transferred from the intended to the actual victim), A's desire to shoot D would be transferred to B.

It is highly unlikely that the State would charge, or be able to prove, first-degree murder, which requires "premeditation, deliberation, and willfulness." On the other hand, the State could assert that A is guilty of second-degree murder because he evidenced a wanton *mens rea* (i.e., consciously engaged in conduct that he knew, or should have known, posed a high probability of death or serious injury to other human beings) by shooting at D while other persons were in the vicinity. Courts have generally been more willing to find such *mens rea* where a firearm is involved; there is even some suggestion that mishandling a firearm, at least when one knows it is loaded, is recklessness or worse. It is unclear from the facts whether A should have recognized the likelihood of hitting someone other than D (this determination would depend on facts such as how good a marksman A was, how far D was from A, how obvious B's presence was to A, etc.).

The State could also contend that A at least acted recklessly (engaged in conduct that posed a substantial risk of death or serious bodily injury to other human beings) by shooting at D while other individuals were in the vicinity and, therefore, is culpable of involuntary manslaughter.

In response, A could contend that the shooting was privileged under the "fleeing felon" justification. Traditionally, a private citizen can use force capable of causing death or serious injury to prevent a felon's escape. Today, however, many jurisdictions require that the felon must have been engaged in a "dangerous" felony (one that involved a risk or likelihood of serious physical harm to others) for this privilege to apply. Assuming D's conduct constituted a felony (discussed below), under the traditional view, A's shooting would be privileged. Even under the emerging view, A could still contend that burglary is arguably a "dangerous" felony, because there is always the risk that the occupant of the home that was invaded would return and a physical confrontation could then result. However, the State could argue in rebuttal that A was aware that D's conduct had not posed a risk of serious harm to others because the house was vacant during D's larceny and any "confrontation" was brought on by A, because D was running away. Furthermore, even if a confrontation were possible, it is dubious whether an *expectable* confrontation would involve firearms. Assuming the modern view is followed, the fleeing-felon justification would probably *not* be available to A.

The defense-of-property privilege is not applicable, because one can never exercise force capable of causing death or serious bodily harm to protect property.

A would assert alternatively that, even if the fleeing-felon privilege was unavailable, the charge should be reduced from murder to voluntary manslaughter. The State would argue that this is a situation in which an otherwise complete "defense of" justification does not exist because of the defendant's unreasonable mistake (thinking that he could use deadly force to prevent the felon from escaping). A would probably prevail in getting the charge reduced to manslaughter, assuming that the jurisdiction does not allow deadly force to be used to prevent such felonies.

(Adequate provocation probably is *not* applicable, because a reasonable person would not think of killing another merely because the latter had stolen the former's property.)

Attempted murder/assault as to D

A could not be prosecuted for the attempted murder of D (the crime of attempt occurs when the defendant has taken a substantial step toward completing the target crime with the intent to commit that crime). Although A's shooting at D with his hunting rifle arguably was at least negligent because A should have recognized there was a substantial certainty that D could die or be seriously injured, attempt requires that the defendant "intend" the consequence, and even if A was reckless, the facts will not support a contention that he intended death.

Alternatively, A could be charged with attempted battery and assault of D, because A presumably placed D in fear of imminent injury when he heard A's original shot. (It is unclear from the facts whether D saw A pointing the rifle at him.)

Assault/battery as to E

The State could conceivably charge A with battery for the stroke suffered by Edith (E). A battery is usually defined as intentionally or recklessly causing bodily injury to, or offensive touching of, another individual. Even assuming that (1) A's intent toward D could be transferred to E (which is unlikely, because the harm suffered by E was dissimilar to that which A desired to cause D), or (2) A's conduct could be characterized as reckless, there was no physical contact with E. Therefore, A probably could not be convicted of battery against E.

An assault occurs where the defendant intentionally places the victim in fear of imminent injury. E probably feared for her own life when she saw that B was suddenly shot. Here, the transferred intent doctrine might apply because the harm suffered by E (fear of imminent injury) would be the same or similar to that suffered by D. Many writers, and some courts, think that the doctrine should be limited, if not abolished, and that a defendant should be guilty of *attempted* murder (or assault, here) as to his actually intended victim, and a "reckless" or "other" level of crime as to the actual victim. If the transferred intent doctrine is found not to apply, an assault conviction cannot be sustained because reckless conduct will not suffice to support a conviction for assault.

CRIMES OF D

Murder/manslaughter

Again, D will not be liable for first-degree murder. But the State could charge D with second-degree murder of Bill under the felony-murder rule (according to which the defendant is deemed to have the *mens rea* for murder, even though he did not intend or desire the victim's death, when, during or as a consequence of the defendant's perpetration of an independent, inherently dangerous felony, a homicide occurs).

The State also could charge D with burglary (the trespassory breaking and entering into the dwelling of another, at night, with the specific intention of committing a felony or, in some states, a theft crime such as larceny, therein) and with larceny (the trespassory taking and carrying away of the personal property of another with the intent to permanently deprive the victim thereof). Because the facts are silent, the State will succeed only if D's burglary occurred at night or if this jurisdiction has abandoned the requirement that burglary occur at night.

The State could contend that D is guilty of second-degree murder under the felony-murder rule, arguing that B's death occurred as a consequence of D's burglary. D, however, could assert in rebuttal that (1) A's wanton intervening conduct extinguished the causal connection between the burglary and B's death, and (2) under these facts D was not engaged in an inherently "dangerous" felony because he was exiting a previously unoccupied home with several items. Courts differ as to whether, in determining if a felony is "inherently" dangerous, they should look at the crime "in the abstract" or "as perpetrated." Here, the State could respond that (1) the causal connection was not broken by A's conduct, because it is reasonably foreseeable that the occupants of a burglarized dwelling might return before the intruder had left, and (2) if this occurs, there is always the possibility of a violent confrontation between a burglar and the returning occupant. Again, whether such a possibility is "foreseeable" will be critical to A's liability. Although these are close issues, the State would probably prevail.

If D's burglary is **not** deemed to be a "dangerous" felony, the State could contend that D is culpable of involuntary manslaughter under the misdemeanor-manslaughter rule (according to which the defendant is held liable as though he had the *mens rea* for involuntary manslaughter when a homicide occurs as a consequence of, and in the course of, the defendant's perpetration of a felony that is not inherently dangerous, or of a misdemeanor or other unlawful act). While D again would contend that there was not a sufficient causal connection between his conduct and B's death, a conviction probably would result if this doctrine were applied.

Finally, given the facts, it is assumed that D would be prosecuted for burglary. If the State cannot show all the elements of burglary, D could be successfully prosecuted for larceny.

CRIMES OF FRED (F)

Robbery

Robbery occurs when the defendant commits a larceny by taking property from the person or presence of the owner using force or fear. Because B protested the removal of his watch, F probably would be deemed to have obtained the item by force. Although B's protestations were faint, given the circumstances, they were adequate to demonstrate that he was not surrendering the watch freely. Thus, F could be convicted of robbery.

Even if F has not used enough force to commit robbery, he has certainly committed larceny—he has taken the property of another with the intent to deprive him permanently thereof. (If F argues that B was already dead and that the watch was no longer B's, it is still the property of B's survivors.)

Answer to Question 2

CRIMES OF CHARLEY (C)

Conspiracy

A conspiracy occurs where there is an agreement between two or more persons to commit a crime. Although there does not appear to have been an explicit agreement to rob Dogge's (D) store, a tacit understanding could be inferred from the following facts: (1) all three drove to D's premises immediately after Baker's (B) solicitation (discussed below), and (2) C and B conducted themselves in a manner that manifested a jointness of action (i.e., C, while armed, positioned himself to cover Able's (A) retreat; B drove the getaway car). Thus, C is culpable of conspiracy. A's participation in the crime would be discounted because her "agreement" was feigned. However, this is not significant because the understanding between B and C would suffice to establish a conspiracy.

Second-degree murder

Under the felony-murder rule, if a homicide occurs during and as a result of the defendant's perpetration of an independent, inherently dangerous felony, the defendant is deemed to have the *mens rea* for second-degree murder (regardless of whether the defendant intended or desired the victim's death). The prosecution could contend that Easey's (E) death was a consequence of C's robbing D's store. C could argue in rebuttal, however, that the felony-murder rule is inapplicable in this instance because (1) E's death was not the result of C's conduct, but rather was caused by A's behavior, for which C is responsible because it could have been anticipated by C, which, in turn, caused D to shoot E; (2) the virus that E contracted at the hospital was the actual and proximate cause of E's death (not the wound sustained in the underlying felony of attempted robbery); and (3) in some jurisdictions, the felony-murder rule is not extended to situations where the victim's death was caused by someone other than a felon. It will be assumed that this state does not require that a felon actually cause the homicide. The prosecution probably could overcome C's causation argument (discussed below under crimes of D). With respect to C's first assertion, the prosecution could argue that, because A's actions were foreseeable (i.e., drawing a gun and demanding money from the cashier), A was, in effect, acting as C's agent or instrumentality. However, because A was under no direct compulsion to feign a robbery, this argument might fail. Thus, the felony-murder rule is probably **not** applicable.

Attempted murder

An attempt occurs where the defendant has deliberately engaged in conduct for the specific purpose of committing a crime (i.e., the target offense). Under common law, the defendant had to be very close to achieving that goal; under the Model Penal Code, the defendant merely has to take a substantial step toward culmination of it. Because C could successfully contend that he did not intend to kill D (only to compel him to stop shooting at A), the prosecution would lose its rebuttal that C must, or should have, recognized there was a substantial possibility that his bullet could have killed D.

In the unlikely event that A were not convicted of attempted murder, C would be culpable of aggravated battery (an intentional or reckless application of force upon another causing serious bodily harm or involving a deadly weapon even if serious bodily harm does not result), because he presumably intended to hit D when he fired his gun.

Robbery/larceny

A robbery occurs when the defendant, by force, or the threat of force, in the victim's presence, commits a larceny (i.e., the trespassory taking and carrying away of another's personal property with the intent to permanently deprive the latter thereof). C could not be guilty of robbery. The only party who took money from D using force was A, and A never intended to permanently deprive D of the cash that D tendered.

Attempted robbery

The prosecution could contend that an attempted robbery occurred when C entered D's store and positioned himself by the door to (presumably) cover A's getaway. While C could argue in rebuttal that no attempt could occur until D was accosted by B or C (which never happened), C did commit a substantial step that would probably suffice under the modern trend toward broader liability.

DEFENSES OF C

Entrapment

C could contend that he was entrapped into the foregoing crimes. This defense exists where a law enforcement official (here, A) induces the defendant to commit a crime that the defendant was not predisposed to commit. Entrapment arguably occurred when A invited B and C to her home and spoke in glowing terms about the recent series of robberies. However,

A probably would ***not*** be deemed to have instigated the crime because A never suggested actually undertaking illegal conduct.

CRIMES OF BAKER (B)

Solicitation/conspiracy

A solicitation occurs where the defendant requests or encourages another to join in the commission of a crime, with the intent to induce the latter to perform the crime. When B suggested to A and C that the drugstore would be a "pushover" (which seems to have been recognized by A and C as meaning it would be easy to rob), a solicitation occurred. However, because A and C indicated their agreement, this crime would probably be merged into the conspiracy (discussed above).

Attempted robbery/attempted murder

A co-conspirator is vicariously culpable for the crimes committed by other co-conspirators, provided such crimes were in furtherance of the conspiracy or were a reasonably foreseeable consequence. Assuming an attempted robbery occurred, it would certainly appear to be within the scope of the conspiracy. The facts are silent as to whether B was aware that C was armed when the latter entered the drugstore, but it would not be unreasonable to assume that B knew C carried some type of weapon given the nature of the crime. Thus, B probably would also be found guilty of the attempted murder of D.

CRIMES OF DOGGE (D)

Attempted murder/murder

The prosecution could contend that D is guilty of the attempted murder of A and the murder of E. D's intent to harm A would probably be applied to E under the transferred intent doctrine (when the defendant intended to commit a criminal act against a particular individual, and, as a consequence thereof, a different person is harmed, the defendant's intention will be transferred to the person harmed, provided the harm the person suffered is the same or similar to that which the defendant intended to cause to the original individual).

As to the murder charge, D would initially contend that no homicide (the killing of one human being by another) occurred because the actual cause of E's death was the virus (i.e., E's health was improving until she contracted the virus). However, the prosecution probably successfully would contend in rebuttal that "but for" D shooting E, E would not have been in the hospital in a weakened condition (which presumably made her more susceptible to the virus).

While D also could argue that the shooting was not the proximate cause of E's death (the virus was an unforeseeable, intervening condition that contributed to E's demise), the prosecution again could contend successfully in rebuttal that one who has been hospitalized for a serious gunshot wound could foreseeably contract a virus that could result in death. (Viruses exist in every hospital.) Proximate cause, of course, is not solely a question of foreseeability, as Justice Cardozo noted in *Palsgraf*, but of policy—do we wish to make all felons responsible for all viral deaths that occur in a hospital to which a crime victim is taken? The defendant will surely argue that the very fact that viruses are widespread in hospitals should require a more nuanced question of liability (suppose, e.g., that D had given E a pinprick, and E had contracted the same virus?). In this particular situation, D's use of a deadly weapon might warrant a stricter view of proximate causation.

D could assert the fleeing-felon privilege (if a citizen reasonably believes that an individual has committed a dangerous felony, and such individual has, in fact, just committed such offense, the citizen may exercise whatever force he reasonably believes is necessary, under the circumstances, to effectuate the offender's arrest) in response to the prosecution's charges. In response, the prosecution could contend that this defense is not available because (1) D's belief that a felony was occurring might not have been reasonable in light of the fact that A's note advised him that A was an undercover agent, and (2) no felony actually occurred because A had not intended to deprive D of his cash. However, D could argue in rebuttal that he reasonably believed that A's note was simply part of a scheme to illegally obtain the store's money, because A drew a gun as she approached D (D did not know that a second person, also involved in the crime, was watching A) and A took the money from D. While D's belief that a felony was occurring was probably reasonable, because A did not (in fact) commit a robbery, this justification might not be persuasive.

If D's belief that A was committing a felony was reasonable, he will be totally exculpated. If the belief was unreasonable, in some jurisdictions, he will be liable for murder, whereas other jurisdictions would allow a reduction to voluntary manslaughter.

Crimes of A

An undercover police officer is ordinarily not culpable for acts that she commits as a feigned accomplice, because such conduct was undertaken for the purpose of obtaining evidence against, and capturing, those who engaged in illegal activity.

Answer to Question 3

Are Bob (B) and Mike (M) guilty of burglary of Smith's (S) garage?
Burglary under common law is the trespassory breaking and entering into, at night, the dwelling of another with the intent to commit a felony (which, in many states, includes theft offenses). Presently, many jurisdictions have eliminated the "nighttime" element and have broadened the "dwelling" element to include any structures on a parcel with living quarters. B would contend that burglary is not appropriate because (1) the door that they opened was unlocked, (2) they entered only a garage not a home, and (3) B and M had *not* formed the specific intention of taking anything when they entered S's garage (the facts indicate that B and H only *sometimes* took tools). As to the "breaking," the State probably could contend successfully that this element ordinarily is satisfied by any forced movement of the structure; the door did not need to be locked. Second, the State would argue that, under the broadened definition, because the garage was "attached" to the home, it should be considered a part of the dwelling. With respect to B, if the State could show that B had taken items in the past, the State might argue that he entered the garage with the intention of taking something if it interested him, and, thus, the "intention" element is satisfied. This doctrine, known as "conditional intent," is questionable. M has an even stronger argument in that he did not possess the specific intention of committing a larceny at the time he entered the garage (even though he arguably did commit one subsequently). He will certainly argue that he was tagging along with the older boys for the first time and presumably was only curious to see what they were doing.

B and M could assert the defense of infancy. At common law, it was conclusively presumed that children under the age of 7 did not have the capacity to commit a crime. With respect to children between 7 and 14 years of age, there was a presumption that they did not have the capacity to commit a crime, but this could be rebutted by showing malice or an awareness that the conduct was wrong. Assuming this is a common law jurisdiction, M could not be prosecuted for burglary, and B could be successfully prosecuted for burglary only if the prosecution rebutted the presumption that B did not understand his actions were wrongful (which is possible).

Are B and M guilty of the larceny of S's watch?
Larceny is the trespassory taking and carrying away of another's personal property with the intent to permanently deprive the owner of his property. Even though M's taking of S's watch was trespassory (he wrongfully took

the watch from S's possession) and M carried away the watch (by taking it home with him), the intent element is not satisfied because M could again assert the defense of infancy (see above).

There appears to be no factual basis (conspiracy or accomplice culpability) for holding B responsible for M's actions, even if M were deemed to be guilty of larceny.

Is B guilty of burglary of Jones's toolshed?

Although burglary at common law was the trespassory breaking and entering into a house, at night, modern law has been expanded to include entry into many structures with the intent to commit a felony or theft offense. While the facts indicate that the requisite "breaking" took place, the facts do not indicate whether B ever actually entered Jones's toolshed. Assuming H stepped into the toolshed first, it is doubtful that B would have any reason to continue in after H was shot. The prosecution could make the argument that H's acts should be imputed to B under a theory of conspiracy between H and B (the agreement between two or more persons to commit an unlawful act) with H's step inside the toolshed constituting the overt act, if this is a jurisdiction that requires one. While the intent to commit the theft offense is clearer here than with S's garage (the facts state that the boys went to Jones's toolshed for the stated purpose of taking a large screwdriver that had previously caught B's eye), the prosecution would again encounter the same defense of infancy. B could be successfully prosecuted for burglary of Jones's toolshed only if the prosecution rebuts the presumption that B did not understand his actions were wrong.

Is Jones (J) guilty of Hal's (H) murder?

A defendant is guilty of first-degree murder where he commits a homicide (the killing of one human being by another) with the intention of causing the victim's death or serious bodily harm, and such killing was premeditated and deliberate. While J probably will contend that he wanted only to scare away potential intruders, one ordinarily may be inferred to have intended the natural consequences of one's actions. Rigging a pistol to discharge when a door is opened certainly has the potential to kill or seriously injure anyone who opens the door. The fact that the homicide was accomplished by a preset instrument is irrelevant, because one is responsible for setting forces in motion that cause a victim's death.

J could assert two defenses. First, some states allow the use of deadly force to prevent another from invading one's home. Because the toolshed was within the curtilage of J's house, such structure was arguably part of J's "home." Second, J could contend that he was preventing the felony of burglary (discussed above). The State could argue in rebuttal, however, that while separate structures on the parcel might constitute part of a dwelling for purposes of the crime of burglary, this is **not** applicable to excuse the use of deadly force in a structure that is not one's actual abode. Second, while one may sometimes kill to prevent a felony, one cannot do so where a lesser degree of force could have accomplished the intended purpose. If J had been in the toolshed, J could have prevented the felony by simply restraining H. Thus, the use of the firearm probably constituted excessive force, and J's defenses should fail.

Answer to Question 4

CRIMES OF SAM (S)

The prosecution could charge S with solicitation, conspiracy, burglary, malicious mischief, and murder.

Solicitation

A solicitation occurs when the defendant requests or encourages another to commit a crime with the intent to induce the latter to perform the crime. When S asked Ace (A) to break into Joe's (J) premises and pour syrup on J's merchandise, a solicitation probably occurred (assuming that the requested acts constituted a crime). Because the crime of solicitation is complete once the defendant makes his request, S will probably be convicted of solicitation.

Conspiracy

The crime of conspiracy occurs where there is an agreement between two or more persons to commit a crime. The prosecution could contend that, because S and A agreed that A would invade J's premises and pour syrup over J's goods, S is guilty of conspiracy to commit malicious mischief (the intentional or reckless injury to or destruction of the property of another). However, S could contend in rebuttal that, because A was mentally handicapped, he did not know the nature and quality of his actions and did not know what he was doing was wrong and, therefore, is legally insane. The fact that A put on a skeleton outfit, which would tend to make him easier to detect than if he were wearing regular clothing, indicates that A did not sufficiently appreciate that he was helping S in the commission of a crime. Because conspiracy requires the participants to share the specific goal of criminal conduct, it is unlikely that S could be convicted of conspiracy. The prosecution could argue that, under the Model Penal Code's "unilateral" theory of conspiracy, S is liable even without A being a conspirator, because, under this theory, only one party's intent is necessary to find the conspiracy.

Burglary

Where a person causes innocent or irresponsible persons to engage in conduct constituting the *actus reus* portion of a crime, the innocent or irresponsible party is looked upon as an instrumentality of the defendant. Because A was S's court-placed ward, and A appeared to be incapable of handling his own affairs, A would be considered the instrumentality of S, and A's conduct would be attributed to S.

Traditionally, a burglary is the trespassory breaking and entering into the dwelling of another, at night, with the intent to commit a felony. Under more modern law, however, the structure need not always be a dwelling, and the intent required is to commit a crime, not necessarily a felony (although some states require it to be a theft crime). Assuming A's actions constitute the "breaking and entering" portions of burglary and assuming this jurisdiction extends this crime to all structures (not just dwellings), A's conviction depends on whether malicious mischief (discussed above) constitutes the requisite crime. If the jurisdiction considers malicious mischief to be a crime, then a burglary conviction depends on whether the jurisdiction requires an intent to commit a theft crime or an intent to commit any crime.

Arson

Arson traditionally is the malicious (meaning intentional or reckless) burning of the dwelling of another. Today, however, many jurisdictions extend this crime to any structure. Assuming this state adheres to the modern view, the prosecution could contend that A committed arson by causing the explosion (an explosion ordinarily suffices to satisfy the "burning" element of arson) in the premises he invaded.

Second-degree murder

In addition, under the felony-murder rule, where a homicide occurs as a consequence of the defendant's perpetration of an independent, inherently dangerous felony, he is guilty of second-degree murder, even though the defendant did not intend or desire to cause the victim's death. Thus, the prosecution could contend that S is guilty of second-degree murder because J's death resulted from the explosion (arson) caused by A.

However, S could raise several counterarguments. First, he would contend that the explosion (even if attributed to him) was the result of negligent, not reckless, conduct (i.e., throwing an unopened can of syrup at the darkened portion of a business premises could not be characterized as conduct that created a high probability of causing an explosion or fire). Therefore, the malice element for arson is lacking, and no conviction could result. Likewise, the underlying independent, inherently dangerous felony necessary for application of the felony-murder rule is absent. Moreover, one ordinarily is not liable for the unintended or unforeseeable conduct of an innocent or irresponsible party. Because S only instructed A to pour syrup over J's merchandise, A hurling the can could not have been anticipated by S (and, therefore, S is not culpable for this aspect of A's conduct). Finally, S could assert that the proximate cause between the alleged felony and J's death is lacking (i.e., it was not reasonably foreseeable that throwing an unopened can of syrup toward the rear of an unoccupied business premises would strike a gas line and cause an explosion resulting in the death of an unknown person next door). S probably **would not** be convicted of second-degree murder.

Involuntary manslaughter

The prosecution might assert that S is guilty of involuntary manslaughter by directly causing J's death through possessing a reckless *mens rea* (undertaking conduct that posed a substantial risk of death or serious injury to others). The prosecution would claim that, because there is always the possibility that a mentally challenged individual will behave in a manner that creates a life-endangering situation to others, S acted recklessly by choosing A to commit malicious mischief. In rebuttal, S could contend that, assuming A had no prior history of violent conduct, S did not act recklessly in assuming that A would refrain from engaging in life-threatening behavior. Thus, S probably would **not** be convicted of involuntary manslaughter simply because he selected A to ruin J's merchandise.

The prosecution could alternatively contend that S could be convicted of involuntary manslaughter under the misdemeanor-manslaughter rule (according to which the defendant is deemed to have the *mens rea* for involuntary manslaughter, even though the defendant did not desire or intend the victim's death, if the death occurs accidentally in the course and as a consequence of the defendant's perpetration of a misdemeanor). With respect to the existence of a misdemeanor, A probably is guilty of attempting to commit malicious mischief to J's merchandise. However, S could contend that the necessary proximate cause between A's attempted misdemeanor (breaking into a store, albeit the wrong store, for the purpose of pouring syrup on J's merchandise) and J's ensuing death is lacking. Thus, no conviction under the misdemeanor-manslaughter rule appears likely.

CRIMES OF DAN (D)

The prosecution could charge D with solicitation and conspiracy. It could contend that D's suggestion to S that someone should "take care" of J constituted a solicitation. However, D probably could argue successfully in rebuttal that (1) no specific illegal conduct was requested (the phrase "take care of" is sufficiently vague to also include legal conduct, such as a purchase of J's business), and (2) assuming S had no prior history of criminal behavior, D probably did not expect S to undertake illegal activity based on his casual statement (especially because the facts indicate that D's statement was made in a half-jesting manner).

D has a much harder case to make in response to the charge of conspiracy (an agreement between two or more persons to commit a crime). The facts indicate that the day after D's first conversation with S (in which he "half-jested" that S "take care" of J), S told D about his plan to have A break into J's store and pour syrup over J's merchandise. D's response was, "Sounds great, but don't ask me to do anything to help." S replied, "All you have to do is sit back and let it happen."

In a conspiracy, it is sufficient if each party, by her actions alone, makes it clear to the other(s) that they will pursue a common goal. The prosecution probably could argue successfully that, once D learned of the plan, his words, "Sounds great," coupled with his decision to "let [the plan] happen" indicated that D and S did share a common goal—ruining J's business. This conclusion is bolstered by the fact that D is a competitor of J, because he has a "stake in the action." If D were simply a stranger to whom S had confided his intention, D's mere knowledge that S was going to commit a crime would not inexorably make him a co-conspirator with S and, hence, not make him responsible for S's subsequent acts.

If this case arose in a jurisdiction that required not only that an agreement be made but also that an overt act be committed, D could argue that he committed no overt act. While S's solicitation of A to commit the crime certainly could be considered an overt act, that took place before D's agreement had been secured. However, the prosecution probably would argue successfully that D's conscious decision to let the plan move forward, together with the facts that S pointed out J's building to A and A moved ahead with the plan (albeit not in the manner anticipated), constituted the necessary overt act. *Any* act committed in furtherance of the conspiracy will suffice as the overt act, and the courts do not require each conspirator to commit an overt act. Rather, the overt act of any individual conspirator will be deemed an act by all conspirators. Last, the prosecutors could argue that if D had not intended for S to ruin J's merchandise, he would have made his objections clear and stopped any further steps in that direction.

CRIMES OF ACE (A)

A may seek to argue diminished capacity, a doctrine recognized by many, but certainly not all, states. This contention requires that A show a mental disease or defect that rendered him unable to form the requisite intent for the crime. The diminished-capacity claim, however, can only lie when the defendant is charged with a "specific intent" offense. Moreover, the claim, which negates wrongdoing entirely, must be distinguished from "diminished responsibility," rarely invoked in the United States, but often referred to in England, which is a form of excuse. Finally, diminished capacity differs from insanity, which requires "total lack of" capacity, rather than "diminished capacity." A person found not guilty of a specific-intent crime due to diminished capacity is exonerated and free; a person found not guilty by reason of insanity, however, is committed, at least for some diagnostic period, after acquittal.

Answer to Question 5

Section 101

No one here committed the *actus reus* for possession or distribution. But Bill and Helen each believed the powder was ecstasy. Under the common law, a claim that the facts were such that the defendant could not commit the crime often meant he could not be guilty of attempting the crime either (factual impossibility). Recent decisions, as well as the Model Penal Code, §5.01, reject this view. Thus, Bill and Helen have attempted to possess or distribute ecstasy. Moreover, because Helen agreed to purchase the drug, and Bill agreed to sell it to her, it appears that they have committed conspiracy to distribute the drug to Helen. A conspiracy consists of (1) an agreement to (2) commit a crime (3) for which an overt act has been taken. It is a specific-intent crime, which is sometimes punished more severely than the target crime itself. Moreover, under the common law, conspiracy does not "merge" with the completed crime—the defendant may be liable for both the conspiracy and the crime. Conspirators are generally held liable only for crimes that they "intend" or "purpose" to happen, but, in some jurisdictions, following ***Pinkerton v. U.S.***, 328 U.S. 640 (1946), they can be held responsible for any acts committed by their co-conspirators that are (1) reasonably foreseeable and (2) in furtherance of the conspiracy. A conspirator is liable for the target crime, unless he "withdraws" by telling ***all*** the co-conspirators he is no longer supporting them. He will still be responsible for the conspiracy. The MPC rejects *Pinkerton* and holds the conspirators responsible only for crimes they intended to encourage. Under §5.03(b) of the MPC, a defendant can avoid liability for the conspiracy if he "thwarts" the target crime. Under the MPC, defendants cannot be punished separately for the conspiracy and the completed crime. However, in some jurisdictions, if the crime requires two people before it can be committed (bribery, sexual offenses), under the so-called "Wharton's rule," there can be no conspiracy if only two people are involved. ***If*** this occurs in such a jurisdiction, can the two of them be involved in a conspiracy with Grace to ***distribute*** the drug? No. Grace had no *mens rea* that the distribution of ecstasy occurred. Thus, she is not a conspirator, and the two "co-conspirators" are off the hook for ***that*** distribution. The charge will then have to be that Bill and Helen conspired to distribute the ecstasy to Dick, rather than to Helen. Failing that, Bill and Helen have conspired that Helen ***possess*** the drug. That offense does not necessitate two persons, and Wharton's rule does not apply. The MPC does not recognize Wharton's rule, and Helen and Bill are conspirators.

Grace is not an attemptor—she knew this was not the proscribed drug.

Section 102

Dick will claim that, although he discharged the gun, he did so while intoxicated. In most jurisdictions, this claim is relevant for specific-intent crimes. "Purposeful" or "knowingly" offenses are deemed to require specific intent. But Dick did "recklessly" cause the gun to "be discharged," and because that offense is a general-intent crime, his voluntary intoxication is not a relevant claim to that crime. Dick, however, will argue it was not the liquor, but the sea salt, that "intoxicated" him and that to that extent his intoxication was involuntary. Whether that claim is sustainable is unclear: a person who knows he is imbibing liquor cannot claim that he didn't realize he was not able to "hold his liquor." Here, however, Dick did not know that he was imbibing any amount of sea salt. His reaction, therefore, may be seen as involuntary, in which case he has a defensive claim even to the "recklessness" count. Essentially, Dick will argue that he was not intoxicated at all by the scotch — he would have been equally affected by sea salt in cola.

Dick's insanity claim will fail. Under the *McNaghten* test, which is the dominant standard in the United States today, a defendant is insane if he suffered from a mental disease or defect that caused him not to (1) know the nature and quality of his act or (2) know that the act was "wrong." Some states have supplemented this standard with a "volitional" test, sometimes referred to as the "irresistible impulse" test, which essentially provides that if the defendant, again because of mental disease or defect, could not stop himself from committing what he knew was "wrong," he should be deemed "temporarily insane." In response to criticisms of these tests, §4.01 of the Model Penal Code asks whether the defendant lacked "substantial capacity" to (1) appreciate (2) the criminality (wrongfulness) of his act or (3) to conform his conduct to the law. Even if the psychiatrist is allowed to testify, Dick did not have a "mental disease."

Sexual crimes

Helen may be charged with attempted rape of Dick. The common law defined rape as the penetration by a male of the vulva of a female (not his wife) against her consent and by force. If the female did not resist "to her utmost," it was not rape. Recent changes in sexual assault law include the following: (1) the crime is now labeled "sexual battery" or "sexual assault," rather than "rape"; (2) a spouse can rape the other spouse; (3) the offense is no longer restricted to males — females can sexually assault males; (4) other forms of sexual relations besides vaginal intercourse may be included; (5) there is no requirement that resistance be "to the utmost"; and (6) other, nonforcible nonconsensual intercourse may be included. Additionally, the procedures at trial have been significantly altered (e.g., there is now no requirement that the victim's claim be corroborated by a witness to the attack, there are "rape shield" laws that prohibit, or restrict, cross-examining the victim on the basis of prior sexual conduct, etc.). Thus, a modern court would not preclude the possibility of rape by Helen. But Helen may argue that she could not factually complete the crime of sexual assault because Dick was not, in fact, affected by the (nonexistent) ecstasy. Helen's claim here—that it was factually impossible for the defendant to commit rape—will fall on deaf ears. Most courts now hold that neither factual nor legal impossibility is a defense to a charge of attempt. The final question, then, is whether Helen has "attempted" "sexual assault." And, once more, the answer is likely to depend on whether the jurisdiction follows the old common law approach or the "new" common law. Under the old common law, a defendant had attempted a crime only if she had gone very far down the road toward achieving it—early steps were deemed "mere preparation." There were many tests that articulated this approach, among them (1) the "probable desistance" test, (2) the dangerously proximate test, (3) the physically proximate test, (4) the last proximate act test, (5) the *res ipsa loquitur* test, (6) the indispensable element test, and (7) the abnormal step test. No matter which test is applied to Helen, she is still very far away from any sexual contact with Dick, much less intercourse. Modern attempt law, however, spurred by the Model Penal Code, focuses not on what the defendant has left to do, but how much the defendant has done—in the words of the MPC itself, whether the defendant has taken a "substantial step" that is "strongly corroborative" of the defendant's ultimate criminal goal. She has—and she's guilty.

Al Maliki's death

Let's begin with Dick. Murder was defined in English common law as a killing with "malice aforethought." The term clearly included intent to kill or intent to commit grievous bodily harm ("express malice"); courts struggled for several centuries to explain what the term meant if the death was unintended ("implied malice"). They often used metaphors such as "depraved heart" or "malignant mind" to capture what the term meant. All murders were capitally eligible in England. In the United States, murder was divided by many state legislatures into two degrees: (1) second degree, which is a lesser included offense of first-degree murder and included all malice-aforethought killings, and (2) first degree, which, in addition to malice aforethought, also required that the killing be done with "premeditation, deliberation, and willfulness." In most states, only first-degree murders were capitally eligible. Although the legislature clearly meant to limit the number of death-eligible murders by the premeditation formula, the courts quickly interpreted the phrase potentially to include anyone who killed: defendants could "premeditate" in the space of five seconds. Dick's intent to kill Helen "transfers" to Al; therefore, he's guilty of homicide. Beyond his claims of intoxication or insanity discussed above, he may claim that he didn't know he was killing a human being, but the "devil incarnate." Short of an insanity plea, however, Dick's claim of mistake of fact is going to be judged on whether it was reasonable or not — and if we ignore Dick's allergic reaction to the sea salt, it is clear that his mistake was unreasonable. He's on the hook for homicide. But at what level? Again, as discussed above, Dick may not have been able to premeditate (and, therefore, commit first-degree murder). For second-degree murder, however, all the prosecution need show is a "depraved heart." Shooting at another human being (remember that Dick's mistake as to the nature of his target is not relevant here) shows a depraved heart, and it is clear that he intended to kill the object at which he shot. Dick is guilty of second-degree murder.

Helen's liability is less clear. She clearly "caused" Dick's acts. And if Dick's reaction had been to the scotch, she might be seen as the "proximate cause" of his acts, because one never knows how another will react to liquor. But Dick's reaction to the sea salt was totally unforeseeable. She can't be said to be reckless or even criminally negligent here. However, that's not the end of the discussion. We have seen that Helen and Bill conspired to distribute ecstasy and that Helen (at least) attempted to distribute it as well. Both these crimes are felonies. Under the original common law, any death that occurred while a defendant was engaged in a felony was murder (and capitally eligible). Today, legislatures typically restrict capitally eligible deaths to those that occur during statutorily articulated "predicate" felonies. These are "first degree" felony murders; all other deaths are "second degree" (not capitally punishable) felony murders. Most state courts have further restricted second-degree felony murders to those that occur during felonies that are "inherently dangerous." The courts are divided on whether that test should apply to the felony "in the abstract" (the way that felony is "typically" committed) or "as perpetrated" (the way in which the felony was committed in this situation). But the conspiracy has already occurred (when the agreement did), and the two never achieved the target crime. Helen's attempt to distribute, however, may be seen to be "continuing," because the effect of the sea salt on Dick was still going on when he fired the gun. If that is accepted, her attempt is still ongoing when Al is killed, and there is a predicate for a felony-murder charge. Now Helen will have to argue that (1) the attempted distribution was complete before the killing occurred, (2) distribution of ecstasy is not a felony "inherently dangerous in the abstract," and (3) the killing was in no way "in furtherance of" the felony of attempted distribution of ecstasy.

Grace is not responsible for Al's death, even though she is clearly a "but for" cause. As discussed above with Helen and Bill, Dick's reaction to the sea salt is simply too tenuous and unforeseeable, and, unlike Helen, Grace never conspired or attempted to distribute ecstasy. Nor is she an accomplice to the crime of attempting to distribute ecstasy because the common law requires that an accomplice have the purpose that the crime occur (sometimes summarized as "having a stake in the action") and that was not her purpose.

Answer to Question 6

CRIMINAL RESPONSIBILTY OF A, B, AND C FOR THE OFFICE BUILDING INCIDENT

Conspiracy

The prosecution could charge A and B with conspiracy to commit burglary and larceny. The crime of conspiracy occurs where there is an agreement between two or more persons to commit a crime. A and B might contend that, while B advised A where a copy of the manuscript was located, they never specifically agreed to take it (i.e., perhaps B simply informed A where the manuscript could be found as a means of expressing his astonishment about the lack of security involving an important manuscript). However, the prosecution probably could argue in rebuttal that, because (1) A and B had discussed how lucrative the sale of excerpts from the manuscript would be, (2) B had described in detail the manuscript's location, (3) B was apparently not surprised when A returned to C's apartment with a copy of the manuscript, and (4) B (together with A) hid when the police arrived at C's apartment, there was sufficient evidence for a jury to infer that a tacit understanding existed between A and B to remove the copy of the manuscript from B's office building.

Burglary/larceny

At common law, the crime of burglary occurred where the defendant, in a trespassory manner, broke and entered into the dwelling of another, at night, for the purpose of committing a felony therein. Presently, however, many states have deleted the nighttime element and have extended the crime to (1) any structure and (2) situations where a theft offense (not necessarily a felony) was intended within the building. Assuming this to be such a state, the prosecution could contend that a breaking occurred when A moved the side door and that she intended to commit a larceny when she entered the structure (as evidenced by the fact that she removed a copy of the manuscript).

Larceny is the trespassory taking and carrying away of the tangible personal property of another with the intent to permanently deprive the owner thereof. A and B could contend that, while they intended to take the manuscript, they did not intend to commit a larceny because (1) no "tangible" personal property was involved, and (2) there was no "deprivation" of property (i.e., the manuscript) because presumably the publishing entity still had the original manuscript or other copies. The prosecution could argue in rebuttal that (1) the manuscript, itself, is tangible personal property, as is the copyright owned in the manuscript's contents, and (2) A and B intended to permanently deprive the publishing company of that copy of the manuscript. Additionally, because A and B probably intended to sell excerpts of it to other publishing entities, there was an intent to appropriate much of the manuscript's value. Although a close question, A and B could probably be successfully prosecuted for both burglary and larceny.

Culpability of C

Under the traditional common law party rules, an accessory after the fact (one who knowingly assists a felon in avoiding arrest or prosecution with the intent or desire to do so) was culpable for the crimes committed by the felon. Today, however, most jurisdictions instead recognize a distinct and separate crime for this type of conduct (usually called "accessory after the fact" or "obstructing justice"). Because the elements of this offense appear to be satisfied (A and B had advised C about what they had done, and C obviously desired that they avoid arrest as evidenced by his untruthful statement to the police that no one else was with him), C could probably be successfully prosecuted for being an accessory after the fact.

CRIMINAL RESPONSIBILITY OF A AND B FOR D'S DEATH

Crimes of B

B would probably have no responsibility for D's death, because A's decision to stab D seems to have been undertaken independently. Furthermore, there is nothing to suggest that A's action was in any way a foreseeable consequence of the conspiracy to steal the manuscript. Thus, B would not be subject to liability as a co-conspirator under these facts.

Crimes of A

A, however, could be charged with murder. A murder occurs where the defendant has committed a homicide (the killing of one human being by another) with malice aforethought (the intent to cause the victim serious bodily harm or death or wanton disregard of the high likelihood of death). The facts are unclear as to whether A had become intoxicated prior to the stabbing incident (the facts state only that A had struck up a conversation with the bartender). If she were intoxicated, she would have a defense to any crime requiring a specific intent (such as first-degree murder), but would still be liable for second-degree murder. If, however, A was not intoxicated, she cannot successfully contend that she lacked the ability to form the specific intent to kill or seriously injure D. Because A appears to have acted spontaneously when she saw several persons attack her friend B, A did not seem to premeditate and deliberate the stabbing. Thus, A would probably be charged with second-degree murder.

A could contend in rebuttal, however, that her actions were justified under the privilege of defense of others (where a person reasonably believes that another is about to cause death or serious injury to a third party, she can exercise force capable of causing death or serious bodily injury to the aggressor). Whether A's actions would come within this privilege would depend on whether she reasonably believed that D and his friends were about to kill or seriously injure B. The facts are silent as to the relative physical sizes of all those involved, whether D and his friends significantly outnumbered A and B, and precisely what D and his friends were doing to B when A stabbed D. (Were they kicking and punching B or merely pushing or slapping him?) Assuming, however, that A reasonably believed that D and his friends were about to seriously injure or kill B, that the degree of force was reasonably necessary to prevent the harm, and that B would have the right to use the same amount of force in his own defense, A would probably have a valid defense to the murder charge. Depending on the jurisdiction, if A's belief was unreasonable, either she would entirely lose the defense-of-others claim and, thus, be guilty of murder, or she would be found guilty of manslaughter.

Moreover, even in a jurisdiction that would preclude any mitigation if her belief were to be found unreasonable, and A's conduct was not justifiable under the circumstances, her homicide charge probably would still be reduced to voluntary manslaughter because she acted in the heat of passion in response to sufficient provocation (i.e., provocation sufficient to cause a reasonable person to lose self-control). A could argue that watching several persons attack her best friend was sufficient provocation. Thus, if the assertion of the privilege described above were *not* successful, A probably would be convicted of voluntary manslaughter only.

CRIMINAL RESPONSIBILITY OF A AND P FOR W'S DEATH

Criminal responsibility of A

The prosecution could contend that A is guilty of second-degree murder of W, if one assumes that A's stabbing of D was *not* privileged, under the felony-murder rule (where a homicide occurs in the course and as a consequence of the defendant's participation in an independent, inherently dangerous felony, the defendant is held liable even though she did not intend or desire the victim's death). There are two potential "dangerous felonies" that might be involved. First, if A does not have a full justification, as discussed above, she might still be "escaping" a homicide. Second, even if the homicide is "complete" before A begins speeding, her driving might be so outrageous as to qualify for a "reckless driving" felony charge. The remaining question, then, will be whether the jurisdiction's felony-murder rule looks at the underlying felony "in the abstract" or "as perpetrated." A has a better chance of avoiding the felony-murder rule if the jurisdiction uses the former, rather than the latter, approach. In the alternative, A could be charged with second-degree murder for causing W's homicide with a wanton *mens rea*. (While a few jurisdictions do not apply the felony-murder rule to situations where someone other than the felon directly committed the homicide, we'll assume that this state is **not** among them.)

A could contend that the felony-murder rule is not applicable because (1) she was not in the process of committing a felony (D's murder had occurred before the incident that caused W's death), and (2) P's reckless conduct in shooting A's tire was an unforeseeable, intervening act that extinguished the proximate causation between A's felonious behavior in the tavern and W's death. The prosecution probably could argue successfully in rebuttal that (1) immediate flight—here, attempting a high-speed escape—is within the commission of the felony, and (2) P's conduct was not "unforeseeable" because a person driving at 80 mph to escape a police officer should recognize that the officer might attempt to use deadly force in overtaking her. Thus, *if* A's murder of D was not privileged (i.e., A was engaged in a felony), she would probably be culpable of second-degree murder under the felony-murder rule.

Even if A's conduct with respect to D was justified, the prosecution could still contend that A acted with a wanton *mens rea* (consciously disregarded a risk that posed a high probability of death or serious bodily injury to others) by driving at 80 mph when P sought to stop her. A again could argue in rebuttal that (1) her conduct was not the proximate cause of W's death, and, alternatively, (2) her conduct was at most reckless (i.e., she engaged in conduct that created a substantial and unjustifiable risk of death or serious bodily injury). Therefore, she could be found culpable of no offense greater than involuntary manslaughter. The prosecution again would contend in rebuttal that (1) P's conduct was not a superseding cause of W's death, and (2) traveling at 80 mph through (presumably) city streets (where the speed limit is usually 35 mph) created a substantial and unjustifiable risk that her car could spin out of control and kill an innocent bystander. Because

A's conduct would probably be characterized as wanton, a second-degree murder conviction appears appropriate.

Criminal responsibility of P

Officer P could be charged with (1) second-degree murder for acting wantonly in shooting at A's tires while engaged in a high-speed chase on (presumably) city streets or, alternatively, (2) involuntary manslaughter if her conduct could be characterized as reckless.

P might argue in rebuttal that if someone is engaged in a dangerous felony, an officer ordinarily is privileged to exercise whatever force (including that capable of causing death or serious bodily injury) she reasonably believes is necessary to effectuate an arrest. Perhaps P would argue that traveling at 80 mph on city streets constitutes a type of dangerous felonious activity (i.e., reckless endangerment, etc.). But the prosecution would respond that deadly force cannot be used against a person who is fleeing arrest for a misdemeanor. Here, P did not know anything about the tavern incident; she began chasing A for ignoring a stop sign (at that point, A was not driving 80 mph on city streets). Thus, P could not successfully assert the law officer's arrest privilege and would be liable for manslaughter.

Assuming P's assertion of the foregoing privilege was not successful, she could contend that, at most, her conduct was negligent (i.e., she failed to act reasonably under the circumstances) because she had to weigh the risk of the escape of a potentially dangerous individual (one who would speed away from a police officer at 80 mph) against the possibility that her efforts to stop the speeding vehicle could result in death or serious injury to innocent bystanders. It is doubtful that P's argument will be persuasive, and, therefore, a successful criminal prosecution against P is likely. Because of the danger involved, many cities in recent years have issued instructions to police not to engage in high-speed car chases in any situation, or at least not unless they know that the suspect has committed a violent, personal crime.

Answer to Question 7

Did Brody (B) and Cole (C) commit a burglary?

At common law, a burglary was the trespassory breaking and entering into the dwelling of another, at night, with the intent to commit a felony therein. Assume, however, that this jurisdiction has extended the crime to (1) cover any structure, (2) include theft offenses within the structure that are not felonies, and (3) not require the incident to have occurred at night. The State might charge B and C with burglary by entering the market and committing a larceny (the trespassory taking and carrying away of another's tangible personal property with the intent to permanently deprive the latter of such property) therein by departing from the store with whiskey C did not pay for.

B and C could contend, however, that the entrance into the store was not "trespassory" because it was open to the public. In addition, each of them might contend that he did not have the intent to commit a larceny when he entered the store because, as a consequence of having been drinking for several hours, he did not have the ability to form such an intent. C might argue, further, that the thought of taking the bottle without paying for it did not occur to him until Brody (B) unexpectedly drew the revolver. The State probably would argue in rebuttal that (1) the entrance into the store was "trespassory" because the owner's consent did not extend to persons entering the structure for the purpose of stealing items; (2) neither B's nor C's actions were those of an intoxicated person, and, therefore, drunkenness did not prevent them from forming the intent required for burglary; and (3) because each entered the store knowing that he had no money, he must have formed the intent to steal the liquor prior to actually entering the building. Even assuming the entrance was "trespassory," mere presence is not enough, and the State would have a difficult time proving that B or C intended to commit a larceny within the structure. C could, of course, assert that he presumed that B, alone, would steal the liquor. But because C picked up the bottle, this argument might prove unavailing. Their best argument is that they formed the intent after entering the store; if so, it is unlikely that either B or C could be successfully prosecuted for burglary.

Vicarious culpability

If B were successfully prosecuted for burglary, the State could assert that C was vicariously culpable as (1) an aider and abettor or (2) a co-conspirator.

The State might contend that C aided and abetted B in the commission of the burglary by accompanying B into the market with the intent to assist in the larceny of the whiskey. However, absent a belief by B that C would actually assist him in stealing the liquor if necessary, this assertion would probably **not** be successful. Thus, C is **not** vicariously culpable for B's burglary (if, in fact, B committed burglary).

A conspiracy arises where there is an agreement between two or more persons to commit a crime. C could contend that no agreement was ever formed with B to steal the whiskey. The State could argue in rebuttal that, because B and C entered the store without money, there must have been at least an implicit understanding that they would steal the liquor. However, without additional evidence of an understanding between B and C, this assertion by the State probably would **not** be successful.

Is C culpable for robbery?

A robbery occurs where the defendant by force, or the threat of force, in the presence of the victim, commits a larceny. B, therefore, is clearly guilty of robbery. Because an aider and abettor is culpable for the crimes of the original perpetrator, the State could contend that C aided and abetted B's robbery by running from the market with the whiskey bottle. C might contend that the "trespassory taking" element of larceny is absent because C had, with the clerk's acquiescence, already picked up the whiskey bottle when B suddenly drew the gun. However, the State probably would contend successfully in rebuttal that a "trespassory taking" did occur because the clerk obviously assumed that the whiskey would be paid for prior to being removed from the store.

C also would argue that he could not form the specific intention necessary to be an aider and abettor because of his prior drinking and that he had lost his ability to function effectively. The State, however, would point out that C had engaged in a gun battle with the police, which might well show capacity, including specific capacity. The State would probably be successful with respect to this issue, too. Thus, C probably could be convicted of robbery.

Is Ames (A) culpable for any crimes of B and C?

Because there is nothing to indicate that A entered into any type of agreement with B and C to steal the whiskey or that A knew that neither B nor C had any money when they entered the market, it is unlikely that A could be culpable for B's and C's crimes as a co-conspirator.

However, the State could assert that, because a crime is not deemed to be complete until the perpetrators have reached a "safe haven," A is culpable for B and C's robbery as an aider and abettor. The State would argue that A assisted B and C in the commission of the robbery by driving the getaway car with the intent to help B and C reach safety.

A could argue in rebuttal, however, that he was not an aider and abettor because (1) he was too intoxicated to formulate the intent to assist B and C in their robbery; (2) not having witnessed or been specifically told by B or C that they committed a robbery, A was not even aware that B and C had actually engaged in criminal conduct; and (3) he acted under duress in helping B and C because B (who was holding a gun) ordered A to drive away. Although A probably did realize that B and C had committed a robbery, it is *not* likely that the State could prove beyond a reasonable doubt that A actually desired to assist B and C in their getaway. Thus, A would probably *not* be culpable for the robbery.

Is C vicariously culpable for Officer Smith's murder?
The discussion about C's culpability must begin with an analysis of whether B could have been successfully prosecuted for first-degree murder had he lived.

Did B commit a murder?
The State could probably contend that B acted with malice aforethought because he (1) deliberately intended to take Smith's (S) life (B shot at S, and a jury may (but need not) infer that a party intended the natural consequences of his actions) or (2) was engaged in an independent, inherently dangerous felony (robbery). A and C could argue in rebuttal that, because of B's earlier drinking, (1) B could not have formed the "deliberate intent" to take another's life, and (2) B did not possess the intent required for robbery. According to the murder statute in the jurisdiction, malice aforethought is present "when there is manifested a deliberate unlawful intent to take the life of a fellow human being." The State's argument — that when B shot at Officers S and Jones (J), killing S, he manifested the requisite deliberate intent to take S's life — probably would prevail because of the presence of mind inherent in B's actions. However, B would point out that the statute requires not merely "intent," but "deliberate" intent to kill, thus paralleling the language of first-degree murder statutes in other states. If so, the State must prove more than "mere" intent. This argument is less

persuasive here than it might otherwise be, because the State also has a first-degree murder statute that uses the same term ("deliberate").

The claim that B was too intoxicated to form the specific intent required for robbery probably would be answered by the State in a similar fashion. Nothing in B's conduct indicated that he was unable to function coherently (i.e., after realizing that neither B nor C had any money, B pointed a gun at the liquor store clerk). Thus, the State would probably be successful on the felony-murder charge even if it did not prevail on the malice-aforethought issue.

Did B commit first-degree murder for which C is liable?

The statute in the jurisdiction defines first-degree murder as "all murder that is perpetrated by any kind of willful, deliberate, and premeditated killing or that is committed in the perpetration of, or in the attempt to perpetrate, robbery or burglary. . . ." Even though the State could argue willfulness and deliberate intent, it does not appear from the facts that B premeditated killing S, because he was involved in a spontaneous gun battle. Consequently, the State would argue that the killing was committed in the perpetration of the robbery. Because a crime is not considered "ended" until the perpetrators have reached safety, it appears that the State would prevail on this issue, too, and B would have been successfully prosecuted for first-degree murder.

Although C did not actually shoot anyone during the gun battle, shooting at the officers probably would constitute assistance to B. Because an aider and abettor is culpable for the perpetration of the crime in which he assisted and for any crimes that were a reasonably foreseeable outgrowth of the one in which he assisted, the State could probably also successfully prosecute C for first-degree murder.

Is A vicariously culpable for Officer S's murder?

In the unlikely event that A was deemed to be an aider and abettor of B and C, A could argue that he withdrew his assistance prior to Officer S's murder. However, for a withdrawal to be effective, it must ordinarily be done voluntarily and communicated to all of the other participants. Because A's purported withdrawal was not voluntary (A presumably fled to avoid arrest), and no effort was made to communicate his withdrawal to B and C, A's assertion of this theory would probably **not** be successful.

Are A and C liable for B's death?

Great controversy surrounds the question as to whether a felon can be held criminally liable for his co-felon's death. Some states preclude liability entirely. Others ask whether the shooting was justified; if so, then the co-felon is not held responsible. Because Jones's shooting of B was clearly justified, A and C would not be held liable. If, however, the killing is merely excused (or not excused), some states will hold A and C liable. Thus, if either of them had accidentally killed B, both might be found liable, in some states, for B's death. There is yet another issue—some states will not hold a co-felon responsible for a death during a felony unless the death is "in furtherance of" the felony. Clearly, B's death would not meet that requirement.

Answer to Question 8

WHO, IF ANYONE, HAS VIOLATED SECTION 101?

Dan has clearly "knowingly" removed the stone. The question is whether his mistake of law, engendered by his reliance on Hermione's advice, would be relevant. Under the common law, the answer is clear—no. No mistake of law, no matter how reasonable, would be an excuse. Under §2.04(3) of the Model Penal Code, however, reasonable reliance on "official interpretation" by someone charged with the interpretation, enforcement, or administration of the statute in question is a defense. Unhappily for Dan, most courts have read those provisions narrowly and required (1) a written opinion, (2) signed by a person in direct authority, (3) specifying the facts on which the opinion is based. Dan doesn't meet those criteria.

What about Hermione? She is clearly a "but for" cause of Dan's criminal act. But she did not know that her advice was erroneous and, therefore, cannot be an "accomplice" to Dan's act. Only persons who have the purpose that the crime occur are accomplices, and she clearly did not have that intent or purpose.

WHO, IF ANYONE, HAS VIOLATED SECTION 102?

Dan

Dan has clearly "destroyed" the artifact. But he has made two mistakes here, either of which could be characterized as a mistake of fact or a mistake of law. First, he does not know that he is on federal land. This could be seen as a mistake of fact ("Where am I?") or a mistake of law ("Is this land on which I stand legally federal?"). As noted above, mistakes of law were irrelevant under the common law, but reasonable mistakes of fact could be relevant to guilt of a general-intent crime. Here, Dan's mistake was reasonable. However, Dan's mistake is relevant only if he has to *know* that he's on federal land. Under the common law, such knowledge is almost certainly not required. Under the Model Penal Code, the first question is whether "knowingly" modifies "federal land." There are two arguments that it does not. First, the federal status of the land might not be a "material element" of the statute. Under §2.0 of the Model Penal Code, *mens rea* words only apply to "material elements of the offense." Under §1.13 of the code, only those elements that are not "related exclusively to . . . jurisdiction" are material elements. If "federal land" is exclusively jurisdiction, then the prosecutor need not prove *any* mental state with regard to the status of the land. Second, even if "federal land" is a material element, and *some mens rea* word applies under §2.02, it is not clear which word applies. The statute does not use "knowingly" until after the phrase "federal land," but under §2.02(4), a declared mental state, such as "knowingly,"applies to all material elements in a statute **unless** a contrary purpose "plainly appears." The prosecutor might argue that by placing the term "knowingly" where it did, the legislature "plainly" indicated a judgment that the term **not** modify"federal land." If that view were accepted, §2.02(3) would apply, and Dan could be convicted if the prosecutor could show that he was **reckless** as to whether he was on federal land. The facts state that Dan "unknowingly" crossed into the park. But a jury might well find that if your hotel is on the edge of a national park, you have "consciously disregarded" the risk that you've crossed the border.

Dan's second mistake is as to the nature of the "rock" that he threw (and destroyed). It is, **as a matter of law**, an "archeological artifact." As discussed above, if this is a question of law, Dan has no defense under the common law. Under the Model Penal Code, he relied on no one and cannot, therefore, take advantage of §2.04(3). If, on the other hand, the nature of the stone is viewed as factual, and not legal, his failure to know (or even suspect) that the item was an "artifact" would certainly be reasonable—and reasonable mistakes are recognized defenses.

However, there is a third issue—can this statute be interpreted as imposing strict criminal liability? Again, there is a difference between the common law and the MPC. Under the latter, a statute cannot be construed as imposing strict criminal liability if there is a possibility of one day's imprisonment. Thus, Dan is not guilty. Under the common law, however, the line is not so clear; some courts have allowed strict criminal liability even where the penalty is very severe. Strict criminal liability offenses—where the government need not prove any **mens rea**, including mere tort negligence, with regard to one or more elements of the crime—have been variously characterized. Initially, they appeared mostly in statutes regulating sexual conduct, foodstuffs, and alcohol or protecting minors. In the 20th century, this group was expanded to include "police" or "regulatory" offenses. The courts have permitted strict liability to crimes that have small punishments and carry minimum stigmatization. Some states have imposed strict liability even where the penalty is severe. Recently, the U.S. Supreme Court declined to hold that a ten-year prison sentence would automatically lead the Court to interpret the offense as a non-strict-liability one. However, in that same decision, the Court defined "public welfare offenses" in which strict liability was permissible as those involving (1) dangerous items (2) that the defendant should expect to be highly regulated.

Dan, of course, will claim that he did not "damage" the artifact with any mental state at all. Moreover, even if he did, he has a claim of self-defense. A defendant acts in self-defense if (1) he acts in response to a threat of personal bodily harm, (2) the harm is imminent, and (3) the defendant was not the original aggressor. The force used must be proportionate—one cannot use deadly force to avoid a slap. In a majority of jurisdictions, the defendant must also have no alternative avenues (no ability to retreat) or be in a place where there is no duty to retreat (such as a home or office). If the defendant is mistaken about any of these requirements, he still has the claim if the mistake is reasonable. In some states, if the mistake is unreasonable, he loses the claim entirely and is guilty of murder; in the majority of states, if the mistake is unreasonable, but honestly held, the defendant is guilty of manslaughter rather than murder. In this instance, Dan used nondeadly force to repel what he believed to be a threat of serious bodily harm or death. Therefore, there's no problem with the amount of force he used. Unfortunately, because Fred was not actually going to use deadly force, Dan did use more force than "necessary." This is not a problem, however—the common law has allowed persons to use force when it seems "reasonably" necessary, even if it turns out that there was no actual necessity. Dan's off the hook.

Fred

Fred has arguably "caused" Dan to throw the "rock" and, hence, is liable under the statute as well, if it is interpreted as imposing strict liability with regard to the nature of the item destroyed. If the statute requires any *mens rea* at all with regard to his "causation," it is unlikely that Fred was even negligent (much less reckless or higher) with regard to the possibility that Dan would throw anything at him.

WHO, IF ANYONE, IS CRIMINALLY LIABLE FOR ANSEL'S DEATH?

As discussed above, even if Dan is not justified in "damaging" the rock, he may legitimately claim that the throwing of the rock was self-defense against Fred. That the result was injury to Ansel rather than Fred does not undermine Dan's self-defense claim.

Fred, on the other hand, can neither claim self-defense himself nor piggyback onto Dan's claim. Fred has "caused" a situation that has resulted in death. Murder was defined in English common law as a killing with "malice aforethought." The term clearly included intent to kill or intent to commit grievous bodily harm ("express malice"); courts struggled for several centuries to explain what the term meant if the death was unintended ("implied malice"). They often used metaphors such as "depraved heart" or "malignant mind" to capture what the term meant. All murders were capitally eligible in England. In the United States, murder was divided by many state legislatures into two degrees: (1) second degree, which was a lesser included offense of first-degree murder and included all malice-aforethought killings, and (2) first degree, which, in addition to malice aforethought, also required that the killing be done with "premeditation, deliberation, and willfulness." In most states, only first-degree murders were capitally eligible. Although the legislature clearly meant to limit the number of death-eligible murders by the premeditation formula, the courts quickly interpreted the phrase potentially to include anyone who killed: defendants could "premeditate" in the space of five seconds. Because the death was not premeditated, it is not first-degree murder. Nor can Fred's practical joke be said to reflect a "depraved heart" (unless, for example, he knew that Dan had a heart condition, and risked the possibility of a heart attack). Even if Fred's actions are "wrong," it is unlikely that they are "criminally negligent," because that requires the defendant to act without being aware of a risk (in this case of death) that most people would see. Practical jokes may be disarming—but they are rarely deadly.

Answer to Question 9

Dr. Jones (J) could be charged with the crime of murder.

Did J have a duty to perform the operation?

Where a defendant is charged with a crime based on his inaction, he must have first had a duty to undertake the conduct in question. A person is under a duty to act where he (1) is contractually obligated to perform the act in question or (2) has commenced to act and subsequently leaves the victim in a worse position as a result of such intervention. J could contend that (1) nothing was said as to payment for the operation so consideration was lacking, and (2) because he never boarded the plane to perform the operation, it cannot be contended that he "commenced to act." However, the prosecution could contend successfully in rebuttal that (1) an implied-in-fact contract arose, whereby J would receive his normal and usual fee for such an operation, and (2) because J had assured the governmental officials that he would perform the operation, they probably ceased their search for another physician to perform it. The State still might be required, however, to show that J would anticipate that the search would be called off. If so, J probably had a duty to perform the operation.

Was J's failure to perform the operation the actual cause of the victim's death?

A defendant's failure to act must have been the "but for" cause of the victim's harm. J could contend that, even if he had boarded the plane on April 11, it is uncertain that the operation could have been performed successfully (especially in light of J's agitated condition resulting from his son's death). However, the prosecution could argue in rebuttal that, because J had perfected the technique involved and the operation was a routine one for him, it could be established beyond a reasonable doubt that J would have been able to perform it successfully. (Assuming J had a history of success with this type of operation, the prosecution should prevail on this issue.)

Was J's failure to act the proximate cause of the victim's death?

Where an unforeseeable cause or factor intervenes between the defendant's conduct and the victim's harm, the defendant's action (or nonaction) is **not** the proximate cause of the victim's misfortune. J could contend that, given his initial reluctance to perform the operation and his obviously agitated condition, the State Department was grossly negligent in not retaining a backup physician in the event J was unable to go through with the operation. However, the prosecution could contend in rebuttal that, at most, the State Department was merely negligent in assuming that J (a responsible surgeon) would abide by the promise he had given to them. Because mere negligence by an intervening entity ordinarily is deemed to be foreseeable, the prosecution should prevail.

Did J commit first-degree murder?

Assuming the *actus reus* portion is satisfied, J must have (1) intended to kill or seriously injure the patient **and** (2) acted with premeditation and deliberation to be culpable of first-degree murder. The prosecution would contend that, given the rule that a jury may infer that a defendant intended the natural consequences of his conduct, J intended the patient to die (or at least knew that her death was substantially certain to occur) because (1) J was told that the patient would die without the operation, (2) his absence was unexpected, and therefore, it was likely that a qualified doctor might not be present, and (3) J had stated "I hope the bastard dies." Additionally, because J had the entire evening to contemplate his conduct, his failure to board the plane was premeditated and deliberate. J could contend in rebuttal that he (1) reasonably assumed that the State Department would have another competent doctor available to perform the operation if he were unable to do so and (2) was too intoxicated (albeit voluntarily) to be able to form the specific intention necessary for first-degree murder. While the facts state that J was intoxicated, there is nothing to indicate that he failed to comprehend that the patient could die in his absence. Moreover, the jury might well find that J's words "if they can" suggest that he believed they could not find a replacement. Here, the nuance and intonation with which the words were spoken may well mean the difference between liability for murder and some other level of homicide (or exculpation). Assume, however, that J might be successful in his argument that the intoxication prevented him from forming the specific intention required for first-degree murder.

Did J commit second-degree murder or involuntary manslaughter?

Where a defendant had a wanton *mens rea* at the time of the homicide for which he is responsible, he is guilty of second-degree murder. An actor has a wanton state of mind where she consciously disregards a risk that she knew (or should have known) posed a high probability of death or serious injury to another human being. Voluntary intoxication is usually **not** a defense to a general-intent crime where the lack of awareness results from the intoxication. Therefore, the prosecution will contend alternatively that

J acted wantonly by becoming intoxicated the evening before he was to board a plane to perform a critical operation. J might argue in rebuttal that he did not act with a wanton *mens rea* because he reasonably presumed that (1) another doctor would be available to perform the operation, and (2) even if he did become intoxicated on the evening of April 10, he would have an entire day to recover because the operation was not to be performed until April 12. Furthermore, J will seek to characterize his *mens rea* as not wanton, but as no more than "reckless." However, the prosecution would probably prevail on this issue. Thus, J probably would be guilty of second-degree murder.

As a third alternative, the prosecution could contend that J is culpable of involuntary manslaughter. This crime arises where the death for which the defendant is responsible occurred while the latter had a reckless *mens rea* (i.e., the defendant acted in a manner that created a substantial risk of death or serious injury to other human beings). The factual arguments described above with respect to whether J acted wantonly would again apply.

If J avoided culpability for second-degree murder, he probably would be prosecuted successfully for involuntary manslaughter.

Mistake of fact
It should be noted that, even if the patient were the Russian general (rather than the wife of the prime minister of Canada), no defense to the crime charged would exist. Mistake of fact is only a defense where, were the facts as the defendant reasonably believed them to be, she would have possessed a defense to the crime charged. In this instance, because the Russian general would have been in the United States with the permission of the State Department, J would have had no justification to cause that person's death.

Culpability of J's friends
The crime of solicitation occurs where the defendant requests or encourages another to undertake a felony or misdemeanor involving a breach of the peace, with the intent to induce the latter to commit such crime. Where a solicitation has occurred, the soliciting party is vicariously culpable for the offense committed by the solicitee. The prosecution could contend that, because the group "encouraged" J not to help the patient, they had solicited the patient's death. However, the group could contend in rebuttal that they were too intoxicated to form the specific intention to induce J to commit the crime in question. Like J, the group may have assumed that

other competent physicians were available to perform the operation if J failed to meet the airplane that would arrive the very next day (because WalterReedHospital is in Washington, D.C., there would presumably be an abundance of capable medical personnel). Finally, the group's lack of desire to persuade J to commit a crime is demonstrated by the fact that at least one of the group urged J to inform the State Department of his decision not to perform the operation. It is, therefore, unlikely that the group could be prosecuted for J's crime.

Answer to Question 10

Crimes of Tom (T)

T could be charged with burglary, larceny, and second-degree murder.

At common law, a burglary occurred where the defendant had, in a trespassory manner, broken and entered into the dwelling of another, at night, with the intent to commit a felony therein. (Assume that this jurisdiction extends the crime to any structure and any theft offense.) While T might contend that no "breaking" occurred because entrance into the building was gained without the necessity of damaging it in any manner, the prosecution probably could argue successfully in rebuttal that this element is usually deemed to be satisfied when any portion of the structure is moved (i.e., opening the door to Xavier's (X's) premises).

There appears to be little question that T committed a larceny (the trespassory taking and carrying away of the personal property of another with the intent to permanently deprive the owner of such property) by placing X's jewelry in a bag and exiting the premises. Because the elements of larceny are subsumed within burglary, T would probably not be convicted for the larceny if the burglary charge were sustained. Indeed, the Double Jeopardy Clause would prohibit at least multiple punishment, if not multiple conviction, on these two charges.

T could also be charged with second-degree murder under the felony-murder rule. Under this doctrine, when the victim's death occurred during and as the result of the defendant's participation in an inherently dangerous felony, the defendant is deemed to have the *mens rea* for murder (regardless of whether the defendant intended or desired the victim's death). States differ on whether to assess the dangerousness of the felony "in the abstract" (i.e., given all the ways the crime *could* be committed) or "as perpetrated" (as it was actually committed in this case). The prosecution's assertion would be that T's burglary of X's store ultimately resulted in Cal's (C's) death. However, T probably could contend successfully in rebuttal that (1) no homicide (the killing of one human being by another) occurred because C caused his own death by firing the defective firearm, (2) many jurisdictions limit the felony-murder rule to situations where an innocent person is killed during the felony, and (3) there is an insufficient causal relationship between T's conduct and C's death (i.e., C's attempt to rob T and C's violent response to the police intervention superseded T's burglary of X's store). Thus, it is unlikely that T will be convicted of second-degree murder.

Crimes of Bob (B)

The prosecution conceivably could charge B with conspiracy to commit robbery, attempted robbery, and second-degree murder as a co-conspirator with Adam (A).

A conspiracy occurs where there is an agreement between two or more persons to commit a crime. Because B initially accompanied A in the car to the jewelry store after A explained the reason for his presence, there must have been at least a tacit agreement to rob T (even if B did not explicitly agree to assist A). The fact that B told A, "I've changed my mind," also indicates that there had been an agreement between them. B, therefore, would be culpable of conspiracy to commit robbery.

B could argue that he withdrew from the conspiracy when he advised A that he no longer wished to go through with the robbery and left. Under the common law, even a (1) fully voluntary and (2) complete withdrawal, (3) communicated to all the co-conspirators, did not relieve the defendant from liability for the conspiracy itself. It did, however, relieve the defendant of liability for further crimes committed by his former co-conspirators. This is consistent with the notion that conspiracy is basically a crime of "encouragement." If the co-conspirators know that A has withdrawn, they can no longer draw encouragement from him. But the common law took the view that the crime of conspiracy was already completed, once the agreement was made, and the bell cannot be unrung. Thus, under the common law, if B did not effectively withdraw, B would still be responsible for A's conduct to the extent that it was within the scope of the conspiracy and a natural outgrowth of it. In such event, B could probably be convicted for A's subsequent robbery of T (discussed below). The Model Penal Code, however, recognizes a claim of "abandonment," which allows a defendant to avoid liability even for the already-committed conspiratorial agreement. The code requires that a conspirator actually thwart the crime. In this case, B would probably not be liable for the attempted robbery of T by C (also discussed below). This is because B could not foresee criminal activity by a new, unanticipated co-conspirator. While it is not necessary that a co-conspirator know the actual identities of all of the members of the conspiracy, it is ordinarily required that he be aware of their likely existence. Also, for similar reasons discussed above relative to T, B would probably not be found liable for the murder of C under the felony-murder rule.

Crimes of A

A could be charged with two counts of solicitation. This crime occurs where the defendant requests or encourages another to join in the commission of a crime, with the intent to induce the latter to perform the crime. A, therefore, committed a solicitation when he asked (1) C (even though he originally thought C was B) and later (2) B to join him in the robbery of T.

A could also be charged with two counts of conspiracy: (1) when he agreed with B to rob T and (2) when he apparently reached a tacit understanding with C to rob T. A could contend that he never agreed with C to perpetrate a robbery; rather, C, having heard of T's intended burglary, was motivated by a desire to obtain the stolen jewelry for himself. It is unclear from the facts whether A should have realized that he had inadvertently spoken with C during his initial telephone call to B. Presumably, when B didn't know why A appeared at B's house, A should have recognized that he had spoken earlier with C (especially if there was no other male in B's home). Regardless, however, a tacit conspiratorial understanding would probably be found between A and C in light of their subsequent jointness of action—A's holding T's arms while C grabbed the bag, and then both running toward A's car.

In most states, a solicitation charge will merge into a conspiracy conviction.

Because a conspirator is culpable for acts committed by a co-conspirator that are within the scope of the conspiracy or a foreseeable outgrowth thereof, A would be culpable for the attempted robbery of T by C. This occurred when C "swiped" at T's bag (a robbery occurs where the defendant, in the victim's presence, by force or the threat of violence, commits a larceny). While A might contend that no robbery was attempted because the property that T had in his possession belonged to X, most jurisdictions hold that a robbery occurs even though the victim had previously stolen the property from another (the rationale being that robbery is a crime against mere possession and does not depend on ownership).

Assuming a conspiracy between A and C was found to exist, A would also be culpable for the subsequent robbery of T (when A held T's arms and C grabbed the bag containing X's jewelry).

If no conspiracy was found (i.e., C was acting only for his individual benefit when he grabbed at T's bag), A would still probably be guilty of attempted robbery based on his conduct in trying to wrest the bag from T (no robbery by A would have occurred in this instance, because it was C who actually carried away the bag containing X's jewelry).

C's death

The prosecution also could charge A with second-degree murder under the felony-murder rule. Points (1) and (2) of the discussion above explaining the inapplicability of the felony-murder rule with respect to T would apply in this instance as well.

Answer to Question 11

The installation

Joe will first attempt to avoid liability for violating the statute by claiming mistake of law because of what he was told over the phone. This will be unsuccessful. At common law, no mistake of law, no matter how reasonable, was a defense to any general-intent offense. Joe, therefore, is guilty of the regulatory offense. He "caused" the air conditioner to be installed. The Model Penal Code, §2.04(3), has created a defense of "reasonable reliance" on "official statements" of the law, but court decisions under the MPC have narrowly construed that provision. Here, the verbal statement by "someone" at the "zoning board office" is unlikely to meet the MPC's requirements.

The deaths of the neighbors

Because it also includes possible jail time, the statute creates a misdemeanor, and Joe may be liable under the misdemeanor-manslaughter rule for the deaths of the two neighbors. Joe will argue that the misdemeanor is "over" before the fire occurs — that the statute does not explicitly prohibit "operating" an excessively hot air-conditioning unit. The state will respond that the whole purpose of prohibiting the installation is to prevent the use of the unit, and the violation is a "continuing" one. The MPC does **not** recognize the misdemeanor-manslaughter rule, and the state would have to prove that Joe was either reckless (for manslaughter) or "criminally negligent" (for negligent homicide) under the code. Joe does not appear to meet either criterion. His reliance on the word of "someone" at the zoning board is probably not unreasonable, and it certainly does not rise to the level of "consciously ignoring" a "substantial and unjustifiable" risk of death to others.

Hilda — duress

Hilda clearly "installed" the air conditioner, and she knew that it violated the statute. She's guilty, unless she can claim duress. But she can't. Both the common law and the MPC allow duress as a claim only if the threat is of personal harm; economic suffering, no matter how severe, is insufficient. Even if she could somehow claim duress, courts have split on whether a defendant under duress can still claim duress when a death, however accidental, occurs. And if that were not enough, Hilda, more than Joe, is likely to be aware of the reason for limiting the output of appliances. If that included the risk of fire, she may have (recklessly) disregarded the risk of death to others.

Answer to Question 12

DID DON (D) COMMIT A BURGLARY?

In the removal of the stereo equipment

Burglary is the trespassory breaking and entering into another's dwelling, at night, with the intent to commit a felony therein. Today, many states extend this crime to any structure and the intent to commit any theft offense within the structure. Because the facts are silent, assume that (1) D acted at night, (2) taking the stereo equipment for the purpose of defrauding an insurance company constitutes a felony, and (3) this jurisdiction extends the definition of burglary to any structure. D could argue that no "trespassory breaking" occurred because he (1) was given the key by Oscar (O) and (2) simply opened the warehouse door with it. The "breaking" element would be satisfied by the fact that the warehouse door was opened (movement of any part of the structure will usually suffice). But D is correct in contending that the "trespassory" element is missing, because O gave him the key to the premises. Therefore, D did not commit a burglary with respect to the removal of the stereo equipment.

In the theft of the vehicle

The State will argue that a burglary occurred when D reentered the warehouse for the purpose of stealing the vehicle behind it. While D might contend that the "therein" element is not satisfied because the car was not *in* the warehouse, entrance into a structure for the purpose of removing something within the fenced-in area behind the structure probably would satisfy this aspect of burglary (i.e., the vehicle would be deemed to be within the curtilage of the structure). Here, the trespassory element is probably met, because O never gave D permission to take the vehicle. Thus, D probably did commit a burglary with respect to the vehicle.

IS D GUILTY OF EITHER SECOND-DEGREE MURDER OR MANSLAUGHTER?

For the State to show that D is guilty of second-degree murder or manslaughter, it would have to prove that (1) Allen (A) is guilty of such a crime, and (2) D is vicariously culpable for A's crime(s).

Second-degree murder/felony-murder rule

Under the felony-murder rule, where a homicide occurs during and as a consequence of the defendant's participation in an independent, inherently

dangerous felony, the defendant is deemed to have the *mens rea* for second-degree murder (even though she did not intend or desire the victim's
death). As noted above, a burglary charge against D and A for entering
the warehouse with the purpose of removing the stereo equipment would
probably be unsuccessful. Thus, this conduct could **not** serve as the underlying felony necessary to trigger the felony-murder rule.

Second-degree murder/wantonness

The State alternatively could contend that A committed second-degree
murder by causing the officer's death while possessing a wanton *mens rea*
(consciously disregarding a risk that posed a high probability of death or
serious bodily harm to others). While A might contend the highway patrol
officer died when she lost control of her car, not as a consequence of A's
conduct, a sufficient causal connection would probably be found between
A's conduct and the officer's death (i.e., "but for" A's driving at an excessive speed and attempted escape, the officer would not have given chase
and crashed). A also could argue that highway patrol officers presumably
receive special training with respect to high-speed driving, and, therefore,
A's conduct did **not** create a high probability of death or serious bodily
harm. However, A should have recognized that, despite a higher than normal level of driving expertise, a lethal accident was entirely possible at 100
mph. Thus, A is probably guilty of second-degree murder.

Involuntary manslaughter/recklessness

Because the State might be unsuccessful with respect to its second-degree
murder assertion, it would alternatively contend that A committed involuntary manslaughter by causing the officer's death while possessing a reckless *mens rea* (acting in a manner that posed a substantial risk of death or
serious injury to others). The same factual arguments described above with
respect to second-degree murder based on a wanton *mens rea* would apply
equally in this instance. If A's conduct was deemed **not** wanton, it should
be considered reckless. Thus, at a minimum, A should be found to have
committed involuntary manslaughter.

Involuntary manslaughter/misdemeanor-manslaughter rule

The misdemeanor-manslaughter rule probably would not be applicable
because driving at an excessive rate of speed (if a misdemeanor) is probably only a **malum prohibitum** (rather than a *malum in se*) offense.

Is D culpable for the crimes of A?

A conspiracy exists where there is an agreement between two or more persons to commit a crime. The facts state that A agreed to help D in D's plan to take the stereo equipment for the purpose of defrauding the insurance company. Therefore, a conspiracy existed between A and D.

A conspirator is vicariously culpable for any crimes committed by other co-conspirators provided such offenses were within the scope of the conspiracy and were a reasonably foreseeable outgrowth thereof. The State could argue that it was foreseeable that (1) the crime might be detected, (2) police would respond, and (3) someone would be killed in the course of an escape. D could contend in rebuttal that a homicide was not foreseeable in light of the fact that A and D had received a key to the premises from the owner and (apparently) no one was armed. The State's argument, however, is too broad—it is always "foreseeable" that a crime may be detected; if foreseeability were so gargantuan a concept, no event would be unforeseeable. Moreover, very few police responses result in death, much less from high-speed car chases conducted by a police officer who only thinks he is chasing a speeder (or even a thief).

IS O VICARIOUSLY CULPABLE FOR D'S CRIMES?

D is probably guilty of burglary (with respect to the vehicle), larceny (taking the vehicle), conspiracy to commit insurance fraud, and second-degree murder or involuntary manslaughter. O was certainly a member of the conspiracy to defraud his insurer. But O probably could contend successfully that the burglary and larceny of the vehicle were not contemplated by the conspiracy. (O presumably thought that D and A would bring their own vehicles.)

Further, with respect to the death of the patrol officer, the State could argue that the officer's death was a foreseeable consequence of the conspiracy to commit insurance fraud, because there is always a possibility of detection and ensuing violence when a stranger enters a warehouse to remove goods from it. However, O would argue in rebuttal that here the possibility of detection and ensuing violence was practically nonexistent because D was not a stranger entering the warehouse, but rather knew O and obtained entry with a key. Thus, D would not have been worried about anyone detecting a "break-in" of the building. The facts indicate that A drove away with the goods without incident and was pursued by the highway patrol car only because he had been driving in excess of the speed limit. By speeding, first when the officer's attention was attracted and then in a high-speed chase in excess of 100 mph, A committed an independent, intervening act that was not a foreseeable consequence of a conspiracy to commit insurance fraud; O would argue that this was beyond what O should have expected D to do (i.e., drive the stereo equipment from O's premises). Thus, while O would be guilty of conspiracy to commit insurance fraud, he probably would not be found guilty of second-degree murder or involuntary manslaughter.

Answer to Question 13

The prosecution would probably charge Dave (D) with murder (the unlawful killing of another person).

Can D assert the fleeing-felon justification?

Where a dangerous felony has been committed in the presence of a private citizen, he may utilize whatever force is reasonably necessary to prevent the perpetrator from escaping. D could contend that, because Bob (B) presumably had just committed a dangerous felony with respect to the museum guard by striking the latter with such force that he was knocked unconscious and bleeding (an aggravated form of battery), D was privileged to use force (the lance) capable of causing B's death to prevent B from escaping. The prosecution could argue in rebuttal, however, that (1) the guard had not actually been attacked in D's presence, (2) B wasn't attempting to escape at the time D killed him, and (3) merely threatening to use deadly force against B might have restrained him until the police could be summoned. While the first argument might not be persuasive, the prosecution's second and third arguments probably would be successful, and, therefore, the fleeing-felon justification should fail.

Can D successfully assert either the self-defense or the defense-of-property justification?

It does **not** appear that D could successfully assert the self-defense or defense-of-property privilege. Self-defense does not appear to apply because there is no indication that B made any type of menacing movement toward D. Indeed, there is nothing in the facts that indicates B even knew D was there. Defense of property (D's paintings) would likewise not apply because one is not privileged to exercise deadly force (i.e., force capable of taking life) in defense of property.

Assuming none of D's defenses are successful, for what degree of murder is he likely to be convicted?

The prosecution could charge D with first-degree murder, arguing that he intentionally took B's life with premeditation and deliberation because D hesitated a moment before throwing the lance. However, because D was "stunned" by the fact that B was slashing D's valuable paintings, the mere passage of a moment or two for D to adjust to the gravity of B's actions probably would not be viewed as a sufficient interval to constitute premeditation and deliberation. The charge would thus be reduced to second-degree murder.

D also would contend that his crime should be reduced from second-degree murder to voluntary manslaughter because he acted with adequate provocation. While the prosecution might contend that seeing someone slash valuable paintings could never constitute adequate provocation (i.e., cause a reasonable person to consider taking life), given the fact that the paintings were irreplaceable, adequate provocation could be found. D probably would be convicted of voluntary manslaughter. There is, further, the argument that D is an art collector and should be judged by the "reasonable art collector" standard. While the common law has resisted "subjectivizing" the provocation standard, the MPC would seem more likely to allow such a move.

What crimes could D be charged with as a consequence of the incident with Amos (A)?

With respect to A, the prosecution could charge D with (1) robbery (where the defendant, by force, or the threat of force, in the presence of the victim, commits a larceny), (2) larceny (the trespassory taking and carrying away of another's personal property with the intent to permanently deprive the victim of that property), (3) assault (deliberately placing another in fear of imminent injury), and (4) battery (intentionally causing bodily injury or offensive touching). These crimes stem from Dave's conduct in sticking a pipe against A's back and pretending it was a gun to recover the memorandum.

One can ordinarily use reasonable, nondeadly force to recover wrongfully taken property, provided the person is in "hot pursuit" of the item(s) (the right of reclamation). D will contend that his action was a reasonable means of regaining possession of his memorandum, and this will be his defense to all of the above crimes. However, because D just happened to see A while driving to the museum, it would not appear that D was in "hot pursuit" (i.e., that he promptly discovered the wrongful taking and immediately set out in pursuit). In addition, the facts state that D only suspected A had taken the memorandum. Thus, this defense probably will fail.

As to the battery and assault charges, D might contend that a pipe is really not a device that can be characterized as forceful or intimidating. However, the prosecution probably could argue successfully in rebuttal that the item used is irrelevant; all that matters is whether a reasonable person in the victim's position would have been intimidated under the circumstances. Because A reasonably believed a gun was pointed at his back, the "force or intimidation" element is satisfied.

As to the robbery and larceny charges, D also might argue that he did not have the intent to permanently deprive A of A's property. This is evidenced by the fact that D threw A's billfold (except for the memorandum, which was D's property) under a streetlight where he expected A to find it. The prosecution would argue in rebuttal, however, that D's decision to return the billfold may have been formed subsequent to the taking and D should have realized that leaving a wallet under a street lamp probably would result in it not being found or returned to A. The prosecution probably would prevail. (If so, the larceny charge probably would be merged into the robbery conviction.)

Thus, D can be convicted of robbery, battery (unless this is a jurisdiction that requires actual physical injury), and assault.

Answer to Question 14

HOW SHOULD THE FEDERAL APPEALS COURT RULE?

Conspiracy

A conspiracy exists where two or more persons agree to commit a crime. Many states require that one of the parties commit an overt act in furtherance of such criminal objective. Both Dan (D) and Paul (P) would contend that neither could be guilty of conspiracy because P never actually agreed with D to rob Bank. While P accepted the pistol, the facts indicate that P feared for his physical safety and that he intended to try to thwart the crime. Neither P nor D ever had an "agreement" with Mike, because Mike was coerced into joining them. Moreover, to the extent that the heart of conspiracy is that each co-conspirator gets encouragement from the voluntary participation by his colleagues, Dan does not fit that description. Therefore, the conspiracy conviction should be overturned. This is probably the correct result even in a jurisdiction governed by the Model Penal Code's "unilateral conspiracy" theory, because, even there, the essence of the crime is the defendant's belief that the other participants want the crime to occur.

The federal statute

Both P and D could contend that they did not commit the crime described in the federal statute because (1) Fred (F) was not "in the performance of his duties" at the time he was shot (arguing that the facts seem to indicate that Fred had *just arrived* at the bank); (2) while the statute appears to describe a general-intent crime (that the defendant only have intended the *actus reus* portion of the statute), D and P would argue that it implies acting "knowingly"; and (3) P and D were not aware F was a federal officer. First, it is necessary to interpret the phrase "in the performance of his duties." The facts state that F "was a federal bank examiner conducting an audit of Bank's accounts," using the present tense. It is arguable that F had already begun this audit and was walking into Bank that day to continue his work. Furthermore, even if P and D's contention is true (i.e., that F had just arrived at Bank to begin his auditing duties), it could be argued that F still would have been killed while performing his duties as a federal bank examiner. Only if F had been killed when he was not on the job as a federal bank examiner should P and D's position prevail. Next, whether Congress desired to punish for this offense only in the event that the perpetrators knew they were assaulting federal officials is a question of statutory intent (to be determined from the legislative history pertaining to this statute).

However, the statutory language appears to reveal a decision to treat the entire class of federal officials in a particular manner, and the defendant's knowledge seems to be irrelevant. Moreover, Congress could have used the word "knowingly" in the statute had it wished to require *mens rea* with regard to the victim's status. Also, it could be argued that "federal officer" and "in the performance of his duties" are merely jurisdictional elements of the statute, to which *mens rea* requirements do not always apply. Finally, under the "greater crime" theory, a defendant who engages in a crime is held strictly liable if it turns out that he actually commits a greater crime than he thought he was committing. In summary, these statutory interpretation contentions by P and D probably would **not** be successful.

Assuming the federal statute was violated, P would contend that (given the absence of a conspiracy) he is not culpable for D's assault with a deadly weapon. An individual is culpable for the criminal acts of another where the former, with the intent to do so, aids or assists another in the commission of a crime. The facts seem to indicate that P probably lacked the intent to aid or assist D (as mentioned above, P apparently helped D because he feared for his safety). Moreover, the crimes committed by the perpetrator must have been reasonably foreseeable by the aider and abettor. While it might have been foreseeable that D would use his pistol if someone obstructed their robbery attempt, it arguably could not be anticipated that D would shoot "a federal officer engaged in the performance of his duties" for no apparent reason. Because the specific-intent element is lacking and because D shooting F was not reasonably foreseeable, P should **not** be guilty of the crime set forth in the federal statute.

In summary, neither P nor D is guilty of conspiracy, and only D would be guilty under the federal statute.

HOW SHOULD THE STATE COURT RULE ON MIKE'S (M) MOTION FOR A DIRECTED VERDICT?

The defense of duress exists where the defendant, as a consequence of threats to cause her imminent death or serious bodily harm, committed the crime with which she is charged, provided, however, the defendant (1) actually and reasonably believed the threatened acts would be carried out and (2) is not charged with intentionally killing another human being. (This latter restriction is rejected by the Model Penal Code.) The facts indicate that (1) D pointed a gun at M and threatened M with death unless M assisted in the bank robbery, (2) M's pistol was unloaded, (3) D always had M "covered," and (4) M "reasonably believed" that D's threats were genuine.

The prosecutor could argue that M, as an aider and abettor to D's killing F, fits into the "intentional killing" exception to the defense of duress. For the same reasons that P should not be guilty of aiding and abetting D's assault with a deadly weapon, M also should be acquitted of this charge; M did not intend to be a part of (i.e., to aid or assist) any intentional killing. Thus, M probably is entitled to a directed verdict.

Answer to Question 15

CRIMES OF ADAMS (A)

Second-degree murder/involuntary manslaughter

Second-degree murder occurs where the defendant commits a homicide (the killing of one human being by another) with a wanton *mens rea* (i.e., consciously disregarding a risk that posed a high probability of death or serious bodily harm to others). However, if the defendant possessed a reckless *mens rea* when the homicide occurred (the defendant engaged in conduct that created a substantial risk of death or serious injury to others), she is culpable only of involuntary manslaughter. The facts are unclear as to the precise conduct undertaken by A (i.e., in what way was operation of the vehicle grossly negligent). To constitute wantonness, A would have had to have been acting in a manner that presented an obvious risk of serious harm to others (e.g., driving at 75 mph through crowded downtown streets). Because A had a prospective customer with her, it is more likely that her grossly negligent conduct would be equated with recklessness. Therefore, A probably could be convicted of involuntary manslaughter.

Note that no conviction under the misdemeanor-manslaughter rule would be appropriate because moving violations are ordinarily *malumprohibitum* misdemeanors (as opposed to *malum in se*) offenses. Only the latter types of crimes are generally the basis for a conviction under the misdemeanor-manslaughter rule.

Larceny by trick/embezzlement

Larceny by trick occurs where the defendant obtains possession, but not title, of the personal property of another, through fraud or deceit, and carries away such personal property with the intent to permanently deprive the victim thereof. If it could be shown that, *at or before* the time A received the $100 payment from Riley (R), A had already decided to sell the vehicle to Williams (W), A probably would be guilty of larceny by trick of W's $100. If, however, it can be proved that A resolved to sell the car in question to W *after* receipt of R's $100 payment, then A probably could be convicted of embezzlement (fraudulently converting the personal property of another at the time when such property was rightfully in the defendant's possession). Thus, more facts are needed to determine whether larceny or embezzlement is the appropriate crime, but it appears that A would be guilty of one of them.

CRIMES OF RILEY (R)

The facts are unclear with respect to how R forcibly took possession of the car from Williams (W). Assuming he merely pushed W away from the vehicle, R probably would be culpable of assault (intentionally or recklessly placing another in fear of an imminent injury), battery (intentionally or recklessly causing bodily injury or offensive touching), and robbery (committing larceny by force, or the threat of force, in the presence of the victim). While R could contend that he believed he had a superior right to the car, and, therefore, his actions were privileged, the prosecution could argue in rebuttal that a mistake of law is ordinarily not an excuse for the commission of a crime. Some jurisdictions, however, permit a mistake of law to negate an element of the prosecution's *prima facie* **larceny** case or other specific-intent crime. If this view were followed here, R probably could contend successfully that no robbery occurred because he lacked the intent to permanently deprive "another" of his personal property (because R believed the car belonged to him). In such event, R probably still could be successfully prosecuted for assault and battery. The State's argument that R should have consulted an attorney before acting on his assumptions about the legal status of the car is probably misguided, but at the most R's acts could be characterized as negligent. If the robbery conviction were sustained, the assault and battery charges probably would merge into that offense.

CRIMES OF HAND (H)

H could be charged with (1) larceny for obtaining an unsigned certified check from the bank (presumably without its authorization), (2) uttering a forged document (the knowing tender of a forged document to another) for giving a document that purported to be a certified check to Black (B), when H knew that the item was worthless, (3) forgery (the fraudulent creation of a false document) for signing the certified check with the signature of a purported bank officer, and (4) false pretenses (the fraudulent acquisition of title to another's property by means of a material misrepresentation of fact) for receiving a certificate of title to the vehicle from B in exchange for an item that H knew was worthless. Probably the only factual contention that H could make is that the larceny prosecution should be unsuccessful because the common law definition of this crime requires that "tangible" personal property be involved. At common law, items such as checks were sometimes deemed to have no intrinsic value (i.e., they only represent a chose in action for the right to acquire money). Today, however, most states extend this crime to documents such as checks. Therefore, whether H could be convicted of larceny would depend on the applicable law of this jurisdiction. In addition, in many jurisdictions, the crime of uttering a forged instrument is merged into a conviction for forgery.

CRIMES OF COOPER (C)

The prosecution could charge C with embezzlement. By giving the finance company a lien upon ABC's car, C has arguably fraudulently converted property of the corporation. However, C could contend that (1) assuming the vehicle was not removed from ABC's premises, there was no conversion of the car (i.e., exercise of dominion or control by the financing entity); (2) there was no "fraudulent" intent to convert the car because he intended to repay the loan (and thereby remove the lien) within three days; and (3) because C held ABC stock, there was no conversion of "another's" property. The prosecution could argue that (1) a conversion occurred because the finance company acquired an interest in the vehicle, and (2) a corporation is a separate legal entity from its stockholders. However, there does not appear to be a successful rebuttal to C's claimed lack of intent unless C did not, in fact, repay the loan within the three-day period. Thus, C probably could ***not*** be convicted of embezzlement.

ABC CORPORATION

Whether ABC could be culpable for the crimes of A depends on the applicable legislation, if any. Many states have enacted laws that permit a corporation to be fined for offenses committed by officers or directors. If such an ordinance exists and A'soffenses fall within it, a monetary fine might be assessed against ABC for A's conduct.

Answer to Question 16

CHARGES AGAINST ALEX (A)

Burglary

At common law, burglary was the trespassory breaking and entering into the dwelling of another, at night, with the intent to commit a felony. Today, many jurisdictions have extended this crime to include (1) structures other than dwellings and (2) situations where the defendant intended to commit a theft offense within the building. The breaking and entering requirements are, respectively, satisfied by A's (1) pushing the window upward and (2) extending the pole into Ben's (B) store (the pole would be deemed to be A's instrumentality). Because B and his family lived upstairs, the pawnshop might be considered a dwelling (i.e., a place of regular habitation), even if the common law definition were to apply.

At common law, the "nighttime" requirement was met if a person's face could not be discerned by natural sunlight. Today, the nighttime element has been eliminated except for higher degrees of burglary in approximately half the states. Had Alex's crime occurred at an earlier time (e.g., 6:00 p.m. during the summer), this might have been an issue, but 10:00 p.m. is certainly "nighttime" everywhere, except possibly Nome in August.

A could still contend that he did not have the intent to commit a felony or theft offense within B's premises. A's attempt to regain his watch might *not* constitute a larceny (discussed immediately below).

Larceny

A larceny occurs where the defendant, in a trespassory manner, has taken and carried away the personal property of another with the intent to permanently deprive the owner of that property. A could contend that (1) because the watch belonged to him, the property "of another" was not involved, and (2) there was no intent to "permanently deprive" B of the watch, because he merely wanted to reobtain it temporarily for the purpose of showing it to his father and would have returned it as soon as his father left. The prosecution could argue in rebuttal that (1) because A had pawned the watch to B, B's interest in the item was superior to that of A, and, therefore, the "of another" element was satisfied; and (2) because A had apparently not decided when he would return the watch to B, the "permanently deprive" element is satisfied. Because the issue is one of intent, a jury might well conclude that A intended to return the item to B as soon as his father had departed. Thus, an interesting issue is raised: whether A is guilty of burglary because he entered the premises with the intent to take the watch, but is not guilty of larceny because he did not intend to permanently deprive B of it (i.e., unbeknownst to A, he did not satisfy all the elements of larceny).

Attempted burglary and larceny

An attempt occurs where the defendant has engaged in conduct for the specific purpose of committing a crime (the target offense), and such conduct represents a substantial step toward the culmination of that crime.

An attempted burglary charge would be inappropriate because A actually entered B's premises. Thus, A's conduct, if criminal, was complete. With respect to the attempted larceny charge, if the conduct A was seeking to accomplish was not criminal, it would be legally impossible for an attempt to have occurred (i.e., there would be no target crime). Thus, if A did not intend to permanently deprive B of the watch (as concluded above), the attempted larceny charge against A would also fail.

CHARGE OF ASSAULT WITH A DEADLY WEAPON AGAINST BEN (B)

An assault occurs where the defendant has intentionally or recklessly caused her victim to be in fear of imminent injury. Where this conduct is accomplished by means of a lethal instrumentality, assault with a deadly weapon occurs. Although B might contend that A never had the opportunity to be apprehensive of an injury (the shot was fired before A realized that B saw him), the prosecution could argue in rebuttal that (1) A must have heard the bullet ricocheting and, therefore, had a moment of apprehension wondering whether it would hit him, and (2) A would have feared a second shot once he heard the first one. The first argument is weak, because of the physics of bullets—it had probably come to rest long before Alex heard it. The second argument is too broad, because it would allow a prosecution for assault long after the event was over (could the putative victim ever be sure there would not be another attempt?). On the other hand, in many jurisdictions, any attempted battery is an assault, and B would have committed such an assault.

B probably could assert the defense-of-home privilege. Under the modern view of the defense-of-home privilege, when a home occupier reasonably believes that an intruder is about to commit a dangerous felony within the premises, she may use deadly force (force capable of causing death or serious bodily harm) to expel the intruder. Because B's pawnshop was part of his home and A appeared to be holding a rifle, B's belief that he and his family were in grave danger probably would be considered reasonable. It is, therefore, unlikely that any prosecution against B would be successful.

B also might assert the self-defense privilege (where a person reasonably believes that he is in imminent danger of death or serious bodily injury from another person, the former may respond with lethal force against the latter). The issue here would be whether B's fear of attack from A as being "imminent" was reasonable, because A was still outside the store and was unaware of B's existence. B, of course, did not know that A was unaware of him and certainly could entertain a fear that A would enter the store or, in responding to B's force, use deadly force himself. Thus, whether the self-defense privilege could be successfully asserted is a close question.

CHARGE OF LARCENY AGAINST CLIFF (C)

Lost or mislaid property is deemed to be in the constructive possession of the person with superior title to it (in this instance, B). Thus, Cliff's act of taking the watch into his possession would be "trespassory," if he had intended to keep it. Moreover, a trespassory taking is not sufficient for liability. The finder must also, at the time of finding, intend to appropriate it **and** know, or have reason to believe, who the actual owner is or that the owner can be later identified. The facts indicate he intended to return it (which might well have been possible because A's initials were engraved on it) at the time he picked it up in front of the store, so there was no intent to permanently deprive the owner of it at the time the "taking" occurred. It is, therefore, unlikely that C could be prosecuted successfully for larceny. (In a few jurisdictions, the crime of embezzlement might extend to situations such as this.)

CHARGES AGAINST DON (D)

Receiving stolen property

The crime of receiving stolen property occurs where the defendant has received stolen property knowing that it has been stolen from another, with the intent to deprive the owner of it. Because (as discussed above) C probably did not commit a larceny, D probably could **not** be successfully prosecuted for receiving stolen property (the watch in question **not** having been the subject of a larceny).

Attempting to receive stolen property

However, most jurisdictions will permit conviction for an ***attempt*** to receive stolen property where, had the facts been as the defendant thought them to be, the target crime would have actually occurred. If, given C's statement that the watch was "hot," D thought the watch was *recently* stolen, D probably could be convicted of an attempt to receive stolen property.

Answer to Question 17

CRIMES OF SAM (S)

Deaths of Mac, Fred, and Tom

Under the felony-murder rule, where a homicide occurs during and as a consequence of the defendant's perpetration of an independent, inherently dangerous felony, each of the felons is deemed to have the *mens rea* for second-degree murder. Because Mac, Fred, and Tom were killed during the robbery (robbery is the trespassory taking and carrying away of another's property, from or in the presence of such person, via the use or threat of force, with the intent to permanently deprive the victim of such property), the State could contend that, under the felony-murder rule, S is culpable for the deaths of Mac, Fred, and Tom. S may contend that Fred's death was not a homicide, but the result of an accident resulting from Fred's ineffectual use of the nitroglycerin. Negligent or reckless killing, however, can still be homicide, and courts have frequently imposed liability on felons for the death of a co-felon caused by his own negligence, most notably in arson cases. Even if Mac's death was a natural consequence of the felony, it was hardly "probable"—it resulted from an independent, intervening event (Eb was unaware of what had transpired inside the casino), and, thus, there was no sufficient causal relationship between the robbery and Mac's death. Finally, Carlo probably was privileged to kill Tom under the fleeing-felon justification. If this jurisdiction follows the rule that the felony-murder rule does not apply to situations where a felon is killed by the victim or other justified actor, S could not be successfully charged with Tom's death.

Attempted murder of Eb (E)/aggravated battery

A murder occurs where one commits a homicide with the intent to kill or cause serious bodily harm to the victim. When S shot E, he probably was attempting to kill the latter (although S might not actually have desired to kill E, the law allows the fact finder to infer that a person intends the natural consequences of his actions, and shooting at someone with a gun certainly has the potential of causing death or serious bodily harm).

If, for any reason, a court or jury held that S did not have sufficient intent to justify an attempted murder conviction for shooting E, S probably could be prosecuted successfully for aggravated battery (causing bodily injury with a lethal weapon).

However, S probably could assert the self-defense justification to these charges (i.e., he reasonably believed he was in imminent danger of serious bodily harm or death), because E had just killed Mac and turned the gun on S. Under the fleeing-felon doctrine, a private citizen can exercise force capable of causing serious bodily harm or death to prevent a felon from escaping where the latter has committed a felony in the former's presence. Thus, E could have been justified in shooting S. If so, then S's shooting of E could not itself be justified. Because E had no knowledge of the felony (he only desired to kill gamblers), whether the fleeing-felon doctrine applies to E has split the courts and commentators. Most courts would find E's shooting not privileged. If so, then S should prevail. On the other hand, Sam did not know, either, that E's shooting was unjustified, and he may similarly lose the claim of justification. The issue of "unknowing justification" has also divided the courts and commentators.

Robbery/larceny
Because S and his co-conspirators threatened Carlo (C) and his employees with force (i.e., they were held at gunpoint), S is guilty of robbery (defined above). While the requisites of larceny (the trespassory taking and carrying away of another's property with the intent to permanently deprive the victim of such property) are also met, this crime would merge into the robbery.

Burglary
The crime of burglary is the trespassory breaking and entering into another's structure, at night, with the intent to commit a felony or theft offense therein. Because S had apparently been permitted ingress into the casino before it closed, the "trespassory breaking" elements do not appear to be satisfied. However, in some states, these requisites are fulfilled where the defendant has trespassorily entered (moved the door of) any room or enclosed area within the structure. Thus, even if S entered the building with consent, he did not have consent to enter Carlos's office, which might also serve as a predicate entry. Additionally, the safe (being of a size in which an individual could stand) could arguably be deemed to be such an enclosed room or area. If so, S could be guilty of burglary because the safe door was blown open for the purpose of taking the money within it (i.e., a larceny).

Arson/malicious mischief
Arson is the malicious burning of another's structure. The State could contend that a "burning" occurred as a result of the explosion and that the safe was actually a "part" of the casino because it could be moved only by heavy

equipment. While in many states an explosion will constitute the "burning" necessary for arson, the facts indicate that the safe was not attached to the building, and there is no indication in the facts that the blast affected any other part of the casino. Consequently, it is unlikely that the "structure" element is satisfied, and a charge of arson probably could not be successfully prosecuted. However, S has committed the crime of malicious mischief (maliciously causing injury to another's property). While the law does not require that the safe be unusable (merely damaged), the extent of the injury is helpful to the State.

Conspiracy

Because S, Mac, Fred, and Tom (apparently) had agreed to commit a robbery (we can infer an agreement to act in concert from their actions of entering the casino, hiding together, and holding the employees at gunpoint while Fred blew up the safe), S could be guilty of conspiracy (an agreement between two or more persons to commit a crime) to commit robbery.

CRIMES OF EB (E)

Murder of Mac

E probably could be successfully charged with the murder of Mac. There is little doubt that a homicide occurred. E showed the necessary malice aforethought (intent to kill or cause serious bodily harm) when he yelled, "Death to gamblers!" and when he fired at Mac. Waiting outside the casino with a gun indicates premeditation and deliberation.

As discussed above, the fleeing-felon justification is probably unavailable to E.

E might contend that he was insane at the time of the shooting because his life was wrecked. Although E apparently understood the nature of his act (by shouting, "Death to gamblers," and then shooting a person whom he thought to be a member of this group) and understood that it was morally wrong (the *McNaghten* test), E might contend that he was acting under an irresistible impulse (i.e., he was unable to control his actions at that moment). The irresistible impulse that affects a defendant's mind may be the culmination of sustained brooding. The State will argue in rebuttal that there is little evidence that E suffered from a "mental disease or defect," a prerequisite for any mental incompetency claim (including under the Model Penal Code). Indeed, E seemed to be in full control of his faculties. While E was obviously upset with his experiences at the casino, there probably is not sufficient proof that the urge to kill gamblers had become irresistible.

A few states recognize the diminished-capacity doctrine. Under this theory, where a mental deficiency (not rising to the level of insanity) prevents the defendant from possessing the specific-intent *mens rea* necessary for murder, his crime is reduced to voluntary manslaughter or second-degree murder. If this were such a state, E might be culpable of only the latter offense if he could show that his brooding hostility vis-à-vis the casino ripened into a mental defect that precluded him from forming the requisite specific-intent *mens rea* necessary for the greater level of homicide.

Attempted murder of Sam (S)
Where a defendant commits some act in furtherance (as opposed to mere preparation) of a criminal offense, an attempt has occurred. Because E was about to pull the trigger of his gun and shoot S, an attempted murder appears to have occurred. While E's actions toward S probably would constitute an assault as well, that crime probably would merge into the greater crime of attempted murder.

CRIMES OF CARLO (C)

Operating a casino
The facts stipulate that C "operated" the casino, and so he would be guilty of a misdemeanor under the state's gambling statute.

Murder
The State probably could not successfully charge C with murder in the killing of Tom. While there is no privilege to exercise force capable of causing death or serious injury in defense of property (the money), C probably could successfully avail himself of the fleeing-felon justification (because Tom had just perpetrated a robbery upon C). The fact that C was responding to the taking of illicit property (the gambling proceeds had been obtained in violation of a criminal statute) would not, in most states, prevent C from asserting this defense.

Involuntary manslaughter
It is conceivable that the State could charge C with the involuntary manslaughter of Tom, Mac, and Fred under the misdemeanor-manslaughter rule. Under this doctrine, where a homicide occurs in the course and as a consequence of a *malum in se* misdemeanor, the perpetrator of the

misdemeanor is guilty of manslaughter for any death that results from that misdemeanor. However, there does not appear to be a sufficient causal relationship between the misdemeanor in which C was engaged (gambling) and the deaths of the three co-felons. These deaths occurred as a consequence of the robbery that they had perpetrated, not because of C's gambling activities. Also, gambling probably is only a *malum prohibitum* misdemeanor. Thus, this assertion by the State should fail.

Answer to Question 18

Regnis

If charged with destruction of the Reo, Regnis will claim duress. Under the common law, a claim of duress requires that the defendant acted (1) in response to a threat of (2) imminent (3) serious bodily harm or death. A threat of future harm or of harm to an economic or property interest was insufficient. A defendant could not claim duress if he killed someone. While similarly restricting the claim to threats of bodily harm, §2.08 of the Model Penal Code allows a claim of duress in homicide cases and in response to a threat of any personal harm. The code also leaves to the jury whether the person of "reasonable firmness" would have succumbed to the threat, even if it were not imminent. Moreover, the defendant must not have brought the situation on himself. Because there was no threat here to Regnis's person, he would lose the claim, even if he acted as a reasonable person. Although the Model Penal Code significantly alters many aspects of the general common law, it continues to adhere to the requirement that the threat be to the person. Therefore, Regnis can't claim duress under either the common law or the MPC.

Regnis may argue necessity. Necessity requires that the defendant achieve a "greater social good" by committing the offense (here, destruction of Quinn's Reo) rather than submitting to the threat (here, the destruction of an irreplaceable cultural icon). Whether a defendant has actually achieved a greater social good is, at least at the first cut, for the judge. If Regnis can convince the judge that a nearly 300-year-old document is more important, socially, than destruction of the car, he may get his case to the jury. The point is that a claim of necessity *might* prove viable even when a claim of duress does not. There is, however, one more caveat—some courts allow a claim of necessity only if the "threatener" is a force of nature (starvation, avalanche, etc.). This restriction seems to have been removed by the Model Penal Code, §3.02.

Quinn

If Quinn is charged with attempted murder, that crime requires specific intent to kill. That will be a jury question, but it is unlikely that a jury would conclude that Quinn "wanted"Regnis to die. He was probably "simply" angry—which would not be enough for attempt.

Quinn's emotional response would seem to raise "heat of passion" issues, but that claim is available only in cases of actual homicide. Because Regnis did not die, Quinn can't take that route. The question, however, asks what might happen if Regnis did die. In that case, Quinn *will* argue heat of passion. Under the common law, a killing "which would otherwise be murder" (i.e., was done with malice aforethought) was manslaughter if it was committed (1) in response to specific, legally adequate provocative acts by the victim(s), (2) in the heat of passion, and (3) without time for the person to "cool off." The events that were considered legally adequate provocation were extremely limited; the most important were (1) finding your spouse committing adultery, (2) being physically insulted (e.g., slapped), and (3) being illegally arrested. Most modern courts have increasingly adopted a more generous approach, asking whether a "reasonable person with [some of] the defendant's characteristics [age, gender, physical disability] would have reacted as the defendant did." Whether the defendant had time to cool off is also now a question of fact for the jury, rather than one of law for the judge. The Model Penal Code, §210.3, subjectivizes the claim even more, leaving to the jury whether the defendant acted "under extreme emotional or mental disturbance" (EED) for which there is a "reasonable explanation or excuse" for someone in the defendant's "situation." The MPC does not expressly require a provocative act; it is enough that the defendant is acting under EED. Even with the MPC, however, it is unlikely that a "reasonable" person would be so attached to his car that he would kill someone who destroyed it. But it might be a jury question—that's the point of the MPC provision.

However, Quinn may argue that he was "mentally irresponsible." Under the *McNaghten* test, which is the dominant standard in the United States today, a defendant is insane if he suffered from a mental disease or defect that caused him not to (1) know the nature and quality of his act or (2) know that the act was "wrong." Some states have supplemented this standard with a "volitional" test, sometimes referred to as the "irresistible impulse" test, which essentially provides that if the defendant, again because of mental disease or defect, could not stop himself from committing what he knew was "wrong," he should be deemed "temporarily insane." In response to criticisms of these tests, §4.01 of the Model Penal Code asks whether the defendant lacked "substantial capacity" to (1) appreciate (2) the criminality (wrongfulness) of his act or (3) to conform his conduct to the law. Because both insanity and "diminished capacity" require a showing that the defendant suffered from a "mental disease," there is nothing specific that would indicate that Quinn was that extreme, but the word "obsessive" might lead at least to a discussion of that question. Assuming that Quinn might persuade a jury that he had such a disease, he would still face problems under the *McNaghten* test of insanity. There is nothing to show that Quinn didn't know the difference between right and wrong. He's sane, at least for the purposes of the law. Finally, Quinn might raise a claim of "irresistible impulse." In most states that recognize that doctrine, the requirement for a "mental disease" is significantly less restrictive than the requirement for insanity.

Quinn has a much better chance under the Model Penal Code if he can show that he suffers from a mental disease. Quinn will argue that he lacked "substantial capacity" to "conform his conduct to the requirements of the law." This articulation of the "volitional prong" of the insanity defense is a much more relaxed test than even irresistible impulse.

Phillip

Phillip is clearly guilty as a principal to the destruction of the Reo. Because he placed Regnis under duress, Phillip is a principal in the first degree. The real issue here is his liability for Quinn's assault on Regnis. Clearly, Phillip did not conspire with Quinn — there was no indication of an agreement and probably insufficient time from which a fact finder could infer an agreement. So far as the facts show, there was no reason to expect Quinn to be present. And even though Phillip said that he hoped Quinn would react just as he in fact did, there is no sign that Phillip actually encouraged Quinn's action. Moreover, his use of the phrase "I hope he kills you" might well be *ad hominem*. Just because Phillip doesn't like Regnis doesn't mean he actually wants him dead. That will be a question for the jury.

Answer to Question 19

Conspiracy

Chain and Walker have clearly conspired to dispose of the oil in violation of Section 101. A conspiracy consists of (1) an agreement to (2) commit a crime (3) for which an overt act has been taken. It is a specific-intent crime, which is sometimes punished more severely than the target crime itself. Moreover, under the common law, conspiracy does not "merge" with the completed crime—the defendant may be liable for both the conspiracy and the crime. Conspirators are generally held liable only for crimes that they "intend" or "purpose" to happen, but, in some jurisdictions, following *Pinkerton v. U.S.*, 328 U.S. 640 (1946), they can be held responsible for any acts committed by their co-conspirators that are (1) reasonably foreseeable and (2) in furtherance of the conspiracy. A conspirator is liable for the target crime, unless he "withdraws" by telling ***all*** the co-conspirators he is no longer supporting them. He will still be responsible for the conspiracy. The MPC rejects *Pinkerton* and holds the conspirators responsible only for crimes they intended to encourage. Under §5.03(b) of the MPC, a defendant can avoid liability for the conspiracy if he "thwarts" the target crime. Under the MPC, the defendants cannot be punished separately for the conspiracy and the completed crime. Here, Chain and Walker have agreed to commit what they know is an illegal act (improper disposal of the oil), and they have taken steps (overt acts) to consummate the crime. But they have also agreed to commit theft. Walker will be committing embezzlement, because the money is from his company; Chain has agreed that Walker will commit that crime and has a "stake in the action." Harry is a co-conspirator to the first offense, but does not, from the facts given, know that Chain and Walker are improperly charging Walker's company. Usually, a co-conspirator has to have a purpose that his cohorts commit such a crime, so Harry doesn't fit neatly into the conspiracy for that crime. But, under *Pinkerton*, a co-conspirator is liable for those crimes committed by his fellow conspirators if those crimes are (1) reasonably foreseeable and (2) in furtherance of the conspiracy. Neither of those requirements seems met here—Chain, Walker, and Harry can dispose of the oil without ever touching Slam Dunk's money. So Harry is still not a co-conspirator for the embezzlement.

Disposing of the oil

Chain, Walker, and Harry are all guilty of the felony of disposal of the oil—it was their target crime, and the first two are responsible, as co-conspirators, for Harry's actions. But what about Ginfield? He did not ***know*** that the barrels contained oil. Here, the construction of Section 101 is critical. Many common law courts would have held that Section 101 does not require that the defendant know that the item "dumped" is oil—merely that he "purposely" or "knowingly" dumped something, which turned out to be oil. The prosecution would further argue that the statute should be interpreted as a "public welfare offense," because damage to the environment is a serious crime, perhaps endangering thousands. Strict criminal liability offenses—where the government need not prove any *mens rea*, including mere tort negligence, with regard to one or more elements of the crime—have been variously characterized. Initially, they appeared mostly in statutes regulating sexual conduct, foodstuffs, and alcohol or protecting minors. In the 20th century, this group was expanded to include "police" or "regulatory" offenses. The courts have permitted strict liability to crimes that have small punishments and carry minimum stigmatization. Some states have imposed strict liability even where the penalty is severe. Recently, the U.S. Supreme Court declined to hold that a ten-year prison sentence would automatically lead the Court to interpret the offense as a non-strict-liability one. However, in that same decision, the Court defined "public welfare offenses" in which strict liability was permissible as those involving (1) dangerous items (2) that the defendant should expect to be highly regulated. The Model Penal Code, §2.05, prohibits strict liability whenever there is a possible imprisonment—even of one day. The substantial penalty for the felony, combined with the misdemeanor provision (which has no *mens rea* requirement and, therefore, **might** be construed as imposing strict liability), would undercut those arguments. If the misdemeanor provision is read as imposing strict criminal liability, Ginfield will be liable, but if any *mens rea* is read into the statute at all, that is unlikely. Colon, however, is more problematic. His statements, as well as his acceptance of $20,000 more to fly the barrels, may well qualify as "willful blindness"—he strongly suspected that the barrels contained some kind of contraband, but strove mightily not to learn precisely what. If so, he is "deemed" to have acted "knowingly" and has committed the felony. If he is not willfully blind, he is still liable for the misdemeanor offense. Note, however, that if the prosecution were governed by the Model Penal Code, even the misdemeanor charge would require negligence as to the contents of the barrels—the MPC precludes strict criminal liability whenever there is a possibility of even one day of imprisonment.

Necessity

All of the parties may claim that the disposal of the oil, as it actually occurred, was necessary and, therefore, justified. An action that would otherwise be criminal is justified if it is the "lesser of two evils" under the circumstances. In this instance, there were several people on board the plane who would have been killed if they had not thrown off the barrels. Disposal of oil in violation of regulations is surely, in the abstract, a lesser evil than causing the (probable) death and/or (certain) injury of several human beings on the plane. The prosecution may respond in several ways. First, there was no actual necessity—the plane was not in actual danger of crashing, and, therefore, the passengers did not "need" to jettison the oil. To this, the defendants will correctly respond that the necessity must be judged by the facts as seen by a reasonable person at the time, not as they turned out to be, and that no reasonable person would have had any concern about the accuracy of the altimeter. That claim will work under both the common law and the MPC; it will be for a jury to decide whether the defendants "believed" that their actions were necessary. The prosecution's second argument will be that a defendant who "causes his own necessity" cannot use that claim as a defensive plea. Here, Harry and Colon decided to fly even though the weather was terrible and, therefore, "caused" the necessity, at least negligently if not recklessly. Had they waited until the weather was better, they would have seen that they were higher than the Rockies and would not have thrown out the barrels. Under the common law, such a finding would bar the defendants from raising necessity as a defense to any criminal prosecution; under the Model Penal Code, however, a reckless or negligent defendant may raise necessity if charged with a "knowing" or "purposeful" crime but not if charged, respectively, with a "reckless" or "negligent" crime. The prosecution will argue, third, that, even if there were a reasonable fear that the plane would hit the Rockies, the defendants lose their claim of necessity because a person was actually killed on the ground, and no death of an innocent person can be justified. Defendants will respond that, even if there is such an exception to the necessity claim, it only precludes "purposefully" or "knowingly" taking the life of an innocent, and that they did not know that people were in the mountains, much less that they would be hit or killed by the barrels.

Death of the two Boy Scouts

None of the parties seems liable for the murders of the Boy Scouts. Murder was defined in English common law as a killing with "malice aforethought." The term clearly included intent to kill or intent to commit grievous bodily harm ("express malice"); courts struggled for several centuries to explain what the term meant if the death was unintended ("implied malice"). They often used metaphors such as "depraved heart" or "malignant mind" to capture what the term meant. All murders were capitally eligible in England. In the United States, murder was divided by many state legislatures into two degrees: (1) second degree, which is a lesser included offense of first-degree murder and included all malice-aforethought killings, and (2) first degree, which, in addition to malice aforethought, also required that the killing be done with "premeditation, deliberation, and willfulness." In most states, only first-degree murders were capitally eligible. Although the legislature clearly meant to limit the number of death-eligible murders by the premeditation formula, the courts quickly interpreted the phrase potentially to include anyone who killed: defendants could "premeditate" in the space of five seconds. Here, no one acted with "premeditation, deliberation, and willfulness" for first-degree murder, and it is hard to say that they acted with a "depraved heart" (common law) or "recklessly under circumstances manifesting extreme indifference to the value of human life" (Model Penal Code, §210.2) so as to render them liable for any lesser degree of murder. Throwing out barrels over a mountain does not raise a "substantial" risk of injury or death. (Compare the case had they disposed of the barrels over Denver.) If they are liable for the homicide at all, it would be for "involuntary manslaughter" under the common law, but even that required "gross negligence," and unless a reasonable person would have been concerned that someone might be hurt by the barrels, it is difficult to argue that this is negligence, much less gross negligence. Similar arguments would be made, and accepted, under the Model Penal Code.

The prosecution will also argue that, even if the defendants are not guilty of "straight" murder, all (except Ginfield) were involved in the felony of disposing of the oil, and that they committed felony murder, which does not require any *mens rea* with regard to the death. Under the original common law, any death that occurred while a defendant was engaged in a felony was murder (and capitally eligible). Today, legislatures typically restrict capitally eligible deaths to those that occur during statutorily articulated "predicate" felonies. These are "first degree" felony murders; all other deaths are "second degree" (not capitally punishable) felony murders. Most state courts have further restricted second-degree felony murders to those that occur during felonies that are "inherently dangerous." The courts are divided on whether that test should apply to the felony "in the abstract" (the way in which that felony is "typically" committed) or "as perpetrated" (the way in which the felony was committed in this situation). Defendants will say the crime is not "inherently dangerous in the abstract." Disposing of oil "in the abstract" may be committed in thousands of ways, few of which are actually dangerous. The image of the "midnight dumper" who pours hundreds of gallons of oil (or other chemicals) into the aquifer is at one extreme; the car owner who disposes of five quarts of oil in a nearby landfill is at the other. Moreover, the defense will contend, whatever danger is created by disposing of *oil* is not the danger that was created here. The danger here was created by disposing of **barrels**. Had the barrels been filled with water, they would have created the same danger as did these barrels. Hence, the predicate felony is not a proper basis for the charge here. Under §210.2b of the Model Penal Code, the defendants have no problem—the code rejects the felony-murder doctrine entirely, except for certain precisely stated offenses, of which "illegal dumping" is not one.

Answer to Question 20

CONSPIRACY

Conrad and Beatrice have clearly conspired to commit robbery. A conspiracy consists of (1) an agreement to (2) commit a crime (3) for which an overt act has been taken. It is a specific-intent crime, which is sometimes punished more severely than the target crime itself. Moreover, under the common law, conspiracy does not "merge" with the completed crime—the defendant may be liable for both the conspiracy and the crime. Conspirators are generally held liable only for crimes that they "intend" or "purpose" to happen, but, in some jurisdictions, following ***Pinkerton v. U.S.***, 328 U.S. 640 (1946), they can be held responsible for any acts committed by their co-conspirators that are (1) reasonably foreseeable and (2) in furtherance of the conspiracy. A conspirator is liable for the target crime, unless he "withdraws" by telling ***all*** the co-conspirators he is no longer supporting them. He will still be responsible for the conspiracy. The MPC rejects *Pinkerton* and holds the conspirators responsible only for crimes they intended to encourage. Under §5.03(b) of the MPC, a defendant can avoid liability for the conspiracy if he "thwarts" the target crime. Under the MPC, defendants cannot be punished separately for the conspiracy and the completed crime. They have also committed an "overt act" for those jurisdictions that require it.

ROBBERY

George

George initially sought to force Rod to give him some money. That the amount was allegedly the market value of the player is irrelevant; the compulsion is enough. George may attempt to claim insanity. Under the *McNaghten* test, which is the dominant standard in the United States today, a defendant is insane if he suffered from a mental disease or defect that caused him not to (1) know the nature and quality of his act or (2) know that the act was "wrong." Some states have supplemented this standard with a "volitional" test, sometimes referred to as the "irresistible impulse" test, which essentially provides that if the defendant, again because of mental disease or defect, could not stop himself from committing what he knew was "wrong," he should be deemed "temporarily insane." In response to criticisms of these tests, §4.01 of the Model Penal Code asks whether the defendant lacked "substantial capacity" to (1) appreciate (2) the criminality (wrongfulness) of his act or (3) to conform his conduct to the law.

Someone like George who (wrongly) believes that he has a child does not seem mentally competent. Here, it is not clear that George meets the initial predicate—that he suffers from a mental disease. Even if he satisfies that requirement, it is arguable that George recognizes that what he is doing is "wrong" —he "needs the money" and pleads for the market value. Even in those jurisdictions that recognize a claim of diminished capacity, George may stumble over the requirement of a mental disease. But if he jumps that hurdle, he may well avoid liability here for larceny, robbery, and any attempts. All those crimes are specific-intent crimes, and diminished capacity will potentially negate that liability.

George may argue that he did not obtain the money because of the threat. If Rod were persuaded by George's dire circumstances, then obtaining the money would not be a crime. But George has committed **attempted** robbery, both under the common law test and under the MPC (§5.01). Under the common law, he has come as close as he could to obtaining the money by force, and he has clearly taken a substantial step under the MPC. Again, however, if George can plead diminished capacity, these are also specific-intent crimes, and he may avoid liability.

Conrad
Conrad has taken some items from the store. It could be argued that he was able to do so because of the force that *he* used and that he has, therefore, committed robbery and not merely larceny. On the other hand, Rod was dead before Conrad took the goods. It is possible that Conrad could be found guilty of only larceny, unless the jury finds that Conrad was able to take the goods only because he killed Rod.

ROD'S DEATH

Conrad has killed Rod. Whether it is premeditated or simply "malice aforethought," it looks like murder. Murder was defined in English common law as a killing with "malice aforethought." The term clearly included intent to kill or intent to commit grievous bodily harm ("express malice"); courts struggled for several centuries to explain what the term meant if the death was unintended ("implied malice"). They often used metaphors such as "depraved heart" or "malignant mind" to capture what the term meant. All murders were capitally eligible in England. In the United States, murder was divided by many state legislatures into two degrees: (1) second degree, which is a lesser included offense of first-degree murder and included all malice-aforethought killings, and (2) first degree, which, in addition to malice aforethought, also required that the killing be done with "premeditation, deliberation, and willfulness." In most states, only first-degree murders were capitally eligible. Although the legislature clearly meant to limit the number of death-eligible murders by the premeditation formula, the courts quickly interpreted the phrase potentially to include anyone who killed: defendants could "premeditate" in the space of five seconds. Conrad will argue heat of passion. Under the common law, a killing "which would otherwise be murder" (i.e., was done with malice aforethought) was manslaughter if it was committed (1) in response to specific, legally adequate provocative acts by the victim(s), (2) in the heat of passion, and (3) without time for the person to "cool off." The events that were considered legally adequate provocation were extremely limited; the most important were (1) finding your spouse committing adultery, (2) being physically insulted (e.g., slapped), and (3) being illegally arrested. Most modern courts have increasingly adopted a more generous approach, asking whether a "reasonable person with [some of] the defendant's characteristics [age, gender, physical disability] would have reacted as the defendant did." Whether the defendant had time to cool off is also now a question of fact for the jury, rather than one of law for the judge. The Model Penal Code, §210.3, subjectivizes the claim even more, leaving to the jury whether the defendant acted "under extreme emotional or mental disturbance" (EED) for which there is a "reasonable explanation or excuse" for someone in the defendant's "situation." The MPC does not expressly require a provocative act; it is enough that the defendant is acting under EED. Unless Conrad can argue that the sight of Rod "rekindled" him, he had 20 years to cool off. Under the Model Penal Code, however, the issue is always one for the jury, which might be sympathetic to Conrad and conclude that a "reasonable person" in Conrad's "situation" would experience "extreme mental and emotional disturbance."

Beatrice has withdrawn from the conspiracy by running out of the pawnshop. She's not guilty of theft, even though Conrad did commit (at least) larceny in the store. By that time, he was no longer being encouraged by Beatrice's participation. For similar reasons, she is not guilty of Rod's death. Even under *Pinkerton*, Beatrice will escape liability because (1) the killing is **not** in furtherance of the conspiracy and (2) the killing is not foreseeable, both because it is related to Conrad's hatred of Rod—and not to the robbery—and because it was Conrad who urged no violence. It is hard, therefore, to say that Beatrice should have foreseen that Conrad would use violence.

George might be seen as a "but for" cause of Rod's death. Had he not assaulted Rod and rendered him unconscious, Conrad might not have been able to kill (or even injure) him. Nevertheless, that is insufficient—even under a tort theory of proximate cause, it is hardly foreseeable that someone will come into Rod's store and kill him.

Answer to Question 21

Samson may have committed rape, and he has almost certainly committed so-called "statutory rape" in most jurisdictions in this country. The common law defined rape as the penetration by a male of the vulva of a female (not his wife) against her consent and by force. If the female did not resist "to her utmost," it was not rape. Recent changes in sexual assault law include the following: (1) the crime is now labeled "sexual battery" or "sexual assault," rather than "rape"; (2) a spouse can rape the other spouse; (3) the offense is no longer restricted to males—females can sexually assault males; (4) other forms of sexual relations besides vaginal intercourse may be included; (5) there is no requirement that resistance be "to the utmost"; and (6) other, nonforcible nonconsensual intercourse may be included. Additionally, the procedures at trial have been significantly altered (e.g., there is now no requirement that the victim's claim be corroborated by a witness to the attack, there are "rape shield" laws that prohibit, or restrict, cross-examining the victim on the basis of prior sexual conduct, etc.). Under the common law definition, Samson has not committed rape. Delilah's equivocal statements are not clearly "nonconsent." Moreover, even if Samson was lying about wanting to marry Delilah, the common law held that "fraud in the inducement" did not render the assault rape, as long as the female knew that she was agreeing to intercourse. In modern criminal law, however, some states have jettisoned the force requirement, while others have moved away from the nonconsent element. Here, Samson may not have used "force" (although his position of superiority over Delilah might obviate that requirement), but her noncertainty about the consent should have alerted him to her nonconsent. Even if Samson has not committed "sexual assault," he has committed "statutory rape," which consists of intercourse with a person under a statutorily established age (in many jurisdictions 16), even if there appears to be "consent." The view is that the minor is simply incapable of giving "true" consent. And a mistake, no matter how reasonable, as to the age of the minor, was irrelevant; strict liability applied. Twenty states now allow reasonable mistake as a relevant defense claim, but even in such a jurisdiction, the issue here would be whether Samson's assumption that any senior "must be" at least 16 is "reasonable."

Delilah's death

Sally's liability is uncertain. She would first argue that she had no "malice aforethought" for murder under the common law, but throwing a bowling ball may well qualify as demonstrating a "malignant heart." She would try to claim her killing was "in the heat of passion," reacting to "adequate legal provocation," thereby reducing it to manslaughter. But the common law restricted the claim to spouses; no matter how "significant" the nonspouse"other," the claim simply was not allowed. Moreover, some courts actually required that the slayer find the spouse (and lover) "in the act" of intercourse; no matter how obvious the liaison was, a slayer who arrived too late would not have the claim (*in flagrante delicto*). Finally, to the extent that the "provocation" claim reflects some notion that the victim "had it coming" because of the provocation, that cannot be the case here, because Delilah was Samson's victim. Sally is likely to fare better under modern criminal law, which allows a "provocation reduction" for any action that might provoke the "reasonable person." Seeing your fiancé unclothed in the presence of another would almost certainly meet that requirement. And modern law would more easily focus on whether Sally's actions were understandable, even if she hit the wrong victim. Under the Model Penal Code §210.3, which does not depend on "provocation," but asks merely whether the defendant was acting under "extreme mental or emotional disturbance," Sally would certainly get to the jury.

Moab's death

Samson will claim self-defense. But his use of deadly force can only be warranted if Sally (1) used deadly force (2) in an unjustified manner. Even so, if Samson was not the initiator of the use of **deadly** force, he can still claim self-defense. Normally, self-defense is allowed only against the actual aggressor. Here, a totally innocent party has been killed. Samson, however, will argue (probably successfully) that, under the doctrine of "transferred intent," his intent (which was justifiable self-defense) follows the bullet, and that Moab's death, however unfortunate, is nevertheless justified.

Sally

Even if Samson has a claim of self-defense, Sally may be liable for Moab's death. If the use of the bowling ball was unjustified, she is the "aggressor" who caused Moab's death. Her assault on Samson would constitute at least a misdemeanor, and "someone's" death is foreseeable manslaughter.

Answer to Question 22

Who, if anyone, has committed criminal trespass (Section 101)?

The statute does not have a *mens rea* word. Strict criminal liability offenses — where the government need not prove any *mens rea*, including mere tort negligence, with regard to one or more elements of the crime — have been variously characterized. Initially, they appeared mostly in statutes regulating sexual conduct, foodstuffs, and alcohol or protecting minors. In the 20th century, this group was expanded to include "police" or "regulatory" offenses. The courts have permitted strict liability to crimes that have small punishments and carry minimum stigmatization. Some states have imposed strict liability even where the penalty is severe. Recently, the U.S. Supreme Court declined to hold that a ten-year prison sentence would automatically lead the Court to interpret the offense as a non-strict-liability one. However, in that same decision, the Court defined "public welfare offenses" in which strict liability was permissible as those involving (1) dangerous items (2) that the defendant should expect to be highly regulated. Because it has jail time, §2.05 of the Model Penal Code would require that some *mens rea* be proven by the prosecution. Under §2.02(3) of the code, when no *mens rea* appears, the prosecutor may prove purpose, knowledge, or recklessness. Mike clearly had the purpose of trespassing. Ike, however, was asleep when the car trespassed on the grounds and may contend that he did not "act" in a way to violate the statute. But §2.01 of the MPC specifies that as long as one's course of conduct "includes" a voluntary act, the defendant cannot claim no *actus reus*. Because Ike knew before he fell asleep where the car was headed, he has "acted" within the meaning of the MPC and the statute. Louis, however, did not know, and he cannot be said to have acted with *mens rea* when he got in the car. By the time he realized where they were, Louis wanted to leave the car, but when Mike gunned the accelerator, Louis will be able to claim that his remaining in the car was involuntary. He may simultaneously argue that it was justified, because any attempt to jump out of the speeding car might have resulted in more harm than the mere trespass. Jules has an even better argument — he had no opportunity to leave the car before the police arrived, and his presence in the car was not a voluntary act.

Who, if anyone, has attempted malicious mischief?

The common law set out various tests to determine whether a defendant had gone beyond "mere preparation" and crossed the line of "attempt." Each of these required that the defendant have the specific intent to commit an offense and be very near his goal. Under any of these common law tests, it is arguable that Mike was close enough and would not have desisted had he not been arrested. Ike similarly knew what the goal was; even though he was asleep when the car neared the target, he is an accomplice of Mike's and, hence, guilty of attempt. Neither Louis nor Jules knew what the goal was and, therefore, could not have shared the purpose of committing malicious mischief. Jules, moreover, has yet another defense—he was intoxicated. In the majority of states, intoxication can be used by a defendant to avoid liability for a specific-intent crime. Attempt is a crime requiring specific intent (purpose) as to the goal, and, hence, Jules will avoid liability this way as well.

Under §5.01 of the Model Penal Code, Mike and Ike again clearly have the purpose and have gone far beyond a "substantial step." On the other hand, neither Jules nor Louis has such a purpose, and they are not guilty. As with the common law, Jules may also claim intoxication. Under the MPC, a defendant may claim intoxication as a defense to a crime of "purpose" or "knowledge." Attempt is such a crime. Intoxication, however, is not a defense to a charge of recklessness, but the charge of Section 102 is not a charge of recklessness.

Answer to Question 23

DAPHNE'S (D'S) LIABILITY AT COMMON LAW

The first possibility is **felony murder**. At common law, the felony murder-makes a defendant liable for murder if he causes the death of another in the course of an enumerated felony.

First, it is clear that D and Velma (V) were engaged in a felony—it is posited in the call of the question. Furthermore, it is clear that the felonious conduct was the but-for cause of the death. If D and V had not engaged in mutual combat, V and Y would be alive today. A more difficult question is whether the deaths of D and Y were reasonably foreseeable. With regard to the death of V, it's hard to see how the answer could be no. D and V were playing a violent game near the edge of the cliff, a game that would only end with one of them passing very near the cliff's edge. With regard to the death of Y, things are more contingent. Yes, there was the possibility that someone falling might fall on someone below, but we would probably need more facts to know just how likely it was that others would be harmed if one of the players fell from the cliff.

Many courts limit felony murder to those crimes that are inherently dangerous. It seems relatively clear that mutual combat is an inherently dangerous felonies; one of the reasons that the legislature has chosen to prohibit people from engaging in it is that it is likely to lead to death in all instances. If that is so, it meets the inherently dangerous standard regardless of whether it is applied to the facts of the crime or to the elements of the offense itself (*compare People v. Phillips*, 64 Cal. 2d 524 (1966) *with People v. Stewart*, 663 A.2d 912 (1995)).

Courts also generally require that the felony be independent of the killing. This is a difficult question on these facts. In many ways, mutual combat resembles an assault statute, and assault is generally held to be a crime that is not independent of the resulting death. (*see, e.g., People v. Burton*, 6 Cal. 3d 375 (1971)). That is, mutual combat is viewed merely as assaulting someone who consents to being assaulted, then calling murder all mutual combat that leads to death seems prohibited for the same reason that allowing all assaultive deaths to be felony murder is generally frowned upon.

Finally, many courts will limit the felony murder to certain killers and certain victims. Here, the outcome depends on how the events leading to death are characterized; either V killed herself (in which case D will not be held liable for V's death) or D's act of assaulting him will be found to be the cause of her death. In either case, the killing was by a co-felon. Similarly, Y was killed by V, a co-felon of D; when courts limit the liability for killers other than the defendant, they usually permit it when the person causing death is the defendant's confederate.

Therefore, felony murder seems appropriate. It is possible, however, that the jurisdiction excludes from felony murder those cases in which a co-felon is killed, which would make D liable for Y's death but not for V's.

Liability based on D's own conduct.

This theory asks whether D committed a culpable act that foreseeably caused the death of another. On these facts, the answer to that question appears to be yes. He was shooting at V as V was getting nearer and nearer the edge of the cliff. Despite the patent risk, D didn't stop, and V fell to his and Y's death. As described above, D's conduct was at a minimum the proximate cause of V's death.

There is also the question of whether V's voluntary decision to both play the game and then leave the playing field severs the causal connection between D's conduct and the deaths. This is a relatively powerful argument on these facts; D did not force V to the edge of the cliff and V's voluntary decision to leave the field in that direction was likely an intervening cause sufficient to absolve D of culpability for V's death. As a policy matter, however, this leaves no one culpable for the death of Y, a situation which the legislature might find repugnant.

Assuming that causation is satisfied, the next question is what level of culpability is appropriate based on **D's mental state**? With regard to V, it's likely that extreme recklessness could be shown and that D would thus be liable for second degree murder. Based on how much space there is between the edge of the field and the cliff, it is quite possible that a jury would find that death was so likely that the defendant acted with an abandoned and malignant heart sufficient to satisfy the common law's requirement of malice aforethought. Similarly, a jury might conclude that the defendant's conduct was reckless, but not so socially repugnant to amount to gross recklessness. In this case, involuntary manslaughter would be the most serious charge his conduct would support. Finally, manslaughter would also be appropriate if the jury were convinced that the defendant's conduct was grossly negligent. If, by contrast, the jury finds that the defendant's conduct amounted to no more than ordinary tort negligence, in most jurisdictions he would not be criminally liable for d's death. With regard to Y's death, by contrast, D's culpability is almost certainly lower. It is difficult to see how a jury could find D more than grossly negligent with regard to the unlikely death of those playing on the beach far below, thus his liability for that killing under this theory is likely limited to involuntary manslaughter.

D may also be liable as an **accomplice in V's homicidal conduct**. D encouraged V to engage in mutual combat in the same way that drag racers encourage one and other to engage in that activity (see, e.g., *Commonwealth v. Root*, 403 Pa. 571 (1961)). However, D did not aid and abet V in the conduct that actually led to death; while it may have been foreseeable that V would go over the cliff, there is no evidence that this is an event that D intended to bring into being. Thus, only in a jurisdiction that follows *People v. Luparello*, 187 Cal. App. 3d 410 (1987) would D be liable as an accomplice. Finally, even in a *Luparello* jurisdiction, D could only be liable as an accomplice in Y's death and not in V's. Because V could not be found liable for causing his own death, D cannot be liable for that death as an accomplice.

It might appear D and V conspired together to commit the crime of mutual combat. They agreed to do it and engaged in many overt acts in furtherance of the agreement. However where a crime requires two participants to be completed, those participants cannot

D's Liability under the MPC

The Model Penal Code has rejected the **felony murder doctrine**. At most, participation in an enumerated felony can give rise to a presumption of extreme recklessness. MPC §210.2(1)(b). Mutual combat is not one of the enumerated felonies, however.

The question then becomes whether, independent of the felony murder rule, **D can be liable for the deaths of V and Y**. The first obstacle to D's liability is that of causation. Again, D's conduct is a but-for cause of both deaths. Under the MPC, the second question is whether the actual result is not so remote or accidental in its occurrence to be fairly attributable to the defendant. *See, e.g.,* MPC §2.03(2)(b). This is, of course, a judgment call, one that a jury would have to pass on; the MPC quite explicitly leaves this question for the jury.

Under the Model Penal Code, an accomplice is only liable for the crimes she encourage or attempts to encourage. MPC §2.06(3)(ii). Here, therefore, D would only be liable as an accomplice in d and Y's deaths if he encouraged the conduct that lead to death. On these facts, that would be difficult to prove. While D encouraged d to leave the field of play by continuing to fire at him as he fled, it is a leap from that conclusion to a finding that he intended for his friend to plunge to his death. Unless it can be shown that D acted with the conscious object of encouraging his friend to plunge to his death, D is not an accomplice in that conduct.

Co-Conspirator Liability

There is no co-conspirator liability under the Model Penal Code. Under the code, co-conspirators are only liable if their conduct amounts to aiding and abetting. Thus, co-conspirator liability is not an independent theory of liability under the Code.

Question 24

A'S LIABILITY AT COMMON LAW

Attempted statutory rape

It is posited in the question that A intended to engage in the prohibited conduct. He did not, however, desire to engage in statutory rape. In fact, that was likely NOT his intent. Nonetheless, according to the doctrine the courts established in *Commonwealth v. Dunne,* 394. Mass. 10 (1985) a defendant charged with an attempt crime need only have the intent to engage in the prohibited conduct; with regard to attendant circumstances he need only have the mental state required by statute. No mental state is specified in the statute, and in the majority of American jurisdictions, statutory rape is a crime of strict liability. Thus, A had the required mental state for attempted statutory rape. There is no question of mistake here, as the mistake could not negate the *mens rea* required by statute.

The question remains, however, whether he did the *actus reus*. At common law, it is generally required that the defendant get dangerously close to completing the crime before he can be charged with an attempt. Here, it appears that A was spotted entering B's home, some time before the crime was to be committed. Thus, it may be that he did not get sufficiently close to completing the crime to be charged with its attempt. However, there is little evidence that he would have desisted had he not been caught. Therefore, although this is a close call the *actus reus* is likely satisfied as well, and D could be convicted of attempted statutory rape.

Involuntary manslaughter

At common law involuntary manslaughter required that the defendant cause the death of another through more than civil negligence. The question, therefore, is whether A caused the death of C and whether he did so in a way that a reasonable person would have realized created a grave risk of death.

Felony Murder

A may be found liable of felony murder if a death occurred while he was engaged in a felony, the felony was inherently dangerous, the death was independent of the felony, and the death satisfies the other requirements regarding killers and victims.

Here, attempted statutory rape, even statutory rape, is likely not an inherently dangerous felony. The felony is looked at in the abstract, and it must be determined whether it can be performed safely. Here, it is easy to imagine a number of consensual statutory rapes which would not be inherently dangerous to human life. Although the law is in place to protect those in their tender years, it is a stretch to argue that statutory rape is always a threat to human life.

If the crime is found to be inherently dangerous, however, it is also independent of the killing. There is an independent felonious purpose B here, the desire to engage in sex with a person under the age of majority. Therefore the killing and the felony do not merge and attempted statutory rape can form the basis of a felony murder conviction.

Finally, A's liability may depend on whether the jurisdiction applies an agency or proximate cause theory of felony murder. *See* ***State v. Canola***, 73 N.J. 206 (1977). Under agency, each felon is liable only for killings done by another felon. Here, to the extent C was killed by anyone, she was killed by her father, who was not in an agency relationship with the defendant. However, in a proximate cause jurisdiction, the question would be whether or not the death was foreseeable, a question addressed in some depth above.

Conspiracy
There was an agreement among A, B, and C that A would engage in conduct that constitutes statutory rape. Furthermore, the parties all took an overt act in furtherance of the agreement; A took B to C's apartment to consummate the act.

However, there are a number of barriers to a conspiracy conviction on these facts. Primary among these is the fact that A and B did not know that C was underage and that the act contemplated by A was criminal. Of course, if the act had been consummated, the fact that A did not know, in fact could not reasonably have learned, that C was under age would afford him no excuse. There is a split of authority regarding whether the same can be said of the conspiracy to commit a strict liability offense.

A'S LIABILITY AT MPC

Attempted Statutory Rape
Then *mens rea* under the MPC is quite similar to the common law approach when it comes to attempts. Thus, he must have the specific intent to engage in the conduct and the mental state with regard to attendant circumstances required by statue. Under the MPC, however, recklessness would likely be

required as to whether C was a minor, as the MPC substitutes recklessness when no mental state is required by statute. Here, it appears that the D was not reckless. MPC §2.02 (3). The question states that he believed that she was not a minor, but that does not resolve the question whether he was reckless with regard to her age. Even if he believed that she was of age, if he was not aware of a risk that he was wrong, he is reckless nonetheless.

Assuming that he was reckless, the question is whether he did the *actus reus*. The Model Penal Code requires that the defendant take a substantial step strongly corroborative of his criminal intent before he can be charged with an attempt. MPC §§5.01(1), (2). Here, a substantial step was clearly taken—A drove to the apartment with B. The MPC was designed to punish attempts at a far earlier point than the common law did, and it would almost certainly impose liability on these facts.

It is clear that A was the but-for cause of C's death. If he had not taken her to B's house, the death would not have occurred at that time and in that way. Proximate cause is more difficult to show on these facts, however. It is true that he was creating a risk by being around C, as D had threatened to kill them both if he saw them together again. The difficulty is that D did not kill C, she dropped dead of fright. Furthermore, the fact that it was D's threats and not A's acts that led to C's death further attenuates his liability. Thus, causation is unlikely to be proven and A cannot be held liable of involuntary manslaughter at common law.

If causation is proven, however, it will also have to be shown that A was at least grossly or criminally negligent with regard to the death of C. On the one hand, a reasonable person in his shoes would be aware that his continuing to see C created the risk that they would both be killed by her father. On the other, this was likely the hyperbole of an over-protective father, and we'd want to know more about the father to know whether his threats were plausible.

Involuntary manslaughter
There is no involuntary manslaughter under the code. Rather, under the code, A can be found liable of manslaughter if it can be shown that he caused a death through recklessness. MPC §210.3(1)(a). Causation under the Code is slightly different than at common law; it requires but for causation, and that the outcome which occurred was not so different from that which is risked that the defendant should not be held liable for it. Here, the harm which resulted is not very different from the harm risked; the defendant risked C being killed by D's rage, but instead, his rage caused her to

die of shock. The Model Penal Code is less than precise about how much attenuation is too much, so it would be left to you to argue the public policy implication of holding defendants responsible on these sorts of facts.

In order for A to be found reckless, he must have disregarded a substantial and unjustifiable risk of C's death. That seems plausible on these facts. A was aware that if he took C out again, they might both be killed by D. Thus, he would likely be found reckless, and guilty of manslaughter if causation is deemed satisfied.

Felony murder

There is no felony murder rule under the Model Penal Code. The closest thing the code has is §210.2(1)(b) which creates a presumption of extreme recklessness based on the defendant's participation in certain enumerated crimes. Statutory rape is not, however, one of those crimes.

Conspiracy

Again, a conspiracy requires an agreement and, likely, an overt act. There was an agreement here for the reasons discussed above, and many overt acts as well.

Here, liability under the MPC is more likely.

B'S LIABILITY AT COMMON LAW

B did not attempt to commit statutory rape. Thus, he cannot be held liable based on his own conduct. However, he may be held for the crime if he was either an accomplice or a co-conspirator. I consider each in turn.

Complicity

One is liable as an accomplice if one encouraged another to engage in a crime with the intent that the other engage in that behavior. Here, B encouraged A to have sex with C at his house and he did so in the hope that they in fact would. Thus, he appears to have the culpable mental state. However, B was not aware of the fact which made the conduct criminal B to wit C's age. Thus, under the doctrine of the Youden case, he cannot be an accomplice.

Conspiracy

As discussed above, it is ambiguous whether a conspiracy existed here. If it did, B is liable for all acts done in furtherance of the conspiracy which are reasonably foreseeable. The attempted statutory rape would certainly be foreseeable, as statutory rape was the object of the conspiracy.

Felony Murder

B is liable for felony murder only if he is liable for the felony and all of the other requirements mentioned above are satisfied. Even assuming that he is liable of the attempt under one of the two theories described above, the requirements of felony murder are not satisfied for the reasons they are not satisfied with regard to A.

B'S LIABILITY AT MPC

Complicity
Under the code, one is an accomplice if one aids or attempts to aid another in the commission of an offense with the intent to aid. MPC §2.06(3)(ii). Here, the same problem arises as at common law B what is one to do about the fact that B did not know of C's age? The MPC seems to imply that it would follow the same rule as the Common Law, hence there is no liability here, as B did not know her age.

Conspiracy
Under the Code, conspiracy is not a theory of liability, it is only a substantive offense. Hence, B cannot be guilty of attempting statutory rape as a co-conspirator.

Felony Murder
There is no felony murder under the MPC.

Question 25

This question is actually easier than it appears. The trick is that because V could not be held liable for homicide based on his own death, D could not be held either vicariously or derivatively liable for that death. Other than that, the question was relatively straightforward.

Common Law

Drag Racing

D was engaged in a competition between two or more people involving speeds above the posted maximums. Thus he satisfies the *actus reus* of the offense. Notice that no *mens rea* is specified by statute. However, because these two clearly intended to engage in a drag race, whatever *mens rea* is required under the statute was definitely satisfied here.

Note also that it is important to establish D's liability for this felony. Many of the crimes that follow are related to this finding.

Felony Murder

We are told in the problem that drag racing is a felony and D's guilt has already been established. Because V died in the course of that felony, felony murder becomes a real possibility.

The first step is to show that the death was caused by the felonious conduct. If the cars had been driving at normal speeds and if the defendant had not tried to prevent his friend from passing, the accident almost certainly would not have occurred. Therefore causation is clearly satisfied.

The next question is whether drag racing is inherently dangerous. In many states the question is whether, looking simply at the elements of the offense, whether this is a crime that can be done without creating risk to human life. *See, e.g., People v. Phillips*, 64 Cal.2d 524 (1966). Very few crimes are deemed inherently dangerous under this standard. Here, a court could easily find that if a course is carefully laid out and the drivers are highly skilled there is little risk of death. In a jurisdiction that looks at the crime as it was committed, by contrast, there is little difficulty in determining that this crime was inherently dangerous. *See, e.g., People v. Stewart*, 663 A.2d 912 (1995). The race was conducted at high speeds, at night, at speeds far in excess of those posted; these factors seem to conspire to create a situation in which death is a likely result.

The next inquiry is whether the felony is independent of the killing. That is, we ask whether the felony is just the means by which the death happened. Here, unlike with some crimes such as assault, there is an independent felonious purpose; D did not plot this race in order to kill V. Furthermore, drag racing is not included in fact or an integral part of the killing; it is not a necessary part of the way the death occurred. Thus, under either test, it does not merge with the killing and may serve as the basis of a felony murder prosecution.

In an agency jurisdiction, a defendant is only liable for deaths that are caused by himself or his confederates. *See State v. Canola,* 73 N.J. 206 (1977). Regardless of whether we attribute this death to D or V, it was caused by one of the perpetrators of the felony, and would therefore be eligible for felony murder in an agency state. Some states, however, have prohibited felony murder prosecutions where one of the perpetrators is the victim, on the theory that the killing is partially justified. *See, e.g., Commonwealth v. Redline,* 391 Pa. 386 (1958). Thus, if this crime took place in such a state, a prosecution would thus be barred.

In sum, this death will likely punishable as felony murder (provided that drag racing is found to be inherently dangerous) likely second degree felony murder as this is not on most lists of crimes that give rise to first degree murder.

Other Homicide
Regardless of whether D is found liable of felony murder he will likely also be punished for homicide under a theory of direct causation.

The first question in such an analysis is whether D was the but-for and proximate cause of V's death. While this is similar to the causation inquiry under the FMR, the two analyses are not identical. With regard to but-for causation, this question is easily answered in the affirmative. Had these two not agreed to drag race on this night, V would not have died at this time and in this way.

The proximate cause question is considerably more complicated, however. As we've seen, courts have resolved the causation in drag racing cases both in favor and against the surviving racer. The biggest impediment to D's liability for homicide is the fact that V made the conscious decision to try to pass at high speeds. Although this result might have been perfectly foreseeable to D, a court might rule that V's choice was an intervening, superseding cause of his own death, thus absolving D of liability. Courts often resolve this issue by considering the policy implications of leaving V's death unpunished.

Assuming causation is satisfied, the next question regards the defendant's *mens rea*. Generally, involuntary manslaughter requires that the defendant act with gross negligence. That is certainly satisfied here. Even if he was not, D should have been aware of the homicidal risks that he created when he attempted to block his friend's passage at more than 40 mph above the posted speed limit. His failure to perceive this risk is a gross deviation from the standard of care that we owe one another and a jury would likely have little trouble convicting defendant of involuntary manslaughter.

The next question is whether he acted with the kind of reckless disregard for human life that would suffice to justify a finding of malice aforethought. It's important here that D knew that he was a better driver than his friend. This could demonstrate that he was aware that he was creating risks to his friend's life and chose to engage in that conduct rather than simply let his friend win. This risk was both substantial—it was a likely risk of death—and unjustifiable—this was not the kind of conduct that served any social utility. This is different than speeding through traffic to reach a hospital; the risks were taken entirely for D's own benefit. Thus, a court would likely find that D acted with gross recklessness and that a finding of malice aforethought is appropriate.

Because there is no indication that D intended to kill, let alone that he premeditated and deliberated V's death, this will not be a case of first degree murder.

Conspiracy

D and V definitely agreed to engage in a drag race. Because their conduct was illegal, their agreement to engage in that conduct, coupled with the numerous over acts in which they engaged would generally be sufficient to make them liable for conspiracy as well as for the substantive offense. However, like dueling, drag racing is a crime that by its nature requires the participation of more than one participant. Thus, Wharton's rule forbids a conspiracy charge on these facts; because the dangers of criminal agreement are inherent in the substantive charge, a conspiracy charge would be unfairly duplicative.

Vicarious Liability

Neither accomplice liability nor co-conspirator (*Pinkerton*) liability is applicable on these facts. First, as just demonstrated, there was no conspiracy on these facts. Second, because V cannot be liable for homicide for causing his own death, D cannot be vicariously liable if V is not liable as a principal.

MPC

Statute
Just as D was liable under the statute in a CL jurisdiction he will be liable in a MPC jurisdiction. He clearly did all of the prohibited acts and did each of them intentionally. Thus, regardless of what *mens rea* is required, D will be shown to have acted with at least that *mens rea*.

Felony Murder
There is no felony murder rule under the MPC. While participation in some crimes can give rise to a rebuttable presumption of extreme recklessness, MPC §210.2(1)(b), drag racing is not one of those crimes.

Other Homicide
As at CL, causation under the MPC is a two-step inquiry. The first is the same: was the defendant a but-for cause of V's death. As above, then answer is yes. The second inquiry is worded slightly differently under the MPC:whether the result that occurred is too remote or accidental to fairly be attributed to D. See MPC §2.03(2)(b). Under the code this is explicitly a policy determination. For the reasons discussed above, a jury considering this question would likely have little sympathy for D, the instigator of the drag race that led to the death of his friend.

With regard to *mens rea*, the MPC identifies a form of liability not found in many CL jurisdictions: negligent homicide. MPC §210.4. Ordinary negligence under the code suffices to convict a defendant of negligent homicide, and D was clearly negligent. The very least that can be said of his culpability is that he should have been aware of the substantial and unjustifiable homicidal risks he was creating. Thus, he will be convicted of at least negligent homicide.

Recklessness is the minimum *mens rea* that must be proven to convict a defendant of manslaughter under the MPC. MPC §210.3(1)(a). Under the code, recklessness requires the awareness and disregard of a substantial and unjustifiable risk. As discussed above, this is a question of fact for a jury. However, the fact that D put his speeding car in V's path, knowing that he was the superior driver, is certainly evidence from which a jury could reasonably conclude that D was aware of a substantial and unjustifiable risk of death.

Murder under the MPC requires at least recklessness manifesting an extreme indifference to the value of this test. MPC §210.2(1)(b). This test is virtually indistinguishable from the abandoned and malignant heart required at CL and the analysis will follow as above.

Conspiracy

D and V agreed to drag race and committed numerous overt acts. Therefore they are guilty of conspiracy. Although the MPC has not adopted Wharton's rule, under the MPC conspiracy and the completed crime merge and a defendant cannot be convicted of both.

Vicarious Liability

As above, vicarious liability has no application to these facts; because V cannot be liable for his own death, D cannot be vicariously liable for that death.

Question 26

V'S LIABILITY AT COMMON LAW

Theft

D knowingly took the property of another with the intent to permanently deny the owner its use. He knew that the iPods were not rightly his but he took them anyhow. Also, it is apparent, although by no means proven, that D had the intent to permanently deprive the Apple store of the iPods; there is no evidence that he was borrowing them, that he was planning to bring them back, etc. The only question, therefore, is whether the statute requires that he know that the value of the thing he is taking exceed $500. It seems ambiguous as written. If knowledge is required, then V will be able to defeat the charges if he is able to convince a jury that he did not in fact know that the iPods were worth that much. It is also possible, at common law, that the statute will be interpreted as strict liability with regard to this element and that V can be convicted regardless of his *mens rea*.

It is important to note that V was guilty of the crime as soon as he took the iPods. The statute did not require that he leave the store with them or reach a place of temporary safety with them in order to have satisfied the elements of the statute. Furthermore, although V was guilty of the crime when he has taken possession of the iPods, the crime was still in progress at the time of the altercation.

Conspiracy.

The core of a conspiracy is an agreement to commit criminal acts or to commit a legal act in an illegal way. The agreement need not be express and may be inferred from concerted conduct. Here, there is certainly concerted effort. D took the iPods while V distracted the guard, enabling (so D claimed) V to leave the store with the devices. However, without more, it is unlikely that a conspiracy could be proven on these facts. V scowled when he saw D watching him before the theft, he did not ask for help, and he was angered when D caught up with him outside the store. In the absence of more evidence, it does not appear that a jury could reasonably conclude that a conspiracy here was proven beyond a reasonable doubt.

Homicide

Unless it can be shown that V was the cause of A's death, he cannot be held for any homicide crime. At common law, it must be shown that V was both the but-for and proximate cause of A's death. V was clearly the but-for cause of C's death, but for V pulling out of the space, C's car would not have struck A, killing her. The proximate causation question is significantly more complicated, however. Clearly if V had simply pulled out into A, the causation would have been clear; it is foreseeable that if you gun your car in a parking lot that you might strike a pedestrian. Here, however, there is the intervening action of C's car striking A after being struck by V. Although this makes the causation more attenuated, it is not the sort of unforeseeable, superseding cause that would preclude a jury from concluding that V was legally responsible for the death of A.

Murder

At common law the dividing line between murder and manslaughter is malice aforethought. Malice aforethought can be satisfied when a defendant intends to kill, intends to do great bodily harm, intends to commit a felony, or shows an abandoned and malignant heart. D did not intend to kill; he did not intend to do great bodily harm. Thus, if he is found guilty of murder it will have to be under a theory of implied malice based on extreme recklessness. In order to demonstrate extreme recklessness, it must be shown, at a minimum, that V disregarded a substantial and unjustifiable risk that his conduct will result in death. If he is able to convince a jury that he was not thinking about the risks and was merely trying to get away from D, then he cannot be convicted of murder. If, however, a jury believes that the risks he created were so patent that he must have been aware of them, he may be convicted of murder. We would need more facts to resolve this issue, particularly with regard to where V was parked, how busy the parking lot was, etc.

Voluntary manslaughter

Even if it is shown that V acted with malice aforethought, he might claim that he was acting out of heat of passion and that as a result his crime should be reduced from murder to voluntary manslaughter. There are at least two problems with this claim. First, voluntary manslaughter is generally only available to reduce an intentional killing to manslaughter, and the killing here was clearly unintended. Second, in many jurisdictions, voluntary manslaughter is only available when the person killed is the person who provoked the killer. Here, A was an innocent and voluntary manslaughter might be completely unavailable.

Felony Murder

At common law, any death that was caused by a defendant's felonious conduct was punishable as murder. And here, it has been demonstrated that

V was guilty of theft as defined by statute. Furthermore, unless it is concluded that V's car was a place of temporary safety, it appears clear that A's death was the result of V's felonious conduct. Over time, however, courts have created a number of doctrines that limit the application of the felony murder in a particular case.

Inherently Dangerous

Many states limit the application of felony murder to those crimes that are inherently dangerous. If a state follows the California approach and examines the statute in the abstract to determine whether the crime can be committed without creating a risk of death, then the crime is not eligible for felony murder. *People v. Phillips,* 64 Cal. 2d 524 (1966). By contrast, if a state looks at the defendant's particular acts, as other states do, then he is much more likely to be convicted. *People v. Stewart,* 663 A.2d 912 (1995). Here, he was speeding away from the crime in what we can presume is a crowded mall parking lot; although theft is clearly not dangerous in every instance, a jury could conclude that the way V committed his necessarily created homicidal risks.

Merger

Felonies that are included in fact or that are integral to the killing may not form the basis of felony murder. *People v. Mattison,* 4 Cal.3d 177 (1971). While this limitation makes it impossible to charge felony murder based on an underlying assault, it likely would not preclude a felony murder charge on these facts. The felony here was not merely the means by which the killing occurred; the killing was entirely incidental to V's criminal conduct and thus there is no merger of the felony and the killing.

Limitations on Killers and Victims

Some states limit felony murder to those killings done by the defendant or a confederate or prohibit felony murder if the person killed is a confederate. Neither limitation is relevant on these facts.

Felony murder is thus something of a stretch on these facts, largely because grand theft is not inherently dangerous.

D'S LIABILITY AT COMMON LAW

Conspiracy

As discussed above, the proof of an agreement between the two here is fairly tenuous. While there is concerted effort, the other facts certainly seem to indicate that there was no agreement either explicit or implicit between the parties. If not, then D cannot be guilty of Conspiracy.

Theft

D did not steal; he did not take the iPods or cause them to be taken. Therefore, he is liable, if at all, either as an accomplice or as a co-conspirator.

Co-Conspirator

As just discussed, D is quite likely not guilty of conspiracy and thus cannot be found liable as a co-conspirator. In the unlikely event that a conspiracy is proven, however, each conspirator is liable for the acts of his co-conspirators that are in furtherance of the conspiracy and are reasonably foreseeable. *Pinkerton v. U.S*, 328 U.S. 640 (1946). Here, just as in Pinkerton, the theft was the very act contemplated by the purported conspiracy; thus, if there was an agreement then D would be liable for the theft as a co-conspirator.

Accomplice

D is liable of theft as an accomplice if he aided in the theft and intended to aid in the theft.

Aid

Here, D appeared to help V commit the crime by distracting the guard so that V could make his getaway. However, when D confronted V in the parking lot, V angrily dismissed his assistance, maintaining that it was no help at all. It should be borne in mind that in order to be an accomplice, a defendant need not offer very much aid at all; D need not even be the but-for cause of the theft in order to be found to have aided in its commission. Given this fact, and notwithstanding V's objections, a jury will likely find that V made the commission of the crime easier and he will likely be found to have aided its commission.

Intent to Aid

Given the inanity of D's question for the guard and D's own contention that it was his goal to facilitate the offence, it will be hard for him to argue that he did not intend to distract the guard to aid in the theft.

Thus, D is likely to be held liable for the theft as an accomplice.

Homicide

The first question is whether D can be held liable for homicide based on his own conduct, that is whether he did a culpable act that caused the death of another person. That seems fairly unlikely on these facts. D did a risky thing in attempting to open V's door as he was starting to drive away, and while that might make him the but-for cause of A's death, the number of steps between his conduct and the death of A make a finding of proximate cause fairly unlikely.

Accomplice liability

D did not encourage V to do the acts that led to death. Therefore he is liable, if at all, under the natural and probable consequences doctrine. If V was D's accomplice in the theft (and he probably was) and if D's killing of A was the natural and probable consequence of that theft, then the natural and probable consequences doctrine will make V responsible for the killing as well. Here, it is not at all clear that the death of A followed naturally and probably from that crime. As discussed, the causal connection between the theft and the death of A is very attenuated, and it seems perhaps more farfetched to assert that that death followed naturally from V's crime.

Co-conspirator liability

Again, the most difficult step here is the finding of a conspiracy itself. If there is a conspiracy then, as discussed above, V is likely for those crimes committed by D that are in furtherance of the theft and are reasonably foreseeable. However, as discussed in detail above, it does not appear that the death of A is one such crime.

Felony Murder

If D is liable for the felony as either an accomplice or a co-conspirator, then he is liable for felony murder to the extent that V is. However, as we saw above, such liability is quite unlikely on these facts.

C'S LIABILITY AT COMMON LAW

C has no criminal liability. Not only is there no evidence that would point to a culpable mental states, but there is no evidence that C did any voluntary act that led to the harms in question here. C was acted upon. She did not act.

V'S LIABILITY AT MPC

Theft

As at common law, V is almost certainly liable for theft. Interpreting the theft statute, the only difference from the common law approach might be the *mens rea* required with regard to the amount of the loss. At common law it is possible that this is a strict liability element; that if D knowingly took the iPods and their value was in excess of $500, then he is liable without any additional showing. Under the MPC, such a reading of statute is not permissible. *See, e.g.,* MPC §2.02(3). Some *mens rea* must be shown with regard to each material element of the offense. However, a jury could reasonably conclude that V selected iPods for his theft because of their high value; even if recklessness is required with regard to the amount of loss, V will likely be found guilty.

Conspiracy

The elements of conspiracy are very similar under the MPC as at common law; there must be an agreement and, in many cases, an overt act done in further of that conspiracy. MPC §5.03(3); MPC §5.03(5). Here, there is no question that an overt act was done (the theft was actually completed) but it will be very difficult to show that V agreed with D to commit this crime. Thus, as above, V is likely not liable for conspiracy to commit theft.

Homicide

As at CL, unless it is shown that V is the cause of A's death, he is not liable for any homicide crime. The MPC requires that V's conduct be an antecedent but for which A's death would not have occurred and that A's death be not too remote or accidental to fairly be attributable to V. On the former question there is no difficulty; on the latter, a jury could probably conclude either way. We would need more facts to know just how likely death was to result from V's conduct. If the mall was nearly empty and A suddenly appeared from behind a pole, the case for V would be considerably stronger.

For an accidental killing to be murder under the Model Penal Code, it must be shown that the defendant acted at least with recklessness under circumstances manifesting extreme indifference to the value of human life. MPC §210.2(1)(b). That would be quite a stretch here. Even if it could be shown that V consciously risked death by pulling out of his parking spot to get away from D, it is hard to believe that a jury would find that this recklessness was sufficiently serious that it could be equated with the intent to kill.

Manslaughter under the MPC is a killing that is done recklessly or which would be murder except that it was done under the influence of extreme emotional disturbance for which there is a reasonable explanation or excuse. MPC §210.3(b). With regard to the former, a jury would have to conclude not just that V was aware of a risk of death when he pulled out of his parking space but that he chose to disregard that risk. As discussed under murder, this is probably a long shot. With regard to the latter, the odds are even longer. As discussed above, it does not appear that V had a sufficiently culpable mental state to make him liable for homicide. Furthermore, it is exceedingly unlikely that a jury will find the desire to get away from a would-be confederate is sufficiently exculpating to reduce the seriousness of a homicide charge.

Felony Murder.
The MPC rejects felony murder and all other forms of strict liability. The closest the MPC comes to felony murder is the assertion that the extreme recklessness necessary to demonstrate murder may be rebuttably presumed if the defendant was engaged in certain enumerated felonies. MPC §210.2(1)(b). Grand theft is not among them.

D'S LIABILITY AT MPC

Conspiracy
Again, conspiracy requires proof of an agreement. There is very little evidence of an agreement on these facts. Although the MPC permits unilateral agreements, that doctrine is generally limited to situations where a defendant agrees with someone who does not in fact agree with him. Even that would be a stretch on these facts. There is nothing to indicate that D believed that V agreed with him to commit theft. At most, D wanted to help and did so without an agreement.

Theft
D's own conduct. D did not steal the iPods. Thus, he is liable for the theft, if at all, derivatively or vicariously.

Accomplice Liability is easier to prove under the MPC than at CL. It need only be shown that a defendant intended to aid and either aided or *attempted to aid* in the commission of an offense. MPC §2.06(3)(a)(ii). This certainly describes D. While V maintains that D did not in fact help him, under the MPC that fact is irrelevant to D's guilt as an accomplice.

The MPC rejects the *Pinkerton* doctrine. Thus, even if a conspiracy between D and V is shown, that fact alone cannot make D responsible for any of the crimes that V commits.

Homicide

The first question is whether D's own conduct caused A's death. While D's conduct is the but-for cause of A's death, it is not clear that that death is fairly attributable to D's conduct to make him legally responsible for that result. Furthermore, it is unlikely that it can be shown that D had a sufficiently culpable mental state *with regard to the death of a third party* to make him responsible for that death.

There is no evidence that D intended to encourage the conduct that led to A's death. Furthermore, because the MPC rejects the natural and probable consequences doctrine, there is no way to make D derivatively liable for that death.

D is also not liable under the Pinkerton or felony murder doctrine, as discussed previously.

C'S LIABILITY AT MPC

As at common law, C neither did a culpable act nor had a culpable mental state.

Multiple-Choice Questions

1. The state of Ames has a statute that defines criminal assault as occurring when one person "causes bodily injury to another." The case law of Ames defines criminal assault as a "general-intent crime."

   George and Kramer are drivers searching for a parking spot at a mall in the state of Ames. Both drivers approach an empty spot at about the same time. They begin to argue over who is entitled to the spot. During the argument, Kramer, intending to scare George away, walks over to George's car and touches George's throat with a screwdriver. Unfortunately, when George twists his head to look at Kramer, he cuts his throat against the screwdriver point and is seriously injured.

   Based on these facts, if Kramer is prosecuted for criminal assault, it is most likely that:

   A. Kramer is culpable because he intended to place the screwdriver against George's throat.

   B. Kramer is culpable because he created an inherently dangerous situation.

   C. Kramer is not culpable because he could not reasonably foresee George's actions.

   D. Kramer is not culpable because he lacked the intent to physically injure George.

2. Responding to a recent trend in gang violence, the California legislature enacted a statute that makes it a capital offense for any motorist to "knowingly" kill another motorist with an explosive device. (Assume that California law follows the Model Penal Code's definition of "knowingly.")

   One day, Freddy, a member of a gang called the Hooters, pulls alongside a car driven by Richie, a member of the Rockers gang. Richie makes a derogatory finger gesture toward Freddy. Enraged, Freddy lights a stick of dynamite, throws the stick into Richie's car, and then races away. Richie is killed when the dynamite explodes. Jack, who was sleeping in the back seat of Richie's car, is also killed. Freddy had no way of knowing that Jack was in Richie's car.

   Based on these facts, can Freddy be successfully prosecuted under the California statute for Jack's death?

   A. Yes, because he knowingly threw the dynamite into Richie's car.

   B. Yes, because Jack was clearly within the zone of danger created by Freddy's conduct.

   C. No, because Freddy did not know Jack was in the car.

   D. No, because Richie's conduct constituted sufficient provocation.

3. Joe, desperately needing money for his drug habit, steals a television from a friend's house. (Assume that, under applicable law, no burglary has occurred.) Three days later, Joe holds a garage sale and offers to sell the TV to Molly for $50. When Molly asks Joe how he could sell the item for "such a bargain," Joe replies that he needs the money "quickly" to relocate to another city. Molly pays Joe $50 and takes the television without ever getting proof of title for the item.

   Based on these facts, it is most likely that Joe could be successfully prosecuted for:

   A. False pretenses because Joe implicitly represented to Molly that he owned the television.

   B. Larceny by trick because Joe received $50 for the television, but gave no instrument of title to Molly.

   C. No crime because Joe made no express representations of ownership to Molly.

   D. No crime because purchasers assume the risk of defective title at events such as garage sales.

4. After Jethro was fired from his job, he decided to "get even" with his ex-employer. So, one night, Jethro broke into Farmer John's barn and set fire to John's favorite tractor. The barn was located approximately 25 feet from the main house.

   One of Farmer John's neighbors, Leroy, saw smoke coming from the barn. Leroy ran over and put out the fire before any part of the barn was destroyed. There was, however, extensive charring to the barn. Also, several of the items in the barn were burned. (Assume that the common law view of arson is adhered to in this jurisdiction.)

   Based on these facts, if Jethro is prosecuted for arson, it is most likely that:

   A. Jethro is not guilty because the barn was only charred.

   B. Jethro is guilty because the fire caused damage to a structure adjacent to the main house.

   C. Jethro is not guilty because he did not specifically intend to damage any structure (only Farmer John's tractor).

   D. Jethro is not guilty because the barn isn't part of Farmer John's house.

5. Mr. Barnes, a senior partner at the We Sue For You law firm, gave a fax machine to Andrew, a file room clerk, to deliver to a repair shop.

Andrew, who felt slighted because he was not given a Christmas bonus by Mr. Barnes, took the fax machine to a local pawnshop and obtained $200 for it. He then told Mr. Barnes that a thug had taken the fax machine from him at gunpoint. Two days later, Mr. Barnes happened to see the fax machine in the pawnshop window and called the police. Andrew was subsequently arrested. (Assume that common law principles are applicable in this jurisdiction.)

Based on these facts, if Andrew is prosecuted for larceny, it is most likely that:

A. Andrew is guilty because he tried to deprive Barnes of his fax machine.

B. Andrew is guilty because he lied to Barnes when he said the fax machine was taken from him.

C. Andrew is not guilty because Barnes voluntarily gave him the fax machine.

D. Andrew is not guilty if he intended to redeem the fax machine from the pawnshop when he was arrested.

6. Anita Badcheck decides that she simply has to have a new Mercedes convertible. She goes to the local Mercedes dealer and writes a check for the price of the car from her personal account. She knows that she only has $50 in her account. Before the salesperson can verify that the check is good, he has a heart attack. After the manager calls for an ambulance, he tells Anita to "take the car" and gives her the car's title documents. Three days after Anita drives off in the new Mercedes, her check is returned to the dealership, marked "insufficient funds."

Based on these facts, if Anita is prosecuted for the crime of false pretenses, it is most likely that:

A. Anita is guilty because she took possession of the vehicle.

B. Anita is guilty because she took title to the vehicle.

C. Anita is not guilty because she received only possession of the vehicle.

D. Anita is not guilty because the vehicle and attendant documents of title were turned over to her voluntarily by the dealer.

7. Erica offered to sell her computer to Jamie for $1,000. Erica told Jamie the computer was worth at least $2,000. However, just the day before, Erica had been told by an expert appraiser that the computer was worth "$500, at most." Jamie, believing that the computer was worth $2,000,

gave Erica a money order for $1,000. Erica, however, lost the money order before she could cash it.

Based on these facts, if Erica is prosecuted for the crime of false pretenses, it is most likely that:

A. Erica is guilty because she fraudulently obtained Jamie's money order.

B. Erica is guilty because Jamie took possession of the computer.

C. Erica is not guilty because she never cashed the money order.

D. Erica is not guilty because her comment about the computer's value was merely her opinion, not a factual statement.

8. Allison was shopping at Bruno Magli, when she spotted an extraordinary pair of loafers. Allison checked the price tag and saw the shoes were marked at $350. She had only $200 in her pocketbook. Undaunted by her shortage of funds, Allison calmly took a $200 price tag from another pair of shoes and switched it with the price tag on the loafers she wanted to buy. The teenage cashier failed to notice the change in price tags. Allison happily took her new pair of shoes home. Two days later, she was arrested when the store manager's inventory check revealed the tag switch.

Based on these facts, if Allison is prosecuted for larceny by trick, it is most likely that:

A. Allison is guilty because she acquired the shoes by deceit.

B. Allison is guilty because she fraudulently switched price tags.

C. Allison is not guilty because she acquired legal title to the shoes.

D. Allison is not guilty because she altered no digits on either of the price tags.

9. Mary asked Brian Beagal if she could borrow his new Toyota. She told Brian that she needed the car to go to a party at a professor's house. When she made the statement, she had no other purpose in mind. Brian gave her the keys and told Mary to have a good time. At the professor's party, Mary had a violent argument with her fiancé and decided that she had to get as far away from him as possible. Mary drove back to her house, put her most valuable possessions in Brian's car, and started on a trip out West. Mary was arrested one week later when a custom's official checked the car's license plate at the U.S.-Mexico border.

Based on these facts, it is most likely that Mary could be successfully prosecuted for:

A. Larceny.

B. False pretenses.

C. Larceny by trick.

D. Embezzlement.

10. Kevin, an 18-year-old with an addiction to silly practical jokes, took a plastic gun from his closet and went outside in search of his friends. Kevin saw his cousin, Mary, and her friend, Pam, walking toward his house. He decided to have a little fun with them and hid behind a bush, waiting for them to walk past. As they walked by, Kevin jumped out and yelled, "Give me your money or I'll shoot." Mary, who knew Kevin's addiction and suspected that Kevin's gun was just an old toy, pretended to be frightened and gave Kevin $5 from her purse. Kevin took the money and ran back into his house. Pam was genuinely frightened, but Kevin ran off before she could give him any money.

Based on these facts, it is most likely that Kevin can be successfully prosecuted for:

A. Robbery.

B. Larceny.

C. Embezzlement.

D. None of these crimes.

11. Tommy Nimblefingers is a professional pickpocket. One evening, he was lounging at a popular tourist resort in California, "checking out" the passing crowd. As he watched, a rich-looking couple walked by, arm in arm. They were obviously focused on each other and not paying much attention to anything else around them. Spying an easy "target," Tommy got up and began walking behind them. When he was close enough, he deftly removed the wallet from the man's back pocket. A nearby shopkeeper saw Tommy take the wallet, and he tackled Tommy before he could get away.

Based on these facts, which crime has Tommy committed?

A. Robbery.

B. Larceny by trick.

C. Embezzlement.

D. None of the above.

12. Kristen works as a live-in maid for Ward and June Cleaver. Feeling that she is underpaid, Kristen decides to steal an antique Chinese vase from the Cleaver mansion. She takes the vase, puts it under her coat, and leaves the house. About an hour later, June Cleaver notices that the vase is missing and calls the police. Police Officer Joe Friday spots Kristen walking in the seedy part of town with a big bulge under her coat. Friday stops Kristen, who admits that she stole the vase. She turns the vase over to Friday.

Kristen tells Friday that she was going to sell the vase to Beaver, a well-known "fence" for antique artifacts. Hoping to earn a few commendation points on his record by catching the notorious Beaver, Friday hands the vase back to Kristen and asks her to go ahead with the sale to Beaver. Beaver, intending to add the vase to his own private collection of rare Chinese antiques, buys the vase from Kristen for a small fraction of its real value.

Based on these facts, if Beaver is prosecuted for receiving stolen property, it is most likely that:

A. Beaver is guilty because the low purchase price establishes that he either knew or suspected that the vase was stolen.

B. Beaver is guilty because the vase was stolen.

C. Beaver is not guilty because Friday had recovered the stolen vase.

D. Beaver is not guilty because he did not intend to resell the vase.

13. Morgan runs the largest "fencing" operation in Broken Arrow. One day, his "employees" call and tell him that a large shipment of stolen televisions has arrived from an adjoining state. Morgan directs his "employees" to place the goods in a warehouse owned by Pete, an innocent third party who is completely unaware of Morgan's "fencing" operation. Two weeks before he can remove any of the stolen televisions from the warehouse, Morgan is arrested by the police, who received an anonymous "tip" about Morgan's operation.

Based on these facts, it is most likely that the most serious crime for which Morgan can be successfully prosecuted is:

A. Receipt of stolen property.

B. Attempted receipt of stolen property.

C. Conspiring to receive stolen property.

D. None of the above crimes.

14. Tom and Alex were both rejected for admission by Avery Law School, although they both had excellent college grades. Tom suspected that the sole reason for their rejection was the blind prejudice of the admissions director against students from Fairmount College. One night, after many beers, Tom asked Alex, "Wouldn't it be great if someone simply got rid of the admissions director?" Alex did not answer, but Tom continued, "If I could just get him alone, I could do it."

    The next day, Tom asked Alex to accompany him to the admissions office "so I can talk to that SOB once more." When they got there, the director was talking with his secretary. Tom asked Alex to get the secretary to leave the office. Alex responded, "Fine." He succeeded in luring the secretary out of the office on the pretext of showing her a mistake on one of the school's bulletin boards. Tom then closed the door to the director's office, took out a gun, and fatally shot the admissions director. Alex knew that Tom owned a gun, but he didn't believe that Tom actually was carrying it with him.

    Based on these facts, if Alex is prosecuted as an accomplice to murder, it is most likely that:

    A. Alex is guilty because he distracted the admissions director's secretary.

    B. Alex is guilty because he helped Tom carry out the murder plan.

    C. Alex is not guilty because he did not participate in the actual murder of the admissions director.

    D. Alex is not guilty because he lacked the necessary *mens rea.*

15. Jimmy Jones is charged with trespass, which is defined as "knowingly entering a private building without permission of the owner." He entered a fenced-in yard. Such a yard is, under state decisional law, a "building." Jones argues that he did not "knowingly enter a building" because he did not know that the yard was a building.

    Jones's claim is likely to succeed:

    A. Under the Model Penal Code.

    B. Under common law.

    C. Under both.

    D. Under neither.

16. Dillinger and Capone were prison cellmates at Alcatraz. Six months ago, Capone was released from prison after serving his three-year term for tax fraud. Dillinger, who is still serving a life term for murder, wants

Capone to kill the police officer who captured him. He sends Capone a letter offering him $50,000 for the hit. Unknown to Dillinger, Capone has been sent to Papillon prison after a new conviction for armed robbery. The letter is forwarded to Capone at his new prison. After Capone receives the letter, he throws the letter in the garbage and mutters, "I'd never help that rat."

Based on these facts, if Dillinger is prosecuted for solicitation of murder in a jurisdiction following the Model Penal Code, it is most likely that:

A. Dillinger is guilty because the letter was read by Capone.

B. Dillinger is guilty because he sent a letter requesting the police officer's murder.

C. Dillinger is not guilty because it was impossible for Capone to kill the police officer.

D. Dillinger is not guilty because Capone had not yet taken a "substantial step" toward killing the police officer.

17. A is the organizer and ringleader of a mob of bank robbers. He hires B and C to rob banks 1 and 2, respectively. Although B and C do not meet, both know of A's position in the mob, and each knows of the other's assignment. At A's instigation, D, also knowing of A's position in the mob, steals a car for use in the robberies. B and C perform their robberies, the former using D's car. Which of the following statements has the *least* support under the common law?

A. There is one overall conspiracy among A, B, C, and D, rather than three separate conspiracies, with A as a partner in each.

B. Under the conspiracy doctrine, A is liable for the robberies of banks 1 and 2.

C. Under conspiracy doctrine, but not under the rules of complicity, B and C are liable for each other's robberies as well as their own.

D. Under the rules of complicity, but not under conspiracy doctrine, B and C are liable for each other's robberies as well as their own.

18. Same facts as above. Which of the following statements has the *least* support under the Model Penal Code?

A. A is liable for the robbery of both banks under the rules of complicity and co-conspirator liability.

B. If D was aware of B and C and their participation in the robberies, he conspired with them, even if they did not necessarily conspire with him.

C. D's punishment for conspiracy to rob bank 1 can be as severe as B's punishment for robbing it.

D. A may be liable for the robbery of banks 1 and 2 as an accomplice, but not as a co-conspirator.

19. Jake met a tough-looking guy named Marty at a bar in the state of Ames. (Ames follows the Model Penal Code.) They hit it off well and began to talk. After determining that they had a lot in common, Jake proposed to Marty that they rob the nearby 7-Eleven together. Marty said, "Okay, let's do it, man." Jake did not know it, but Marty was actually an undercover police officer.

Jake and Marty entered the store together. Jake pointed his gun at the cashier and demanded "all of the cash in the register." Marty then pointed his gun at Jake and advised Jake to "drop the gun and put your hands in the air." Jake dropped the gun and was arrested by Marty.

Under the Model Penal Code, which result is most likely:

A. Jake is guilty because he agreed to rob the 7-Eleven with Marty.

B. Jake is guilty because he had undertaken a "substantial step" toward commission of the crime.

C. Jake is not guilty because he was entrapped.

D. Jake is not guilty because Marty's agreement was feigned.

20. Amanda and Corrine are friends at Portside High School. One day, Amanda says to Corrine, "Let's rob the Gap and get some cool clothes." Corrine, assuming that Amanda is joking, responds, "Sounds like fun. Let's do it." Amanda, who has a reputation as a gang tough, pulls two guns from her purse and hands one to Corrine. Corrine wants to run away, but she's afraid that Amanda will hurt her if she doesn't go through with the plan. Corrine goes with Amanda to the Gap & Snap Mall. Before going into the Gap, Corrine says she has to go to the bathroom, hoping somehow to get away. While Corrine is in the bathroom, a security guard sees a bulge in Amanda's purse and suspects it's a gun. He arrests Amanda, who tells him that Corrine is her accomplice. Corrine is arrested as she leaves the ladies' room.

Based on these facts, if Corrine is prosecuted for conspiracy to commit robbery, it is most likely that:

A. Corrine is guilty because she took the gun and went with Amanda to the mall.

B. Corrine is guilty because she did not renounce the crime after separating from Amanda.

C. Corrine is not guilty because she never entered the Gap.

D. Corrine is not guilty because she never agreed with Amanda to rob the Gap.

21. Bill and Ted are partners in a major drug distribution operation. They agree to sell ten kilos of cocaine to Mickey, a drug dealer in the town of Bedrock. One night, Bill and Ted drive over to an abandoned warehouse to make the sale to Mickey. Bill notices several police cars cruising the neighborhood, and he becomes alarmed. He tells Ted, "I don't want any part of this one. It's too dangerous. You should pull out, too." Ted responds, "You no-good wimp. I can do this without your help." Bill leaves, and Ted goes through with the sale to Mickey. Unsurprisingly, Ted is arrested on the spot. Hoping to make a deal for a lighter sentence, he tells the police that Bill helped him to plan the sale.

Based on these facts, if Bill is prosecuted in a Model Penal Code jurisdiction for conspiracy to sell illegal drugs, it is most likely that:

A. Bill is guilty because he agreed with Mickey to sell drugs.

B. Bill is guilty because Ted completed the drug deal.

C. Bill is not guilty because he withdrew from the conspiracy and attempted to dissuade Ted.

D. Bill is not guilty because he didn't participate in the actual sale of the drugs.

The following facts apply to questions 22-23:

Having heard that B intended to burglarize C's house on a particular night, A deliberately left a ladder in back of C's house in order to help B break in. B came that night and entered C's house by picking the front door lock, never learning of the ladder's presence.

22. Under the **common law**, which statement is correct?

A. A did not in fact aid B and therefore cannot be B's accomplice.

B. Without some prior agreement or understanding with B, A cannot be convicted as B's accomplice.

C. A is an accomplice to B's burglary.

D. A only attempted to aid B and therefore is liable only for attempted burglary.

23. Under the **Model Penal Code,** which statement is correct?

   A. A did not in fact aid B and therefore cannot be B's accomplice.

   B. Without some prior agreement or understanding with B, A cannot be convicted as B's accomplice.

   C. A is an accomplice to B's burglary.

   D. A only attempted to aid B and therefore is liable only for attempted burglary.

24. Barker and Samantha are violence-prone computer hackers. They decide to rob a local Geek City Software store. Each uses a handgun. They agree in advance to split up after the robbery and to meet at Samantha's home one hour later to divide their booty. The robbery goes off without a hitch, but on her way home, Samantha is stopped by Frank, a local police officer. She begins to run, but is brought down by Kipper, Frank's police dog. Samantha reaches for a knife concealed in her left stocking and slashes Kipper across the throat. Kipper dies immediately. (Assume that, in this jurisdiction, killing a police dog during commission of a felony is itself a felony.)

Based on these facts, if Barker is prosecuted for the killing of Kipper, it is most likely that:

   A. Barker is guilty because it was reasonably foreseeable that Samantha would use force to avoid capture.

   B. Barker is guilty because conspirators are culpable for the acts of their co-conspirators.

   C. Barker is not guilty because Samantha's killing of a police dog was not reasonably foreseeable.

   D. Barker is not guilty because the conspiracy was concluded when the robbery of the Geek City Software store was concluded.

25. Liz Taylor has obtained what she believes is a valid divorce. Her lawyer has told her so. She then marries Larry King. She is prosecuted for bigamy because her divorce was, in fact, invalid because she had not signed the proper forms in red ink, as required by domestic relations law. She claims mistake of law.

Liz's *best* argument under the common law is:

   A. She relied on her lawyer.

   B. The requirement of red ink has nothing to do with the legitimacy of her divorce.

    C. Her mistake is not one of criminal law.

    D. The judge who officiated at the wedding considered the divorce decree (which he saw) valid.

26. Frank was devastated when his girlfriend, Louise, broke up with him. He tried for months to win her back, but she rebuffed him every time. Finally, Frank decided that if he couldn't have Louise, no one else would, either. He bought a gun and drove to her apartment, intent on killing her. When he got there, the janitor told Frank that Louise had moved to the North Side. Frank asked for the address, but the janitor said he didn't know it. Frank drove to the North Side with the gun in his pocket, hoping to spot Louise. As he cruised through the neighborhood, Frank was stopped by a police officer for going through a red light. A check revealed a warrant for Frank's arrest for robbery. Frank was arrested, and the gun was confiscated. (Assume this jurisdiction follows the Model Penal Code.)

    Based on these facts, if Frank is prosecuted for attempted murder, it is most likely that:

    A. He's guilty because he intended to kill Louise.

    B. He's guilty because he made every effort to locate Louise with the intent of killing her.

    C. He's not guilty because he never actually shot at Louise.

    D. He's not guilty because he never found Louise.

27. Ivan Georgski and his wife, Raisa, both new immigrants to the United States, were vacationing in a state that has adopted the Model Penal Code, when Raisa confessed to having an adulterous relationship with Boris Gudunov. Georgski, in keeping with his religious faith, killed Raisa.

    Ivan's *best* claim for avoiding a murder conviction is:

    A. Common law provocation.

    B. The "cultural defense."

    C. Extreme emotional disturbance.

    D. Diminished capacity.

28. On her way home one night, Margot saw Thomas sleeping in a cardboard box outside the entrance to her luxury apartment building. Margot hated the presence of homeless people in her wealthy neighborhood. Determined to send a message to the homeless, she took out a pair of scissors from her purse and stabbed Thomas several times

in the neck and back. Margot's intent was not to kill Thomas, but to frighten the homeless away from her posh neighborhood. However, the wounds she inflicted were deep enough to kill any ordinary man. The autopsy revealed not only the extent of the stab wounds but also the fact that Thomas was already dead when Margot stabbed him. He had died an hour earlier from dehydration and hypothermia.

Based on these facts, if Margot is prosecuted for murder, it is most likely that:

A. She is guilty because she stabbed Thomas with the intent to seriously injure him.

B. She is guilty because her stab wounds would have killed the average person.

C. She is not guilty because she did not intend to kill Thomas.

D. She is not guilty because Thomas was already dead.

29. Harry has been convicted of drug dealing on several occasions. One day, he is standing on a street corner waiting for the bus to take him to his new job. Matthew, a plainclothes police officer, recognizes Harry as a convicted drug dealer. He approaches Harry and asks, "Know where I can get some crack?" Harry replies, "If the price is right, sure." Harry has no crack in his possession at the time, but knows where he can get some. Matthew immediately arrests Harry for attempting to sell an illegal substance.

Based on these facts, if Harry asserts the defense of entrapment, it is most likely that:

A. Harry is guilty because he was predisposed to sell drugs.

B. Harry is guilty because the defense of entrapment is not available to former convicts for the same or a similar crime.

C. Harry is not guilty because Matthew proposed the transaction to him.

D. Harry is not guilty because he did not intend to sell drugs until Matthew approached him.

30. Merlin is charged with breaking into a store, a crime that has been determined to be a general-intent crime under the common law and that carries the *mens rea* of "recklessness." Merlin seeks to show that he had a blood alcohol content (BAC) of .21 at the time of the break-in.

Is the evidence admissible *in the majority of states*?

A. No, because when you're drunk you take the chance that you'll commit a crime.

B. Yes, because no one knows that he'll commit a crime while drunk.

C. Yes, because he has to know that it's not his store.

D. No, because intoxication, even where allowed to negate *mens rea*, is only relevant to specific-intent crimes and not general-intent crimes.

31. Looking for an easy mark, Carl decided to burglarize the home of Mary Murphy, an 80-year-old recluse who lived alone. Carl suspected that Mary was away visiting her sister in another state. The lock was not as easy to pry open as Carl thought it would be. Determined to get in, Carl broke the lock and used a crowbar in his effort to pry the door. Despite all his strength and efforts, he could not get the door to open, and he finally left in disgust.

   Unknown to Carl, Mary was actually home and heard all the noise. She hid in a closet until the noise stopped. She then tried to leave the house by the only available exit—the front door. However, Carl had succeeded in jamming the door against the doorjamb. Mary was unable to get out of the house, though she tried for two hours to get the door open. She finally called the police, who broke the door down and rescued her. The jurisdiction defines kidnapping as "the intentional and unlawful confinement of another for a substantial period of time."

   Assuming that the "substantial period of time" element is satisfied, if Carl is prosecuted for kidnapping, it is most likely that:

   A. Carl is not guilty because Mary was able to call the police and obtain help.

   B. Carl is not guilty because he didn't know Mary was home.

   C. Carl is guilty because Mary was confined to her home by Carl's actions in jamming the door.

   D. Carl is guilty because Mary was unable to leave her home for two hours.

32. One summer evening, Alison decided to go swimming in the rooftop pool of her apartment building. She stepped out onto the roof to find only Jamie, her neighbor's seven-year-old. Alison watched in horror while Jamie fell into the deep end of the pool and began to thrash around. Alison had been a lifeguard in high school and could easily have saved Jamie without any risk to herself. Fearing that she might be accused of pushing Jamie in the first place, she decided not to intervene and went back downstairs. She did, however, call the police when she got back to her apartment. The police came immediately, but Jamie had already drowned.

Based on these facts, if Alison is prosecuted for homicide, it is most likely that:

A. Alison is not guilty because she was under no legal duty to save Jamie.

B. Alison is not guilty because she made a reasonable effort to save Jamie by calling the police.

C. Alison is guilty because she could have saved Jamie without serious risk of harm to herself.

D. Alison is guilty because there is a special duty to help minors in danger.

33. Kevin's Furniture Store was facing bankruptcy. The store occupied the first floor of a two-story building. One evening, Kevin set fire to the building. He planned to collect on the store's insurance policy. Unbeknownst to Kevin, Ben, a 42-year-old homeless derelict, was asleep on the second floor, which was vacant. Ben was burned to death. Before the fire could be put out, the entire building was destroyed. Tormented by this tragedy, Kevin confessed his crime to the police.

Based on these facts, if Kevin is prosecuted for murder, it is most likely that:

A. Kevin is not guilty because he did not intend to kill Ben.

B. Kevin is not guilty because it was not reasonably foreseeable that someone would be killed by the fire.

C. Kevin is not guilty because he was only attempting to commit insurance fraud (a felony that is not inherently dangerous).

D. Kevin is guilty because Ben was killed in the fire Kevin started.

34. Seth asked Daniel if he could borrow his DVD player to watch a DVD with his girlfriend. Daniel loaned Seth his DVD player, but before he could get it back, the two had a big argument. Daniel demanded his DVD player back, but Seth responded, "I'll get to it when I get to it." The next evening, Daniel opened an unlocked window at Seth's home and went inside, intent only on recovering his DVD player. Inside Seth's house, Daniel saw and instantly decided to take Seth's new Macintosh PowerBook. Daniel loaded the DVD player and the PowerBook into his van and drove home. A neighbor, who had seen Daniel climb through the window, called the police and gave them Daniel's license plate number. He was arrested shortly thereafter.

Based on these facts, if Daniel is prosecuted for burglary, it is most likely that:

A. Daniel is not guilty because he entered Seth's home only for the purpose of retrieving his DVD player.

B. Daniel is not guilty because no "breaking" occurred.

C. Daniel is guilty because he had no legal right to enter Seth's house.

D. Daniel is guilty because he took the PowerBook with the intent to permanently deprive Seth of its possession.

35. David has been telling malicious lies about his sister, Janice, to their parents. Janice is convinced that David is out to get them to disinherit her. Home from college on Christmas vacation, Janice decides to "excise David, once and for all." She makes a batch of poison-laced cookies, puts them on a plate, and leaves the plate on David's desk. Janice then drives downtown to finish her holiday shopping. The holiday music at the mall fills her with remorse and guilt. She calls home to tell David what she's done, but the line is busy. Janice rushes home, intending to throw the poisonous cookies away, but she finds that David has already eaten the cookies and is lying unconscious. She rushes David to the nearest hospital, but David dies in the emergency room.

Based on these facts, if Janice is prosecuted for murder, it is most likely that:

A. Janice is not guilty because the *mens rea* element necessary for murder was lacking when David ate the cookies.

B. Janice is guilty of voluntary manslaughter, not murder, because Janice was provoked by David's malicious lies.

C. Janice is guilty of murder because she intended to cause David's death.

D. Janice is guilty only of attempted murder because she tried to warn David about the cookies.

36. Jonathan and Peter are classmates at Podunk Law School in the state of Pretoria. One evening, they begin to discuss the proposed Pretoria legislation forbidding any school to promote or utilize affirmative action as a basis for admission. Before long, Jonathan and Peter are on their feet, arguing and shouting at one another. Peter calls Jonathan "a warped, opinionated, prejudiced, calloused, stupid idiot who doesn't belong in law school." Enraged by these remarks, Jonathan pushes Peter, who loses his balance and falls backwards, hitting his head against the edge of an oak table. Peter dies instantly. (Assume that common law principles are applicable in Pretoria.)

Based on these facts, if Jonathan is prosecuted for homicide, it is most likely that:

A. Jonathan is guilty of first-degree murder.

B. Jonathan is guilty of voluntary manslaughter.

C. Jonathan is guilty of involuntary manslaughter.

D. Jonathan is **not** criminally culpable for Peter's death.

37. Erica and Pat are law school roommates. They live in a large duplex located in a nice, quiet section of Houston. They argue constantly about Pat's tendency to let dirty dishes pile up in their sink and her refusal to share in the housekeeping. One day, Erica decides to "teach Pat a lesson." She leaves Pat's new mountain bike unlocked and unattended on the sidewalk in front of their apartment house. Erica keeps an eye on it from the apartment hallway, but, when she returns to the apartment for a moment to get a cigarette, the mountain bike is stolen. Pat is definitely **not** amused by Erica's excuse and explanation. She decides to flex her law-school-student muscles and files a charge of larceny against Erica.

Based on these facts, if Erica is prosecuted for larceny, it is most likely that:

A. Erica is guilty because it was reasonably likely that the theft would occur.

B. Erica is guilty because her actions were undertaken for the improper purpose of teaching Pat a lesson.

C. Erica is not guilty because she didn't participate in taking Pat's mountain bike.

D. Erica is not guilty because her intent was only to teach Pat a lesson.

38. A tells C that she is thinking of leaving him to live with another man. C threatens to commit suicide if A leaves. A knows C well and perceives the risk of his doing so as genuine and substantial. Indeed, C's threat makes up her mind: she stands to inherit some property if C dies. She leaves C and moves in with the other man. C thereupon carries out his threat and kills himself. Suicide is not a crime in this jurisdiction, neither is causing another's suicide. If A is not guilty of any crime it is because:

A. She did not cause C's death.

B. She lacked the required *mens rea* for a homicide crime.

C. She did not do a voluntary act.

D. Her motive for leaving C is irrelevant to her guilt.

39. Molly and Samantha were neighbors. Molly became convinced that Samantha was having an affair with her husband. This was not the case. One day, Molly, an employee of Wow Chemical, hid a bottle of acid under her smock as she left work. When Molly arrived home, she saw Samantha sunbathing on her porch. Molly uncorked the bottle and splashed acid on Samantha's face, intending to disfigure her. Reacting quickly, Samantha ran to the pool in her backyard and dove in to dilute the acid. In her panic, she dove into the shallow part of the pool and fractured her cheekbone. Her fracture healed, but, despite excellent plastic surgery, her smile was permanently, although only slightly, distorted, due to the injury from her dive into the pool.

    The crime of mayhem is defined in this jurisdiction as "the intentional infliction of a disfiguring bodily injury."

    Based on these facts, if Molly is prosecuted for mayhem, it is most likely that:

    A. Molly is guilty because she intended to cause a disfiguring bodily injury to Samantha.

    B. Molly is not guilty because Samantha's response was a supervening cause of her injury.

    C. Molly is not guilty because her conduct was not the proximate cause of Samantha's injuries.

    D. Molly is not guilty because the acid caused Samantha no disfigurement.

40. Dustin Hoffperson knows that Dinah Saur is a pet lover. Dustin threatens to kill all of Dinah's pets unless Dinah helps him embezzle $5,000. If she assists Dustin in the embezzlement, Dinah:

    A. Has no claim of duress because the harm inflicted is greater than the harm avoided.

    B. Has a claim of duress because a "person of reasonable firmness" would do just what she did.

    C. Has no claim of duress because there was no threat of personal injury to anyone, including herself.

    D. Has a claim of duress because she was in a "maelstrom of circumstances" and could not be said to have acted voluntarily.

41. David destroyed a gas meter in his mother-in-law's basement in order to obtain the change contained inside; as a result, gas escaped from the pipes and reached the mother-in-law where she was sleeping 3 floors above. David is charged with recklessly injuring his mother-in-law. He will most likely be:

    A. Acquitted if a reasonable person would not have perceived the danger to his mother-in law.

    B. Acquitted, regardless of whether a reasonable person would have perceived the danger or not, so long as he did not in fact perceive it.

    C. Acquitted, because he did not intend to harm his mother-in-law and injuring another is a specific intent crime.

    D. Convicted, because the injury occurred during the course of another felony.

42. Assume that the jurisdiction in this case does not permit a claim of imperfect self-defense.

    Steve and Jenny have been married for five years. Steve has a "temper problem" and has beaten Jenny many times during their marriage. One Saturday night, Steve begins to yell at Jenny when she suggests that he get counseling for his temper. Jenny has never seen Steve so enraged. Steve hits Jenny several times and then says, "Your time is almost up." Steve then turns away and goes to sleep. Two hours later, Jenny, fearing that Steve intends to kill her when he awakes, quietly removes a gun from the kitchen cabinet and shoots Steve in the temple, killing him instantly.

    Based on these facts, if Jenny is prosecuted for murder, it is most likely that she would be convicted of:

    A. Murder.

    B. Voluntary manslaughter.

    C. Involuntary manslaughter.

    D. No crime at all.

43. Jeremy works as a prosecutor in the Juvenile Division of the Euphoria State Attorney's Office. In response to a series of anonymous death threats, Jeremy has started carrying a gun. One night, when Jeremy leaves work, he spots a teenager running toward him carrying a gun, which he points toward Jeremy's chest. The youth, who appears to Jeremy to be about 15, is 18 feet away from Jeremy when he first sees

him. When the boy shouts, "Look out, fool," Jeremy shoots him, killing him instantly. When the police come, they find the boy is only 12 and that the "gun" is only a toy rubber gun. Later, they discover that the boy was taking part in an initiation by a local gang.

Based on these facts, if Jeremy is prosecuted for homicide, it is most likely that he will be convicted of:

A. Murder.

B. Voluntary manslaughter.

C. Involuntary manslaughter.

D. No crime at all.

44. Phi Rho fraternity has a long tradition of making its new pledges run through a wall of fire at the conclusion of "Hell Week." Because other fraternities had been sued by pledges for Hell Week injuries, Phi Rho required that its pledges sign a consent and waiver form, specifically relieving the fraternity and its individual members of responsibility for injuries resulting from hazing.

Biff, Phi Rho's current president, supervised this year's wall of fire activities. After the wall of fire was built, Biff instructed Morton to run through it. Though scared, Morton was determined to become a member of Phi Rho. He ran toward the fire, but tripped and fell as he reached the "wall." Before he could be pulled away, he had received life-threatening second-degree burns over much of his body. An ambulance was called which took Morton to the hospital where he died that night. The cause of death was a contaminated blood transfusion negligently administered by the hospital staff.

Based on these facts, if Biff is prosecuted for involuntary manslaughter, it is most likely that:

A. Biff is guilty because he acted negligently.

B. Biff is guilty because he manifested a reckless disregard for Morton's safety.

C. Biff is not guilty because Morton signed a waiver.

D. Biff is not guilty because Morton's death was caused by the hospital's negligence.

45. Barney was exposed to Jordan's driving ambition and ruthlessness when they were classmates at Harpert Law School. Years later, when Jordan, after a meteoric but unprincipled career, announced his candidacy for governor of Utopia, Barney felt it was his patriotic duty to

stop him before he destroyed the state. Barney read in the local paper that Jordan was going to be making a speech in the public square of Harpert Village the next day. Barney also knew that there was an abandoned office building located opposite the square, where he could position himself in order to fire at Jordan.

About 30 minutes before Jordan's speech, Barney entered the building facing the square, carrying a high-powered rifle. A vigilant police officer saw Barney at the window holding what appeared to be a rifle, "casing" the square. The officer immediately broke into the building and arrested Barney. (You may assume that the Model Penal Code is operative in Utopia.)

Based on these facts, if Barney is prosecuted for attempted murder, it is most likely that:

A. Barney is guilty because he undertook a substantial step toward the assassination with the intent to kill.

B. Barney is not guilty because he was waiting for Jordan to begin his speech.

C. Barney is not guilty because Jordan had not yet arrived.

D. Barney is not guilty if his rifle's range could not reach the spot at which Jordan would be standing.

46. D is charged with felony murder for the poisoning death of her husband. Poisoning is defined as the "knowing administration of a toxic substance to another with the purpose of causing his death or injury." Which of the following is the most likely outcome:

A. D will be convicted of felony murder because the felony is independent of the killing.

B. D will be acquitted of felony murder because the felony is not independent of the killing.

C. D will be convicted of felony murder, but only in a jurisdiction that follows the Model Penal Code.

D. D will be acquitted of felony murder, but only if it is shown that she did not have the intent to kill.

47. Larry and Francine saw a neighborhood "thug" selling drugs to several young children at a local schoolyard. Larry, who knew that Francine always carried a gun in her purse, said to her, "Someone should kill the scum." Francine nodded. Larry then suggested that they wait behind a trash bin so that Francine could shoot the dealer as he walked past.

While they were waiting behind the trash bin, Larry had second thoughts about participating in a murder. Without saying anything to Francine, he quietly slipped away. Unaware that she was alone, Francine shot and killed the drug dealer.

Based on these facts, if Larry is prosecuted as an accomplice to murder, it is most likely that:

A. Larry is guilty because he aided Francine in the murder and intended to do so.

B. Larry is guilty because he left the area without specifically advising Francine not to kill the drug dealer.

C. Larry is not guilty because it was Francine who shot the drug dealer.

D. Larry is not guilty because he had already left the vicinity before the shooting occurred.

48. Peewee Herman — 108 pounds, 5 feet tall, and 56 years old — while in the movies one night, is approached by Hulk Hogan, who threatens to "punch out his lights" because Herman is talking too much. Herman shoots Hogan dead. At his trial, Herman attempts to show Hogan's height (6′3″), weight (265 pounds), and age (24). The evidence is:

A. Admissible, to show the reasonableness of Herman's fear of great bodily harm.

B. Admissible, to show the likelihood that Hogan would strike Herman.

C. Inadmissible, because the reasonable person — or even the reasonable male — would not shoot someone who threatened to hit him hard.

D. Inadmissible, because Herman's cowardice is irrelevant to self-defense.

49. Ethan borrowed $10,000 from Carl, a professional loan shark. When Ethan missed his first payment, Carl decided to teach Ethan a lesson. He went to Ethan's house and threw Ethan against the wall. Carl smashed several vases and then told Ethan, "If you don't pay up, this is what's going to happen to you." At this point, Ethan called Carl "a no good SOB." Carl stared menacingly at Ethan for several seconds, but finally turned and left, slamming the door behind him.

Ethan was so frightened that he had a massive heart attack and died. Ethan's death was the last thing Carl wanted because it meant that now he would never get his money back. Carl had only wanted to scare Ethan into making his future loan payments on time.

Based on these facts, if Carl is prosecuted for Ethan's death, it is most likely he will be guilty of:

A. First-degree murder.

B. Second-degree murder.

C. Voluntary manslaughter.

D. Involuntary manslaughter.

50. Late one night, Jim was walking home alone from the library. Ilya, the "Chicago Slasher," began to trail him. Ilya's plan was to kill Jim as soon as they reached a secluded area. Ilya knew of a dark alley that would be "the perfect spot." When Jim was only a block away from the alley, Ilya took a knife from his knapsack and began to run toward Jim. A police officer saw Ilya holding the knife as he moved closer to Jim. Ilya spotted the police officer out of the corner of his eye. He quickly put the knife into his pocket and began walking in the opposite direction.

Based on these facts, if Ilya is prosecuted for attempted murder, it is most likely that:

A. Ilya is not guilty because he didn't take a substantial step toward commission of the murder.

B. Ilya is not guilty because he terminated his plan to murder Jim prior to his arrest.

C. Ilya is guilty because he intended to kill Jim.

D. Ilya is guilty because he drew the knife from his knapsack with the intent to kill.

51. Angie, a 22-year-old cover model, married a wealthy 80-year-old widower. Seven years later, Angie's husband was still in good health, and it appeared he would easily live several more years. Impatient to collect her inheritance, Angie decided to speed up the old man's death.

She asked her favorite bartender if he knew anyone who could "do a hit." The bartender gave her a phone number and told her to ask for Danny. She called the number and made arrangements to meet with Danny to discuss the deal. When they met, Angie offered to pay Danny $20,000 upon the successful "elimination" of her husband. Danny then informed Angie that he was an undercover police officer and arrested her.

Based on these facts, if Angie is prosecuted for conspiracy to commit murder, it is most likely that:

A. Angie is guilty because she offered to pay Danny to have her husband killed.

B. Angie is guilty because she specifically intended to have her husband killed.

C. Angie is not guilty because no actual agreement occurred.

D. Angie is not guilty because a substantial step had not yet been taken to carry out the murder.

Questions 52-54 are based on the following fact situation:

Frederick, who had a local reputation for unreasonable violence, threatened Bruce with a severe beating unless Bruce wrote, signed, and mailed a letter to the president of the United States threatening the president's life. Bruce complied. A statute makes it a felony "knowingly to mail to any person a letter that threatens the life of the president of the United States."

52. Is Bruce guilty of violating that statute?

   A. Yes, because Bruce knowingly mailed the letter.

   B. No, because he acted under duress.

   C. Yes, if Bruce believes that Frederick will carry out his threat against the president.

   D. Yes, because Bruce was not threatened with loss of his life.

53. If Frederick and Bruce are prosecuted for violating the statute and Bruce is acquitted, may Frederick be convicted?

   A. Yes, under the doctrine of transferred intent.

   B. Yes, because a person can commit a crime through an innocent agent.

   C. No, because Frederick did not write or mail the letter.

   D. No, because Frederick cannot be vicariously liable for Bruce's act.

54. If Frederick and Bruce are charged with the crime of conspiracy to violate the statute, they will most likely be found:

   A. Not guilty, because the conspiracy was merged into the completed crime.

   B. Not guilty, because Bruce was not a willing participant.

   C. Guilty, because Bruce participated in the commission of the crime.

   D. Guilty, because Bruce complied with Frederick's threat.

55. Bank had a substantial increase in the number of robberies at its main office. During one of these robberies, a teller was wounded when the robber became impatient with the speed with which she handed over the money. Bank hired Sharp, a former FBI agent, and placed him at a position where he could observe the entire bank floor through an opening in the ceiling. Several days after Sharp was hired, Rob entered the bank, pointed a gun at a cashier, and demanded money. When Sharp saw Rob point a gun at a cashier, he fired at and killed Rob.

What criminal offense, if any, did Sharp commit?

A. None, because Sharp reasonably believed his act was necessary to prevent a dangerous felony.

B. Voluntary manslaughter, because Sharp used deadly force to protect private property.

C. Voluntary manslaughter, because Sharp did not first warn Rob.

D. Murder, because Sharp deliberately aimed to kill Rob.

56. Mike was employed as a salesperson in Leo's store. Leo owned a beautiful clock that Mike had often admired. The clock needed repairs, and Leo asked Mike to take it with him on his way home and leave it at the repair shop. Mike saw an opportunity to keep the clock for himself. He took the clock, did not deliver it to the shop, and did not return to work for Leo.

Did Mike commit larceny?

A. Yes, because Mike decided not to take it to the repair shop after he received the clock.

B. Yes, because Mike was a mere employee of Leo.

C. No, because Leo personally handed the clock to Mike.

D. No, because Mike did not induce or trick Leo into giving him the clock.

Questions 57-58 are based on the following fact situation (assume the jurisdiction follows the Model Penal Code):

Deft intended to kill Vic. Deft deliberately shot at Vic, but missed and hit Cal. Cal was wounded only slightly. Cal was able to get up and saw Deft running away. Cal yelled at Deft, "Stop or I'll shoot." When Deft continued to run, Cal took out his gun and shot Deft, killing him instantly.

57. Is Deft guilty of the attempted murder of Cal?

A. Yes, because Deft attempted to kill Vic.

B. Yes, because Deft acted with premeditation and malice toward Vic.

C. No, because Cal was wounded only slightly.

D. No, because Deft intended to kill Vic, not Cal.

58. What crime, if any, did Cal commit?

A. Manslaughter.

B. Murder.

C. Negligent homicide.

D. No crime.

Questions 59-60 are based on the following fact situation:

Borrower owed Lender $5,000. Payment was overdue, and Lender retained Ace, Inc., to collect the debt. Washington, the president of Ace, Inc., assigned Little, an employee of Ace, to collect the account. At the time Washington assigned Little to collect the debt, Washington and Ace were also indebted to Lender for $5,000. Washington intended to apply the funds paid by Borrower in discharge of the debt owed by him and Ace to Lender. Little collected the $5,000. The amount collected was immediately remitted to Lender by Washington as payment of the debt for which Ace, Inc., and Washington were jointly liable. Lender was not told that Little had collected Borrower's debt.

59. Based on these facts, it is most likely that Washington can be successfully prosecuted for:

A. Embezzlement, because Lender's money was entrusted to Ace, Inc.

B. False pretenses, because, at the time Little collected the funds, Washington intended to use them for his own benefit.

C. Larceny, because, at the time the funds were collected, Washington intended to use them for his own benefit.

D. No crime, because Lender received all of the funds that were due from Borrower.

60. If a crime was committed by Washington, can Ace, Inc., be convicted for the same offense?

A. Yes, because Washington was president of Ace, Inc.

B. Yes, but only provided Washington is also convicted for the same offense.

C. No, because a corporation cannot be imprisoned.

D. No, if the crime involved requires a specific intent.

61. Agent was an undercover police officer. Agent received information from a reliable source that Deft, recently released from prison after serving a sentence for selling narcotics, was again selling narcotics, but that he was being very cautious and would sell only to persons who knew a designated code word. Agent's source told Agent the current code word.

Agent approached Deft, offered to make a buy of narcotics "at the going rate," and said the code word. Deft agreed to the sale and to the time and place of delivery. When Deft accepted the cash for the narcotics, he was arrested.

If Deft claims he was entrapped, will he prevail?

A. Yes, because Deft would not have made the sale if Agent had not said the code word.

B. Yes, because Agent approached Deft and offered to make a buy.

C. No, because Deft was already predisposed to sell narcotics.

D. No, because Deft accepted the Agent's cash.

62. Roger, walking down a city street, found a wallet on the sidewalk. He picked up the wallet and examined its contents. He found a driver's license containing the owner's name and address. In the belief that the law was "finders keepers," he removed the cash from the wallet, put it in his pocket, and tossed the wallet into the trashcan.

Did Roger commit a theft crime?

A. Yes, because Roger kept the money, knowing the owner's identity.

B. Yes, because Roger had lawful possession when he formed the intent to keep the money.

C. No, because Roger did not commit a trespassory taking.

D. No, because he was right on the law and was entitled to keep the money.

63. Mike, Leo, and Frank planned to rob a local liquor store. The agreement was that Mike would supply the guns and ammunition, and Leo and Frank would actually commit the robbery. Mike told Leo and Frank that all he wanted was to be paid for the guns and ammunition, that he would have nothing to do with the actual robbery, and that he would not be present at the time or share in the proceeds. Mike supplied Leo and Frank with guns and ammunition, which they then used to rob the liquor store.

Can Mike be held criminally liable for the robbery of the liquor store as:

I. A co-conspirator?

II. An accessory before the fact?

A. No, neither I nor II.

B. Yes, I but not II.

C. Yes, II but not I.

D. Yes, both I and II.

64. Intending to get Art arrested, Bob and Sam threatened him at gunpoint and told him, "If you don't immediately hold up the bank on the corner, we will kill you." They handed Art a loaded gun. Bob and Sam then positioned themselves so they could observe Art's actions. Art entered the bank and pointed the gun at a teller. Before the teller could respond, Art saw that a bank guard was pointing a gun at him and was about to shoot him. Art dropped his gun and held up his hands in surrender.

    Did Art commit the crime of attempted robbery?

    A. Yes, because Art carried a loaded gun.

    B. Yes, because he took a substantial step toward the completion of the robbery.

    C. No, because he surrendered before the robbery was completed.

    D. No, because Art did not intend to take the bank's funds.

Questions 65-66 are based on the following fact situation:

When Dave saw his girlfriend, Sally, walking down the street holding hands with Abel, he was infuriated. Dave drove to Sally's house, hid in the bushes outside, and waited. A short time later, Dave saw Abel and Sally sitting at the kitchen table, drinking coffee. Still angry, Dave went to his car and got a pistol. When he returned, Abel and Sally were still sitting at the kitchen table. Intending only to scare Abel by shooting in his direction, Dave fired through the window.

65. The bullet from Dave's pistol missed Abel, but struck the coffee cup Abel was holding, shattering the mug in his hands. Which of the following crimes did Dave commit?

    A. Battery.

    B. Assault with a deadly weapon.

    C. Battery and assault with a deadly weapon.

    D. Attempted murder.

66. If the bullet from Dave's pistol struck and killed Abel, the most serious crime with which Dave could be charged is:

    A. First-degree murder.

    B. Second-degree murder.

    C. Voluntary manslaughter.

    D. Involuntary manslaughter.

67. Georgia O'Keefe becomes intoxicated one night and strangles her arch-enemy, Mary Surratt. O'Keefe believes that she is squeezing a lemon. What is O'Keefe's **best** defense to a charge of first-degree murder?

    A. Although she knew the nature and quality of her act, she suffered from a mental disease.

    B. She did not know the nature and quality of her act, but suffered from no mental disease.

    C. She did not have the capacity to premeditate.

    D. Mistake of fact.

68. Ferdinand pours ecstasy into Daisy's orange juice, hoping that he'll "get lucky" with her. She goes into immediate convulsions and dies. She is one of 1 percent of the population to have an allergic reaction to this drug. If Ferdinand claims that he didn't realize that anyone, much less Daisy, could be so allergic, would he nevertheless be guilty of reckless homicide?

    A. Yes, because any ordinary person would recognize that another person might be allergic to anything.

    B. Yes, because he should have considered the possibility of an allergic reaction.

    C. No, because he didn't have the purpose to kill Daisy.

    D. No, because Ferdinand never realized he might harm or kill Daisy.

Questions 69-70 are based on the following fact situation:

Art talked Bob into giving him $200 to buy a gun and ammo for the robbery of a bakery and the theft of its receipts, in return for a one-quarter share of the proceeds. On his way to complete the purchase after receiving the $200 from Bob, Art changed his mind. He never bought the gun or committed the robbery. Instead, he gave the $200 to the local YMCA.

69. Did Art commit the common law crime of conspiracy to commit robbery?

    A. Yes, when Art asked Bob for the money.

    B. Yes, when Bob furnished the money to buy the gun and ammo.

    C. No, because Bob did not agree to take part in the robbery.

    D. No, because Art never bought the gun.

70. If Art did not return the $200 to Bob, did he commit a crime by using it for another purpose?

    A. No, because the contract between them was for an illegal purpose.

    B. Yes, larceny.

   C. Yes, embezzlement.

   D. Yes, obtaining property by false pretenses.

Questions 71-73 refer to the following set of facts:

It is against the law in West Dakona to sell the drug Xtol if the seller sells it "know-ingly" or "under the belief" that the drug is Xtol. Defendant Druggist takes the drug Ytol off her shelf, believing it to be Xtol, and sells it to Customer.

71. If the defendant is prosecuted for the sale of Xtol, which of the follow-ing is true?

    A. Defendant is not guilty of selling Xtol because her mistake negates any knowledge.

    B. Defendant is guilty of selling Xtol because her mistake was unreasonable.

    C. Defendant is not guilty of selling Xtol because an element of the crime is lacking.

    D. Defendant is guilty of the sale of Xtol if West Dakona holds that legal impossibility is no defense to the crime of attempt.

72. If Druggist is charged with **attempting** to sell Xtol to Customer, which of the following is true:

    A. Defendant is not guilty of attempting to sell Xtol because her mis-take negates her *mes rea*.

    B. Defendant is not guilty of attempting to sell Xtol because it was impossible for her to sell that drug to customer.

    C. Defendant is not guilty of attempting to sell Xtol because the thing she in fact sold, Ytol, is not a prohibited substance.

    D. Defendant is guilty of attempting to sell Xtol because she intended to do so and took steps indicating her intent to do so.

73. It is also against the law in West Dakona to "knowingly" sell the drug Xtol without reporting the sale to state authorities. Defendant believes the law is unconstitutional and refuses to report his sales of Xtol. His attorney advises him that she also believes the law to be unconstitu-tional. The law is later declared to be constitutional. Which of the fol-lowing is true?

    A. The opinion of the attorney is irrelevant because a misunderstand-ing of the law is never a defense to a crime.

    B. Defendant's belief that the law was unconstitutional is a defense because it negated the *mens rea* for the crime.

C. Defendant has a defense if the attorney's opinion was reasonably based on her interpretation of lower court decisions in that jurisdiction.

D. Defendant acted under a reasonable mistake of fact rather than a mistake of law.

74. Dr. Alexandra X told Defendant Jimmy James (a pharmacist) that she had inadvertently prescribed a banned (but not ordinarily dangerous) drug for Mrs. Jones. Pharmacists are under a statutory duty to report violations of the drug laws, and failure to report is a misdemeanor. Defendant did not report Dr. X's violation. He did try to contact Mrs. Jones at the address she had given him, but the address was obviously wrong. Mrs. Jones took the drug and died. Defendant is charged with involuntary manslaughter. Defendant's **best** defense would be:

A. He did not do anything culpable.

B. He could not reasonably foresee the death.

C. Dr. X alone is responsible.

D. He tried to contact Mrs. Jones.

75. The applicable jurisdiction requires a defendant to prove an affirmative defense to a criminal charge by a preponderance of the evidence. Which of the following defenses would the State be required to **disprove** beyond a reasonable doubt?

A. That the defendant was insane at the time he committed the crime.

B. That the defendant was acting under duress at the time he committed the crime.

C. That the defendant honestly believed his victim was about to kill the defendant's wife.

D. That the defendant's conduct was reflexive (i.e., he was not fully conscious of his actions at the time of the crime).

76. Arthur and Dan were walking on a mountain road, arguing about affirmative action, when Arthur called Dan a "stupid idiot." Dan, enraged by this remark, pushed Arthur as hard as he could. Unfortunately, Arthur's head snapped backwards and struck a rock. As a consequence, Arthur died a few days later. Which of the following is true?

A. Dan is guilty of involuntary manslaughter.

B. Dan is not guilty of involuntary manslaughter because he did not intend Arthur's death.

C. Dan is not criminally responsible for Arthur's death.

D. Dan is guilty of voluntary manslaughter because Dan's insult was adequate to provoke a reasonable person.

77. Dick was planning to rob Bailey's Bank. He asked John if he would drive the getaway car in exchange for one-third of the loot. John agreed on condition that they use toy guns to avoid the risk of injury to anyone. When they got to the bank, Dick got out of the car and began to walk toward the bank. Realizing that the moment of truth was approaching, John got cold feet, left the car, and hailed a taxi back home. Unaware that John had left the scene, Dick entered the bank and pulled out his toy gun. A bank guard saw him and ordered him to put up his hands. Dick turned toward the guard without lowering his gun, and the guard fired. His shot missed Dick, but struck and killed an innocent bystander.

If John is charged with felony murder, he will be:

A. Acquitted, because he did not participate in the robbery.

B. Acquitted, because he withdrew from the conspiracy before any criminal acts were completed.

C. Acquitted, because John's desire to use toy guns indicates he wanted to avoid violence.

D. Convicted, because John was a co-conspirator in the robbery.

78. Forrest's mother, Ena, is terminally ill—the doctors say she has only a few more days to live. Although the doctors have tried everything to ameliorate her pain, Ena continually moans. She asks Forrest to end her misery. Forrest comes into the hospital with a revolver and aims it at Ena, who says, "Please, now." Forrest pulls the trigger four times.

A. Forrest is guilty of first-degree murder.

B. Forrest is guilty of second-degree murder.

C. Forrest is guilty of manslaughter.

D. Forrest is not guilty of any level of homicide.

79. Bill works as a teller in USA Bank. One day, Jim comes into the bank and hands Bill an envelope containing $10,000 in payment of a loan he owes the bank. After Jim leaves, Bill takes the envelope and puts it in his pocket. At the end of the day, Bill deposits the money in his personal account at USA Bank. What crime did Bill commit?

A. Embezzlement.

B. Larceny.

C. False pretenses.

D. Larceny by trick.

Questions 80-82 are based on the following fact situation:

Mick confided to Maud while they were having lunch one day that he had recently made a lot of extra money robbing supermarkets. Mick told Maud that if she would drive the getaway car, while he "knocked over" Jim's grocery, he would take care of her rent for a year. Maud said that she could use some extra money, but that her license had recently been revoked for "drunk driving." Sue, their waitress, heard Mick brag about his record and his plan to rob Jim's grocery. Sue said, "I hate that SOB, Jim. If I weren't working now, I'd drive that car for you in a minute." Bill, who was sitting in the booth behind Mick and Maud, overheard the entire conversation. Bill went over to Mick and offered to drive the getaway car for a third of the proceeds. Mick accepted, and they went off together to rob the grocery. After the robbery, Mick went back to the restaurant and gave Maud $1,000 just to show her how lucrative a life of crime could be. Maud accepted the money.

80. If Maud is charged with conspiracy to commit robbery, she will probably be found:

   A. Guilty, because she never advised the police of Mick's plans.

   B. Guilty, because she knowingly received part of the proceeds from Mick's robbery.

   C. Not guilty, because she didn't participate in the robbery.

   D. Not guilty, because she didn't agree to commit a robbery with Mick.

81. If Sue is charged with aiding and abetting in the commission of a robbery, she will probably be found:

   A. Guilty, because Sue knew of Mick's plans to rob Jim and failed to warn Jim.

   B. Guilty, because Sue failed to tell the police of Mick's robbery plans.

   C. Guilty, because she told Mick she would participate if she could.

   D. Not guilty.

82. If Mick and Bill are tried separately on charges of robbery and conspiracy to commit robbery and Bill is tried first and is acquitted of both charges, Mick could be convicted of:

   A. Conspiracy only.

   B. Robbery only.

   C. Both crimes.

   D. Neither crime.

Questions 83-87 are based on the following fact situation:

John believed that Michael, who lived down the street, had taken several tools from his truck. One night, John found his power saw missing. Outraged, John grabbed a hammer and ran to Michael's home. He entered it through the front door, which was wide open. John saw Michael in the backyard, ran outside, and hit Michael repeatedly with the hammer, killing him. Anne, Michael's wife, fainted when she saw Michael fall to the ground. As she fell, she struck her head against a porch step, knocking herself unconscious. Thinking that both Michael and Anne were dead, John quickly pulled them into the house and placed them on a sofa in the living room. He then set fire to the sofa. He hoped the fire would destroy the sofa and conceal how Michael and Anne had died. He then left. Firefighters extinguished the fire quickly; the only damage was a charred wall, but Ellwood, who was the first firefighter to arrive on the scene, died of smoke inhalation as he tried to pull the dead bodies of Anne and Michael outside. The autopsies showed that the cause of Anne's death was smoke inhalation.

83. Is John guilty of burglary?

  A. Yes, because he intended serious injury to Michael when he entered Michael's house.

  B. Yes, because his action occurred at night.

  C. No, because there was no breaking.

  D. No, because John did not intend to commit a larceny.

84. John's killing of Michael is most likely to be characterized as:

  A. Voluntary manslaughter.

  B. Involuntary manslaughter.

  C. Murder.

  D. Justifiable homicide.

85. Is John guilty of arson?

  A. Yes, because John maliciously burned Michael's house.

  B. Yes, because John was involved in the commission of a burglary.

  C. No, because the house was only charred.

  D. No, because John did not intend to burn the house.

86. John's killing of Anne is probably:

  A. Voluntary manslaughter.

  B. Involuntary manslaughter.

  C. Felony murder.

  D. No homicide crime because John believed she was already dead.

87. Is John guilty of Ellwood's murder?

    A. Yes, if John's suspicion that Michael had taken his power saw was incorrect.

    B. Yes, because he set fire to Michael's sofa.

    C. No, because John did not intend to kill Ellwood.

    D. No, because the missing power saw constituted reasonable provocation for John's actions.

Questions 88–89 are based on the following bigamy statute of North Dakona:

    I. Every person who has previously married a person of the opposite sex and who marries any other person, except in the cases specified in the next section, is guilty of bigamy.

    II. The previous section does not extend to any person

        a. who has no living spouse;

        b. whose prior spouse has been absent for five years without knowledge by such person that such prior spouse is still living;

        c. whose prior marriage was dissolved by divorce or annulment; or

        d. who reasonably believes that the prior marriage was dissolved by divorce or annulment in another state.

    III. Every person who marries another person with knowledge of circumstances that would render such other person guilty of bigamy under the laws of this state is also guilty of bigamy.

    IV. Bigamy is punishable by a fine of not more than $2,000, imprisonment in the county jail not to exceed six months, or both.

88. Fred, lawfully married to Agnes, left his home late one night to purchase an evening paper and did not return. Agnes never heard from Fred again. Agnes concluded that Fred was dead, and four years later married Clyde. Before their marriage, Agnes told Clyde she had previously been married but that her husband was dead. Fred reappeared one year after Agnes's marriage to Clyde. Under these circumstances, if Agnes and Clyde are charged with bigamy, the statute should be applied so that:

    A. Neither Agnes nor Clyde is guilty.

    B. Both Agnes and Clyde are guilty.

    C. Only Agnes is guilty.

    D. Only Clyde is guilty.

89. Victor was lawfully married to Susan, who left him and moved to another city. Victor proposed to Peggy and falsely told her that Susan was dead. Irwin, another suitor for Peggy's hand, told her that Susan was still alive and produced a recent letter from Susan to support his contention. However, Peggy was intoxicated at the time and did not understand or remember what Irwin told her. Thereafter, Peggy married Victor. On these facts, if Peggy is charged with bigamy, she is:

A. Not guilty, only if her intoxication was voluntary.

B. Not guilty, only if her intoxication was involuntary.

C. Not guilty, regardless of whether her intoxication was voluntary or involuntary.

D. Guilty, regardless of whether her intoxication was voluntary or involuntary.

Questions 90-93 are a series.

90. The Jets, a gang consisting of several former football players, decide to paint a "40" on every sign posting a speed limit of 10, using a paint that is indistinguishable from the legitimate paint. Joe Namath, the founder of the group, goes to the local hardware store and buys a gallon of paint. Namath and the Jets are guilty of attempting to vandalize government property:

A. Under the common law.

B. Under the MPC.

C. Under both.

D. Under neither.

91. Assume that Namath buys the paint, and, at midnight, he and the Jets drive to the corner where they intend to start the defacing. Namath picks up the paintbrush and moves toward the sign, but suddenly, for no apparent reason, decides he'd rather play football and orders everyone back to the car. He (and the Jets) is guilty of an attempt:

A. Under the common law.

B. Under the Model Penal Code.

C. Under both.

D. Under neither.

92. Assume that Namath and the boys are not stopped until they (literally) painted the town red. Under the common law, they are guilty of:

    A. Conspiracy to vandalize, attempt to vandalize, and vandalizing.

    B. Attempt to vandalize and vandalizing.

    C. Conspiracy to vandalize and vandalizing.

    D. Vandalizing, but not conspiracy to vandalize.

93. Assume that Namath and the Jets are not stopped until they (literally) painted the town red. Under the Model Penal Code, they are guilty of:

    A. Conspiracy to vandalize, attempt to vandalize, and vandalizing.

    B. Attempt to vandalize and vandalizing.

    C. Conspiracy to vandalize and vandalizing.

    D. Vandalizing, but not conspiracy to vandalize or attempt to vandalize.

94. Bernie Maddon perpetrates a massive securities fraud (a felony) on thousands of people, inducing them to invest millions of dollars in stocks he knows are worthless. Two of these investors, having lost their life savings in this scam, commit suicide. The prosecution argues that this is felony murder.

    What is the strongest defense rebuttal to that theory?

    A. Maddon was not a "but for" cause of the suicides.

    B. Maddon was not a proximate cause of the suicides.

    C. Fraud is not, in the abstract, an inherently dangerous felony.

    D. The death "merges" with the felony fraud.

95. Matilda needs money. She buys a gun, loads it, and approaches Delores, on the street, intending to demand her money. At that moment, however, within five feet of Delores, Matilda changes her mind and walks away. If Matilda is *not* guilty of attempt under the common law, that is because:

    A. She has not reached the point of probable nondesistance.

    B. She has not taken a substantial step.

    C. She has abandoned her attempt.

    D. She has yet to commit the last act within her control.

96. Assume the same facts as above, but assume the jurisdiction is a Model Penal Code state. If Matilda is not guilty of attempt, the **best** explanation is:

    A. She has not reached the point of probable nondesistance.

    B. She has not taken a substantial step.

    C. She has abandoned her attempt.

    D. She has yet to commit the last act within her control.

97. Nancy wishes to enroll her son, Harry, in a very expensive private school, but she cannot afford the tuition. She meets with Gary, the principal, and pleads with him to admit Harry, but he is adamant. "However," says Gary, "if you become my lover, we'll find a way to admit Harry." Nancy agrees and for several years has sex with Gary. Gary:

    A. Has committed rape because he forced Nancy to consent.

    B. Has committed rape because he was in a superior position to Nancy.

    C. Has not committed rape because he did not threaten Nancy with serious bodily harm or death.

    D. Has not committed rape because Nancy is an adult.

98. Alex and Patrick see Gregory, whom they believe had taken Alex's iPod several weeks earlier. Intending to beat Gregory and then turn him in to the police, they scream, "Give us back that iPod!" at Gregory, who starts running away, with Alex and Pat in hot pursuit. After a vigorous five-minute chase, with Gregory running in between moving cars and across several streets, Gregory is hit and killed by a car.

Alex and Patrick are most likely:

    A. Guilty of first-degree murder.

    B. Guilty of second-degree murder.

    C. Not guilty of murder, because they did not intend that Gregory die.

    D. Not guilty of murder, because Gregory's death was fortuitous.

99. Assume the same facts as above. Are Alex and Patrick guilty of conspiracy to commit murder?

    A. Yes, because their intent to harm Gregory is clear.

    B. No, because it is not clear that they agreed on any crime.

    C. No, because it is not clear that they had the intent that Gregory die.

    D. Yes, because chasing Gregory among moving cars is highly reckless.

100. Abdullah, a native-born American, is a devout Sikh. This requires him to wear traditional clothing, including a turban. For years, Abdullah has endured jibes about his clothes. On several occasions, he has come close to hitting his taunters. One day, Abdullah is walking across campus when Billy Jack mutters, as he is passing by, "Hey towel head. We're in America now." Abdullah grabs BJ by the throat and strangles him.

Under the common law, Abdullah:

A. Is guilty of first degree murder because he had time to premeditate the killing.

B. Is guilty of second degree murder.

C. Is guilty of manslaughter because no reasonable person can be expected to ignore racial, religious, ethnic, or other such taunts.

D. Is guilty of no crime.

Multiple-Choice Answers

1. **A** A general-intent crime requires proof only that the accused intended to commit the act that served as the *actus reus*, not that he intended the injury that might result. Because Kramer intended to place the screwdriver against George's throat, and George was hurt when he twisted his head, Kramer is culpable of criminal assault. Choice **A** is correct. Choice **D** is incorrect because proof that the accused intended injury is unnecessary for a general-intent crime. Choice **C** is incorrect because George's reaction was a reasonable response to Kramer's actions, and Kramer should reasonably have expected that his placing an object against a person's neck might lead the victim to turn his head to view the source of the pressure. Finally, choice **B** is incorrect because the critical issue is not the inherent danger of the perpetrator's actions, but his intent to commit the act that causes the danger. Kramer would be innocent if he had not intended to place the screwdriver on George's throat.

2. **C** Under the Model Penal Code, a defendant acts "knowingly" if "he is aware that it is **practically certain** that his conduct will cause that result." MPC §2.02(b)(ii). Because Freddy was unaware that anyone except Richie was in the car, he could not reasonably be considered "practically certain" that his conduct would cause Jack's death. The correct answer is choice **C**. Choice **D** is incorrect because, as applied to capital crimes, the "provocation" must be such as would lead a reasonable man to lose his self-control. It seems extremely unlikely that a reasonable man would throw dynamite in response to a derogatory finger gesture. Choice **A** is incorrect because the definition of "knowingly" relates not only to the act committed but also to the consequences of the act. The accused must be considered "practically certain" that his actions will produce the result produced. Choice **B** is incorrect because, although Jack was clearly within the zone of danger created by Freddy's conduct, Freddy did not have actual knowledge that Jack was in the car.

3. **A** The correct answer is choice **A**. The crime of false pretenses occurs when the defendant obtains title to the property of another by knowingly misrepresenting a material fact. Here, Joe obtained "title" to Molly's $50 by misrepresenting his ownership of the television. Selling a television at a garage sale implies ownership of the item by the seller. Choice **B** is incorrect because in larceny by trick only possession of the property is obtained. If ownership of property is obtained, the crime is false pretenses. Because Molly did not intend to get back her $50, she was giving up ownership rather than mere

possession of the money. The fact that the television did not come with title is irrelevant to the issue. Choice **C** is incorrect because Joe implicitly represented to Molly that he owned the TV by conducting the garage sale. Finally, choice **D** is incorrect because purchasers at a garage sale do **not** (despite the relative informality) assume the risk of defective title.

4. **B** Common law arson occurs where the defendant, at night, maliciously burns the dwelling house of another. Charring ordinarily satisfies the "burning" element, and arson occurred because the barn would be considered part of the dwelling house. Although the barn was a separate structure located 25 feet from Farmer John's house, it is regarded as part of the dwelling because of its proximity to the main building. In this sense, it comes within the definition of *curtilage*, which was originally applied to all the buildings adjacent to a main dwelling and surrounded by the same fence as the dwelling. This definition of dwelling also applies in the crime of burglary. Choice **B** is the correct answer. Choice **C** is incorrect because no specific intent is necessary for the crime of arson to occur. The defendant must only have acted maliciously (i.e., **intentionally** or **recklessly**). Choice **A** is not correct because the charring of a building is sufficient to constitute arson. Finally, choice **D** is incorrect because arson extends to structures located within an area adjacent to the house that can reasonably be fenced in.

5. **A** The crime of larceny occurs if the accused, in a trespassory manner, takes and carries away personal property of another, with the intent to permanently deprive the owner of the item. The "taking and carrying away" element is satisfied here because Andrew, as a minor employee, has only custody of the fax machine (possession remained with Mr. Barnes). In most states, the "permanently deprived" element is satisfied if the accused pawns the item, even if he intends ultimately to redeem and return it to the rightful owner. Thus, Andrew is culpable of the crime charged. Choice **A** is the correct answer. Choice **B** is incorrect because Andrew's lie to Barnes about the thug's theft of the fax machine is irrelevant to the crime of larceny. Choice **C** is incorrect because Andrew was a low-level employee with temporary custody and under specific instructions about the repair of the machine, and the machine is still deemed to be in Mr. Barnes's possession. Finally, choice **D** is incorrect because, even if Andrew intended to redeem the fax machine, the majority view is that his actions have still "permanently deprived" Mr. Barnes of the item.

6. B The crime of false pretenses occurs when the accused has fraudulently obtained title to another's property. Because Anita knew that she had insufficient funds to cover the check to the Mercedes dealer, she obtained title to the vehicle by fraudulent means. Thus, she is guilty. The correct answer is choice **B**. Choice **A** is incorrect because, to commit false pretenses, the defendant must obtain title to (rather than mere possession of) the item involved. Choice **C** is incorrect on the facts as stated, which tell us that Anita received the car's documents of title as well as the car. Finally, choice **D** is incorrect because Anita knew that the dealership would not have given her the car and the title documents if it had known her check was bad.

7. A The crime of false pretenses requires that the accused, with the intent to defraud, knowingly make a misrepresentation of a material fact that causes the person to whom it is made to give the accused title to his property. The statement is material if it would induce a reasonable person to part with title to the property. Erica's statement is material because a reasonable person would not pay $1,000 for a computer worth $500. Because Erica knew her statement was false, and she obviously made it to get more money for the computer, she committed the crime of false pretenses when she permitted Jamie to give her the $1,000 money order for the computer. The fact that Erica was not able to cash the money order is irrelevant. Erica had title to the money once she received the money order. Choice **A** is the correct answer. Choice **B** is incorrect; Jamie took possession only because he was induced to do so by Erica's fraudulent statements. Choice **C** is incorrect because the fact that Erica never cashed her money order is irrelevant. Her crime was complete when she took possession and title to the money order. Finally, choice **D** is incorrect because Erica's statement that the computer's value was $2,000 was not an opinion but an outright lie; she knew the actual value was lower.

8. C Larceny by trick occurs when, with the intent to steal, the accused has fraudulently obtained ***possession*** of (but not ***title*** to) another's personal property. When the defendant has obtained ***title*** to the property, she cannot be convicted of larceny by trick. She can only be convicted of false pretenses. Therefore, the key issue here is whether Allison obtained title to the shoes. The rule is that a transfer of title occurs when the victim parts with property as the result of a ***sale***. Because Allison bought the loafers from the store, she acquired title, and, therefore, she cannot be successfully prosecuted for larceny by trick. She is, however, guilty of false pretenses. The correct answer is choice

C. Choice **D** is incorrect because, whether or not Allison altered the numbers on the price tags, Allison could be convicted of larceny by trick if she obtained possession of the shoes by switching the tags, and of the crime of false pretenses if she obtained title to the shoes. Finally, choices **A** and **B** are incorrect because, as discussed above, Allison cannot be guilty of the crime of larceny by trick because she acquired title to the shoes (rather than mere possession of them).

9. **D** The crime of embezzlement occurs when the accused has fraudulently converted the property of another at a time when the property was lawfully in her possession. If the accused obtained the property lawfully, she cannot be guilty of embezzlement. Because Brian had voluntarily loaned the car to Mary at a time when her intent was only to use it to drive to a party, Mary committed the crime of embezzlement when she appropriated the car for her escape to the West. The correct answer is choice **D**. Embezzlement and larceny are distinct crimes that cannot overlap. Choice **A** is incorrect because the crime of larceny requires a trespassory taking; it is a crime against possession and cannot occur when possession is obtained lawfully. Choice **B** is incorrect because the crime of false pretenses requires that title to property pass as the result of a false misrepresentation of a material fact. Mary made no misrepresentation, and she never acquired title to Brian's Toyota. Finally, choice **C** is incorrect because an individual cannot be convicted of larceny by trick if she was in rightful possession of the property at the time she appropriated it for her own use. Larceny by trick is simply one way in which the crime of larceny can be committed.

10. **D** Each one of the crimes listed requires the unlawful taking of property by the accused. None of these crimes was committed against Pam because Kevin did not get any money from her. While Mary did give $5 to Kevin, she was not frightened into giving Kevin the money, but did so voluntarily to go along with Kevin's prank. Mary's impulsiveness in playing along with Kevin's game does not create an unlawful taking. In addition, it is reasonably clear that Kevin did not intend to deprive Mary of her money. Kevin was only playing a game. He cannot be convicted of any of these crimes unless it is proved that he had the intent to steal. If Kevin had acted with the intent to steal, and either Mary or Pam had been frightened into giving Kevin her money, he would have committed the crime of robbery. A robbery occurs when the accused, by force or the threat of force, takes and carries away from her person or presence the personal property of

his victim, with the intent to steal. The correct answer is choice **D**. Choice **A** is incorrect because the facts do not establish the crime of robbery. Choice **B** is incorrect because the crime of larceny requires a trespassory taking, and no trespassory taking occurred. Finally, choice **C** is incorrect because no embezzlement occurred. Kevin did not have lawful possession of Mary's money before he took it from her.

11. **D** The correct answer is choice **D**. Tommy is not guilty of any of the three listed crimes. Larceny by trick is a form of larceny, but it requires two ingredients that are not necessary for simple larceny: (1) the property taken by the accused must be **converted** by him (i.e., it must be destroyed, sold, or otherwise deprived of its utility to the victim), and (2) title to the stolen property must not have passed to the accused. Larceny by trick also requires that the property be taken by fraud or deceit. None of these requirements is present here, and choice **B** is, therefore, incorrect. Choice **A** is incorrect because the wallet was not obtained by Tommy by force or the threat of force, an essential element of the crime of robbery. Finally, choice **C** is incorrect because Tommy did not convert property that was lawfully in his possession. The crime of embezzlement can occur only with respect to property that is lawfully in the possession of the accused when it is fraudulently converted. Lest we conclude that no crime is committed by pickpockets, let us state that Tommy has committed the crime of common law larceny, which requires only a trespassory taking and carrying away of the property of another with intent to steal.

12. **C** The best answer is choice **C**. The crime of receiving stolen property occurs when the accused receives **stolen goods** that he knows to be stolen, with the intention of permanently depriving the owner of the goods. The low price that Beaver paid for the vase justifies the conclusion that Beaver knew he was purchasing stolen property. Further, Beaver's intent to keep the vase establishes that he intended to deprive the true owner of the vase. However, we are lacking one essential element of the crime of receiving stolen property. The key issue is whether the vase was **stolen property** at the time of the sale to Beaver. The rule is that once the police recover the property in question, it ceases to be "stolen." Because the vase was recovered by the police when Friday took it from Kristen, Beaver cannot be convicted of receiving stolen property. He may be successfully prosecuted for **attempted** receipt of stolen property, but, even here, he may be able

to assert the defense of legal impossibility, on the theory that what he tried to do could not have been construed as a crime because the goods were not stolen when offered to him. ***People v. Jaffe***, 185 N.Y. 497 (1906). (Under the Model Penal Code, Beaver would easily be convicted.) Choice **D** is incorrect because the crime of receiving stolen property occurs whether or not the accused intends to resell the article; he may, as here, simply wish to retain it. Choice **A** would be correct if the vase had not been recovered by the police. Once the property is no longer considered stolen goods, the accused is not guilty, even if he believed he was purchasing stolen property. Finally, choice **B** is also incorrect because the vase had ceased to be "stolen." In addition, even if the vase were considered stolen, choice **B** would be incorrect because it fails to include one of the essential elements of the crime of receiving stolen property (i.e., that the accused know (or have reason to believe) that the goods were stolen).

13. **A** The crime of receiving stolen property occurs when the accused has voluntarily taken into his possession goods that he knows to be stolen, with the intention of permanently depriving the owner of the goods. The key issue here is whether Morgan can be convicted of receiving stolen property even if he never personally handled the television sets himself. The accused need not handle the goods. He is guilty if he exercises control over the goods. On these facts, Morgan exercised control over the goods when he directed his "employees" to deposit the goods in Pete's warehouse. The correct answer is choice **A**. Choice **B** is incorrect because ***attempts*** are ordinarily merged into the completed crime and carry a lesser penalty than the completed crime. Choice **C** is incorrect. The crime of conspiracy requires agreement by two or more parties to carry out an unlawful act or to carry out a lawful act by unlawful means. The requirements are not met here because the facts fail to indicate that Morgan agreed with anyone else to receive the TV sets. Also, conspiracy to commit a particular crime ordinarily carries a lesser penalty than the completed crime, and the question calls for the most serious crime committed by Morgan. Finally, choice **D** is incorrect because, as explained above, Morgan is guilty of receiving stolen property because he took custody of the sets by depositing them in Pete's warehouse even though he did not handle the goods and did not own the warehouse.

14. **D** A person becomes an accomplice when he aids, abets, encourages, or assists another in the commission of a crime. It is generally said that the accomplice's state of mind must be essentially the same as that of

the perpetrator of the crime (i.e., he must have the same *mens rea* as the perpetrator). (But there are exceptions—if A purposely enrages B, who kills C in the heat of passion, A may be liable for purposeful murder, even if B is guilty only of homicide.) Here, Alex knew that Tom was angry with the director and that he intended to "have words with him." But he did not know that Tom was carrying his gun, and, as we are told, he didn't believe that Tom intended to murder the director. Thus, even though Alex did help Tom to commit the crime by luring the secretary out of the office, he lacked the *mens rea* necessary to the crime. The correct answer is choice **D**. Choice **A** is incorrect because it's not enough that a person commit an act that helps the perpetrator; he must ***intend*** that that act result in the crime itself. Choice **B** is incorrect for the same reason. Choice **C** is incorrect on the facts because, in the strictest factual sense, Alex did "participate" in the crime. He is not guilty as an accomplice, however, because an accomplice must also intend that the criminal act itself occur.

15. **D** Jones knew he was entering "something," and whether that "something" constitutes a "building" is not a factual, but a legal, question. He doesn't claim that he knew the legal definition of the word "building" and mistakenly applied that definition to the yard. His claim is ignorance (not mistake) of law. Instead, he is arguing that he didn't know the definition of "building." The common law did not recognize a claim of ignorance of law. Thus, choice **B** is incorrect (and, perforce, choice **C** is also incorrect). The Model Penal Code, §2.04(3), does provide a limited claim of reasonable reliance on official statements made by certain kinds of state actors, but this is not Jones's claim. Therefore, choice **A** is incorrect. Consequently, the correct answer is choice **D**.

16. **B** The crime of solicitation occurs when the accused requests another to commit a crime, with the specific intent that the crime be committed. Under the Model Penal Code, the accused is guilty of solicitation even if he "fails to communicate with the person he solicits." MPC §5.02(2). This means that, when Dillinger sent the letter asking Capone to kill the police officer, all the elements for solicitation were satisfied. Choice **B** is the correct answer. Choice **A** is incorrect because Dillinger would still be guilty even if Capone never saw or read his letter. The crime was complete when the letter was mailed. Choice **C** is incorrect because there is no general defense of impossibility to a solicitation charge. It doesn't matter that the solicitee

cannot actually commit the crime; all that's necessary is that the solicitor believe that the crime can be committed. Finally, choice **D** is incorrect because there is no requirement that the solicitee take any action for the crime of solicitation. As soon as the defendant makes the request, the crime is complete.

17. **D** Although determining the scope of a conspiracy is often difficult, there is a good argument to be made here that there is a single conspiracy proven on these facts. Here, there is a level of interdependence among the parties; each knows of the others' involvement and understands that he is part of a larger whole. Thus, while arguable, there is a case to be made that the facts parallel those of *United States v. Bruno*, 105 F.2d 921 (1939). Therefore **A** is incorrect. **B** is also incorrect because there is no evidence that A and B did anything to facilitate D's car theft. Although the theft might have facilitated the robberies, there is no evidence that the robberies facilitated the theft. Therefore there can be no aiding and abetting liability. Similarly, while A and B can be said to be in a conspiracy together, there is nothing to show that they facilitated each other's crimes. Therefore choice **C** is also incorrect. **D**, the flipside of **C**, is the correct answer. Because, as explained above, it is possible to conceive a single conspiracy on these facts, each of the participants can be charged with the crimes others do in furtherance of the conspiracy that are reasonably foreseeable. *Pinkerton v. United States*, 328 U.S. 640 (1946).

18. **D** Choice **A** is incorrect. The MPC has rejected the co-conspirator doctrine and therefore A cannot be liable under both theories. While this might be the correct answer at CL, it's quite wrong under the MPC. Choice **B** is tempting but also incorrect. Under the MPC, the defendant must have the "purpose of promoting or facilitating" the crimes of another in order to be liable as an accomplice. MPC §2.06(3). The wording of this question says that D *knows* that he is facilitating the crimes of another. Under the MPC knowledge is a different, and lesser, *mens rea* state than purpose and therefore is insufficient to make D an accomplice. Choice **C** is a correct statement of the law under the CL, but not under the MPC. Under the MPC, a defendant may be convicted either of conspiring to commit a crime or of committing it, but not both. See MPC §5.05(3). Therefore of these statements, only the one in **A** correctly states the law under the MPC.

19. **A** The crime of conspiracy requires the agreement of two or more persons to commit an unlawful act or a lawful act by unlawful means.

The key word is "agreement." The traditional rule was that a conspiracy could not be found unless there was an actual agreement of two or more persons to commit a crime. Under this traditional view, a conspiracy could not exist when one party, such as an undercover police officer, feigned agreement. The more modern view, however, holds that a defendant can be convicted of conspiracy even if the other party lacks the intent to commit the object crime. This means that a defendant can be convicted of conspiracy if he agrees with a police officer to commit a crime, even though the police officer is feigning agreement. The Model Penal Code has adopted this modern view. The code reaches its conclusion by reasoning that any person who agrees with another, whatever the circumstances, to commit a crime is guilty of conspiracy. Under this approach, conspiracy is not defined as an agreement between two or more parties, but, rather, as the commitment of one defendant to the other(s). MPC §5.03(1)(a). Because Jake agreed to rob the 7-Eleven, he is guilty of conspiracy. The correct answer is choice **A**. Choice **C** is incorrect because the defense of entrapment is available to an accused only if the police officer *induces* commitment of the crime. Here, Jake proposed the robbery, not Marty. Choice **D** is incorrect because, as explained above, under the modern view, it does not matter that Marty never really agreed or intended to rob the store. Finally, choice **B** is incorrect because it is not necessary for the crime of conspiracy that a "substantial step" be taken toward commission of the target crime. (The "substantial step" requirement can be a factor in assessing "attempt" crimes; the term in conspiracy is "overt act," which is usually a much less significant act.)

20. **D** Under common law principles, a conspiracy occurs when there is an agreement between two or more persons to commit an unlawful act or a lawful act by unlawful means; the U.S. Supreme Court has made clear that whether an "overt act" is required depends entirely on statute. Half the jurisdictions also require an overt act by one of the conspirators in furtherance of the conspiracy. The Model Penal Code requires an overt act only in the case of minor crimes. In the case of felonies of the first or second degree, the code does not require an overt act because it wishes to encourage "preventive intervention." In this case, the robbery was aborted before any act could be committed. In at least half the states, the overt-act rule would prevent Corrine from being convicted of conspiracy. Further, the general rule is that a defendant cannot be charged with conspiracy unless she

has agreed to join in the commission of the crime. (Even under the Model Penal Code, which has adopted the "unilateral" approach to conspiracy, Corrine could not be the one charged because she never agreed with Amanda to rob the Gap.) She went with Amanda to the mall only because she feared that Amanda would harm her. Because she did not voluntarily agree to commit the crime, she cannot be convicted of conspiracy. The correct answer is choice **D**. Choice **C** is incorrect because the act of entering the store is not a necessary element of this crime. Even if this jurisdiction is one that requires an overt act, the overt act probably occurred when Amanda pulled the two guns from her purse and handed one to Corrine. Choice **A** is incorrect because Corrine took the gun and went to the mall only because she felt threatened, not because she intended to rob the store. Finally, choice **B** is incorrect. Because Corrine did not intend to commit a crime, she did not have to repudiate it in order to avoid culpability.

21. **A** Bill and Ted formed a criminal conspiracy when they agreed to sell cocaine to Mickey. The key issue is whether Ted can escape culpability for the crime of conspiracy because he left the scene before the deal was consummated. The common law rule is that an act of withdrawal is not a defense to a conspiracy charge because the conspiracy is complete once the agreement has been made. The Model Penal Code does permit a withdrawal defense, but only if (1) the accused's renunciation was voluntary, and (2) the accused thwarts the success of the conspiracy. MPC §5.03(6). Ted's withdrawal satisfies neither view: it was not voluntary because it was motivated only by a desire to avoid arrest, and it did not thwart the success of the conspiracy. The correct answer is choice **A**. Choice **B** is incorrect because completion of the drug sale is not required. If Bill dropped the bag with the cocaine and was unable to complete the sale, Ted and Bill would still be guilty of conspiracy. Choice **C** is incorrect because Bill's withdrawal cannot be motivated by the desire to avoid arrest, especially because the success of the conspiracy was not thwarted. (Under the common law rule, a voluntary withdrawal would not save Ted from culpability in any event.) Finally, choice **D** is incorrect because a co-conspirator need not participate in the target crime to be culpable of conspiracy.

22. **A** At common law, one was liable as an accomplice when he, with a sufficiently culpable mental state, aided another's criminal conduct. It was not necessary to show that the accomplice was the but-for

cause of the principal's conduct; rather it was merely required that the accomplice's conduct made the commission of the offence easier or more likely. See, e.g., *Wilcox v. Jeffery*, 1 All E.R. 464 (1951). Under the posited facts, A did not in any way facilitate the commission of the offense and therefore is not liable as an accomplice, making **A** the correct answer. Choice **C** is incorrect because on the facts as stated A did nothing to help with the burglary and does not have a sufficiently culpable *actus reus* to make him liable as an accomplice. Choice **B** is incorrect because the law has never required an agreement, either explicit or implicit, before a defendant can be held liable as another's accomplice. Finally, choice **D** is incorrect. At common law, a would-be accomplice's mere desire to aid was insufficient to make him liable for an attempt crime.

23. **C** Under the MPC, one is liable as an accomplice when, acting with a sufficiently culpable mental state, he either aids or intends to aid in another's commission of an offense. MPC Sec. 2.06(3). Thus, choice **A** is incorrect. While at common law it was generally required that the accomplice provide at least some actual aid, the MPC, with its focus on *mens rea*, did away with that requirement. Answer **B** is also incorrect. The law has never required an agreement before an accomplice can be convicted for aiding another's criminal conduct; agreement is a strict requirement for conspiracy (and co-conspirator liability) but not for accomplice liability. Choice **D** is tempting. Under the MPC, A could be found liable for an attempt if he tried to aid a crime that was never attempted or if he aided a crime that was attempted but not completed. However, under the code, where he tries to aid a crime that is committed, he is liable for the completed crime as an accomplice even if his attempt to aid is not in fact successful.

24. **A** A conspirator is liable for the criminal acts of a co-conspirator that occur in the furtherance of the conspiracy and that are a reasonably foreseeable outgrowth of it. Because Barker and Samantha agreed to rob the store at gunpoint, it is reasonable to conclude that Barker foresaw that some violence would ensue, including the use by Samantha of a deadly weapon. The correct answer is choice **A**. Choice **B** is incorrect because it is too broad. Conspirators are **not** always liable for the acts of their co-conspirators. The modern view is that a conspirator will not be liable simply because he is a member of the conspiracy. This view imposes liability only if the crime committed is (1) within the scope of the conspiracy or (2) a reasonably foreseeable outgrowth of it. MPC §2.06(3), Comment 6(a).

Choice **C** is incorrect because, under the circumstances, the killing of Kipper was reasonably foreseeable. Finally, choice **D** is incorrect because the conspiratorial objectives would not be concluded until the money taken from the store had been divided between Barker and Samantha. Also, this choice cannot be right because it would enable co-conspirators to limit their liability by defining their target crime in such a way as to eliminate the possibility of liability for other crimes growing foreseeably out of the target crime.

25. **C** Under the common law, mistake of law (*ignorantia juris*) was no excuse. Reliance on persons assumed to know the law (lawyers, judges) — no matter how reasonable — was irrelevant. Thus, facially, none of the claims that Liz wants to make will help her. However, some courts have concluded that the purpose of the doctrine is to make people understand the ***criminal*** law, not all law. Here, Liz knew that it was a crime to be married to two people at once — her mistake was one of domestic relations law, not of criminal law. While it might not be a winning argument, choice **C** is Liz's best contention. But she might want to pack a few clothes for prison — just in case.

26. **B** The Model Penal Code imposes attempt liability if (1) the accused intends to commit the crime that is attempted, and (2) the accused has taken a substantial step toward completion of the crime. MPC §5.01(1). The intent element is satisfied under these facts, which tell us that Frank was "intent on killing her." Although Frank never found Louise, he did cruise around the neighborhood hoping to spot her. Under the Model Penal Code, this conduct is sufficient to constitute the required "substantial step" toward completion of the crime. The code example is "lying in wait, searching for or following the contemplated victim, of the crime." Thus, Frank is guilty of attempted murder. (Note, however, that the act of searching for the victim is not enough to constitute a substantial step under the more traditional "proximity test" used by some courts. ***People v. Rizzo***, 158 N.E. 888 (N.Y. 1927).) Choice **A** is incorrect because the intent to kill, without more, is insufficient to satisfy the *actus reus* of attempt. Choice **C** is incorrect because the crime of attempted murder can occur without the firing of a shot. Under the Model Penal Code especially, the crime of attempted murder occurs many steps ahead of the actual gunshot. Choice **D** is incorrect because, as noted above, the crime of attempt occurs as soon as the accused, intending to commit the crime, begins to search for his intended victim. The correct answer is choice **B**.

27. **C** The common law recognized finding a spouse *in flagrante delicto* as "adequate legal provocation" to reduce to manslaughter a killing that would otherwise be murder. However, a **confession** of adultery was not enough—on two grounds: (1) the defendant had to actually "see" the adultery (some courts even required that he find the two "coupled," and (2) words alone were almost never adequately legal provocation. Thus, choice **A** is incorrect. Choice **B** is also incorrect because American courts have been very reluctant to recognize a "cultural defense" as grounds for avoiding, or even mitigating, criminal liability. Any consideration that might be given to the defendant's culture will occur at sentencing, not at the guilt stage. Choice **D** is also incorrect for several reasons. First, many states do not recognize a claim of diminished capacity. One must be "insane" to claim any lack of mental capacity. Second, the claim still requires that the defendant demonstrate that he suffered from a recognized "mental disease." There is nothing in the problem that suggests this. Third, even in those jurisdictions that permit a diminished-capacity claim, it is limited to crimes of specific intent. Murder does not require **specific** intent to kill; indeed, it does not require such intent at all. Choice **C** is correct—not only by default but also because the Model Penal Code, §210.2(b), does allow extreme mental or emotional disturbance to reduce a killing to manslaughter. The defendant has to show that his actions were reasonable for a person in the defendant's "situation," but the code makes clear that virtually any aspect of the defendant's character may be considered part of his "situation" —at least to allow the jury to consider it.

28. **D** The crime of murder cannot occur unless a life has been taken. The crime requires proof that the action, or inaction, of the accused caused another's death. Because the autopsy revealed that Thomas was already dead when Margot stabbed him, she did not cause his death, and, therefore, she cannot be guilty of murder. The correct answer is choice **D**. Under these facts, the prosecution could have prosecuted Margot successfully for attempted murder because she stabbed Thomas with the intent to inflict serious bodily injury. A killing caused with intent to inflict serious bodily injury satisfies the *mens rea* for murder. Choice **C** is wrong because a person can be guilty of murder even if she did not intend to kill. The *mens rea* requirement for murder is satisfied if the accused had the intent to cause serious bodily harm. Choices **A** and **B** are incorrect because, as explained above, Thomas had already died. Thus, no homicide occurred despite Margot's actions or intent.

29. A Courts use one of two tests to determine whether entrapment of the accused by a police officer has occurred. A majority of courts, including the Supreme Court, use the "predisposition" test. Under this test, entrapment exists where (1) the government proposes the crime and induces the defendant to commit it, and (2) the defendant is "innocent" (i.e., not predisposed to commit the crime). In this case, Harry immediately offered to sell drugs "for the right price" in response to the officer's request. This offer, combined with Harry's prior record, establishes a predisposition to sell drugs. Therefore, Harry's entrapment defense will fail. In the minority of courts that use the "police conduct" test instead of the "predisposition" test, the defense will also fail on these facts. Under this test, the government's inducement and participation must be such as to lead "innocent" or unpredisposed individuals to commit the crime, whether or not the defendant himself is actually predisposed. Harry's entrapment defense would fail under this test because, clearly, Harry was not an "innocent" or unpredisposed person. An innocent person would have remained silent, walked away, or said "no." The correct answer is choice **A**. Choice **B** is incorrect because there is no legal rule that says that the defense of entrapment is unavailable to former convicts for the same or a similar crime. Evidence of the same or similar prior crimes can be used as evidence of predisposition, but it would not be dispositive. Choice **C** is incorrect because it is not enough to show that government inducement initiated the crime; under the majority view, the defendant must also show that he was not predisposed to commit the crime. Finally, choice **D** is incorrect because Harry can still be convicted even if he did not have the immediate intent to sell drugs. If he was ready and willing to accept the first offer to buy drugs, it doesn't matter that he didn't intend to sell drugs until the officer approached him.

30. D This is a tricky question. The correct answer is choice **D**. Ten states do not recognize the "general" - "specific" division and preclude the introduction of evidence of intoxication no matter what the crime charged. In those states, choice **A** would be correct. But the question asks for the rule in the *majority* of states. In the majority of states, intoxication is allowed to "negate" a specific-intent crime. The facts, however, tells us that this is a general-intent crime, for which intoxication is irrelevant. Choice **B** is not correct because, even in the majority of states, the common law imposes liability for general-intent crimes by drunks. Choice **C** is more plausible — but a requirement that he know that it's not his store would mean that the crime is a specific-intent crime, and the facts tells us that the crime has been interpreted to be a general-intent crime.

31. **B** The kidnapping statute at issue requires that the accused commit the confinement of another "intentionally." Under common law principles, intent (*mens rea*) is satisfied when the accused (1) intended the result that occurred or (2) should have realized that the result would be substantially certain to follow from his actions. Here, Carl intended to commit a burglary. He did not intend to commit the crime of kidnapping as defined in the statute. On the contrary, he believed that Mary was visiting her sister in another state. When a person commits one crime with the requisite intent but inadvertently and unintentionally also commits the acts defining another crime, he is not guilty of the second crime because there is a failure of "temporal concurrence" — that is, the concurrence between the mental state (*mens rea*) and the act (*actus reus*). The correct answer is choice **B**. Choice **A** is incorrect because it is not the best reason to find Carl not guilty. Mary was unlawfully confined for a substantial period of time. Nothing required her to call the police before attempting to free herself. The better answer is choice **B**, which relies on Carl's lack of intent. Finally, choices **C** and **D** are incorrect because Carl never intended to cause Mary's confinement.

32. **A** The American legal system does not generally impose criminal liability for a failure or omission to act. Under some circumstances, however, there may be a duty to act to avoid or prevent an undesirable result. An accused will be found guilty if (1) she had a legal duty to act, (2) was aware of the facts or circumstances that obliged her to act, and (3) was capable of performing the act required. A legal duty to act can be based on (1) the personal relationship of the parties, (2) statutory law, (3) contract, (4) a voluntary assumption of care, (5) creation of the risk or danger by the accused, or (6) status as a landlord. Because the relationship between Alison and Jamie does not fall within any of these categories, Alison had no legal duty to rescue Jamie, and she is not guilty of murder (or any other crime). The correct answer is choice **A**. (However, it is probably safe to say that Alison will not win the "Good Citizenship" award for this or any month; nor would she be well advised to use the pool again.) Choice **B** is incorrect because this is not the basis for exonerating Alison; even if Alison had made no effort to call the police, she would still ***not*** be guilty of murder. Choice **C** is incorrect because, as explained

above, although Alison could have saved Jamie without any risk of harm to herself, she was under no legal duty to do so. Choice **D** is incorrect because there is no special duty in the general public to come to the aid of a minor. The duty would arise, for example, because of the special relationship between a minor and his parents or by virtue of a statute.

33. **D** If a defendant kills another, even accidentally, during the commission of a felony, he becomes guilty of murder under the felony-murder rule. Although Kevin's ultimate intent was to commit the felony of insurance fraud, a felony that is not inherently dangerous, he elected to do so by committing arson, a felony that is very dangerous. In most jurisdictions, arson has now been extended to include commercial buildings. (Under common law, it was limited to a residence and its adjoining structures.) To hold the defendant guilty of the killing resulting from commission of the felony, there must be a causal relationship between the two. The defendant will be liable only when the death is the "natural and probable consequence of his act." The key issue is whether Kevin's act of arson satisfies the proximate cause element despite his ignorance of the fact that Ben was in the building. The rule with respect to arson is that the requisite causal relationship exists with anyone who is in the building at the time the fire is set and who dies in the fire. Therefore, Kevin is guilty of murder. The correct answer is choice **D**. Choice **C** is incorrect because Kevin committed arson, an inherently dangerous felony (as well as attempting insurance fraud). Choice **A** is incorrect because the felony-murder rule does not require that the defendant have a specific intent to kill. Finally, choice **B** is incorrect because it was reasonably foreseeable that a human being might die as a consequence of his actions (e.g., a firefighter rather than an unknown derelict). Choice **B** is also wrong because the felony-murder rule does not depend on foreseeability, except, perhaps, as foreseeability of injury or death making the predicate felony inherently dangerous.

34. **A** Common law burglary requires several specific ingredients: (1) a breaking, (2) and an entry, (3) into the dwelling of another, (4) at night, and (5) with the intent to commit a felony. The intent to commit a felony must be present at the moment of breaking and entering. It cannot be formed after the accused enters the dwelling. When Daniel entered the house, his sole purpose was to retrieve his DVD player. Obviously, the act of retrieving your own property is not a felony. Because the intent to take the computer was not formed until

after he was in the house, Daniel cannot be convicted of the crime of burglary. The correct answer is choice **A**. Choice **B** is incorrect because the facts tell us that Daniel opened the unlocked window, and the slightest opening created by the accused constitutes a "breaking" for purposes of this crime. Choice **C** is incorrect because it does not state all the ingredients of the crime of burglary: (1) the illegal entry must be a "breaking," and (2) the defendant must intend to commit a felony once inside the house. Finally, choice **D** is incorrect because the fact that Daniel took the PowerBook after he entered the house would make him guilty of larceny (the trespassory taking and carrying away of the personal property of another with intent to steal), but not burglary.

35. **C** The crime of murder requires three essential ingredients: (1) an affirmative act by the accused (*actus reus*), (2) resulting in a death, and (3) committed with malice aforethought (*mens rea*). In addition, there must be a causal relationship between the act and the death (i.e., the act must be both the "cause in fact" and the "proximate" cause of the death). Janice laced the cookies with poison and placed them on David's desk, with the intent to kill, and David died as a result of eating the cookies. Thus, all the elements for a murder conviction are satisfied. It doesn't help Janice that she relented and attempted to undo her actions. The correct answer is choice **C**. Choice **A** is wrong because Janice had the necessary *mens rea* when she committed the acts that caused her brother's death. Choice **D** is incorrect because the time to measure Janice's state of mind was at the moment she committed the acts that led to David's death — at that time, she had the necessary *mens rea* (i.e., the intent to kill). A subsequent change of heart does not absolve Janice of responsibility for the murder. Choice **B** is incorrect. The provocation that is required to justify the reduction of a homicide from murder to voluntary manslaughter is not satisfied by Janice's impulse to preserve her interest in her parents' estate, whether or not David was telling malicious lies.

36. **C** The crime of involuntary manslaughter results when the accused, through grossly negligent or "merely" reckless conduct, causes the accidental death of another person. It also results when the accused has committed a misdemeanor or other unlawful act that causes the accidental death. The latter is called the ***misdemeanor-manslaughter rule***. The reasoning behind the rule is similar to the reasoning behind the ***felony-murder rule***. (The Model Penal Code rejects the misdemeanor-manslaughter rule in its entirety, and it has been criticized

by others because it often converts conduct that cannot be characterized as more than mere negligence into a homicide.) In this case, however, the correct answer is choice **C** because Jonathan committed a criminal battery. Simple battery, a misdemeanor, occurs when the accused intentionally causes either (1) bodily injury or (2) offensive touching. The crime can be committed intentionally or, in some states, recklessly or with criminal negligence. Jonathan committed a battery when he pushed Peter, and he is guilty of involuntary misdemeanor manslaughter. Choice **A** is incorrect because Jonathan did not intend to kill Peter, and the crime of murder requires malice aforethought. Choice **B** is incorrect because voluntary manslaughter also requires an intentional killing. The crime occurs when an act that would otherwise constitute murder is reduced to manslaughter because of provocation, "heat of passion," or the relationship in time between the provocation and the killing. Finally, choice **D** is incorrect because, as discussed above, Jonathan is criminally responsible for Peter's death under the misdemeanor-manslaughter rule.

37. **D** A larceny occurs when the defendant, in a trespassory manner, takes and carries away the personal property of another, with the intent to deprive that person permanently of the property (merely borrowing doesn't constitute larceny). The "intent" element is crucial to the crime, which cannot be committed negligently or recklessly. The facts make it clear that Erica intended only to "teach Pat a lesson," not to deprive her permanently of the bike. Erica's lack of larcenous intent is shown also by her vigil in the hallway. Thus, Erica is not guilty of larceny, and the correct answer is choice **D**. Choice **C** is incorrect because the fact that Erica did not take part in the actual removal of the bike is immaterial to the issue of her intent. Choice **A** is incorrect because the issue is Erica's intent, not the consequence of her actions. Finally, choice **B** is incorrect because the crime of larceny requires the intent to steal, not the intent to inconvenience someone or "teach her a lesson." Erica intended to return the bike, and the intent to return is inconsistent with the intent to steal.

38. **A** A has the intent to kill C; she believes and hopes that by leaving him, she will cause his death. Therefore, choice **B** is incorrect; C's *mens rea* can fairly be described as intent. For this reason, choice **D** is also incorrect; it's true that C's motivation—acquiring money—is irrelevant to her guilt for a homicide crime. However, it is also true that C has sufficient men rea to make her guilty of murder. Choice **C** is simply incorrect. C did many overt acts; in particular, she moved out on A

and moved in with another lover. The question here is not whether she acted, but whether her acts were the cause of the harm. This case closely resembles *People v. Campbell*, 124 Mich. App. 333 (1983) in which a defendant was acquitted for engaging in conduct that very predictably caused another's suicide. The court reasoned there that the deceased's conscious decision to take his own life was the cause of his death, rather than any conduct of the defendant.

39. **A** The common law crime of mayhem resulted from the need to punish the commission of batteries that resulted in great bodily harm (the common law did not recognize aggravated assault or battery). The crime required both permanent injury to the victim and intent by the accused to cause the injury. The statute quoted here conforms to the general requirements at common law, but might be interpreted as requiring something less than "great" bodily injury. However, a defendant will not be held liable for the injury she causes if the injury occurs through a completely bizarre, unforeseeable chain of events. She is liable, however, if she intends one injury, but the actual injury occurs in a slightly different way or is slightly different from the injury she originally intended. In this case, Molly clearly intended to disfigure Samantha, and her actions caused Samantha to jump in the pool to wash the acid away. The fact that Samantha was injured in a desperate attempt to escape the acid was not a bizarre or unforeseeable event under the circumstances, and Molly is guilty of mayhem as defined in the statute. The correct answer is choice **A**. Choice **B** is incorrect because a victim's attempt to avoid injury will rarely be a supervening event without the occurrence also of some bizarre and unforeseeable event. Samantha's attempt to remove the acid by jumping in the pool was obviously not an abnormal reaction to Molly's action. Choice **C** is incorrect because Molly's conduct was the proximate cause of Samantha's injuries. Her actions caused Samantha's injuries without the intervention of any other event or conduct and the result was foreseeable. Finally, choice **D** is incorrect because, as explained above, Molly is still culpable even if the injury is different from the injury intended or is caused in a different manner.

40. **C** Choice **D** is incorrect. The common law concluded that even an act done at the point of a gun to one's head was "voluntary," because the defendant could have accepted death. Therefore, the choice to commit the "requested" crime was voluntary. While choice **A** seems correct—most persons would, in fact, take the money rather than see

their beloved pets injured — it confuses the claim of duress with the claim of necessity. Most courts, including the U.S. Supreme Court, have held that a claim of duress is an excuse, rather than a justification, and does not require weighing the harm avoided with the harm actually done by the person under duress. Choice **B** appears correct, perhaps for the same reason that choice **A** was appealing. But both the common law and the MPC require that the threat to which a person of "reasonable firmness" succumbs is a threat to the person. A threat to any piece of property (which is what pets are, no matter how devoted we may be to them) is insufficient as a matter of law. The correct answer is choice **C**.

41. B This question should bring to mind the seminal case of *Regina v. Cunningham*, 2 Q.B. 396 (1957). Although in that case the defendant was charged with maliciously wounding his mother-in-law, here the statutory language has been updated to recklessness (which is how the English court read maliciously in *Cunningham*). Answer **A** is incorrect because it confuses recklessness and negligence. Recklessness is a subjective test; it focuses on whether the defendant perceived a risk or not. By contrast, negligence is a subjective test. It focuses on whether a reasonable person would have perceived that risk. Choice **C** is incorrect because recklessness does not require intent. Even if David wished no harm to befall his mother-in-law, he is nonetheless culpable if he was aware of a risk that his conduct would cause that result but proceeded with his conduct regardless. Finally, Choice **D** is incorrect as well. In *Cunningham* the court explicitly rejected the assertion that the defendant is liable for any crimes that result from the crime he meant to commit. While the law occasionally recognizes such a principle (in felony murder, say), where the legislature has specified a *mens rea* for a particular statute, that *mens rea* must be demonstrated beyond a reasonable doubt before the defendant may be convicted. Thus, only choice **B** is correct. It acknowledges that recklessness is a subjective standard and that a defendant will not be absolved merely because a reasonable person would not have discerned the risk.

42. A The courts have recently been confronted by many cases involving battered wives who claim that they acted in self-defense in killing their abusive husbands. Although sympathetic to these wives, the courts have consistently applied the traditional requirements for self-defense. A person may use deadly force when she reasonably believes that she is in imminent danger of being killed or is being threatened with serious bodily harm. Although Jenny is clearly a battered woman and legitimately frightened, she must still show that the danger of her death was imminent. The general rule is that, when the batterer goes to sleep, and the defendant shoots him while he sleeps, the defendant's self-defense claim fails because the danger is not sufficiently imminent. The logic behind this rule is that the defendant had ample time to protect herself by other means, such as calling the police or leaving the house. From another angle, the "beating" episode is over, and a new episode has begun, in which Jenny is the aggressor. These cases of "preemptive strikes" also arise in other contexts, such as international conflicts where one country, fully expecting a warlike strike from another country, or believing that the other country has weapons that it could use to begin war, acts first. The international law is similar to the domestic law. Although Jenny's self-defense claim fails, some jurisdictions allow the intentional homicide to be reduced to voluntary manslaughter when the accused honestly, but unreasonably, believes she is killing in self-defense. However, most jurisdictions follow the rule of the jurisdiction in this question and do not permit a claim of imperfect self-defense to reduce murder to voluntary manslaughter. (Note: An "imperfect" self-defense is one that does not constitute a complete defense to homicide. It arises when the defendant has killed because of an unreasonable mistake as to the need for force, when she is the initial aggressor, or under other circumstances that do not provide a complete defense against the homicide, but mitigate against the crime of murder.) Therefore, Jenny is guilty of murder, and the correct answer is choice **A**. Choice **B** is incorrect because Jenny did not meet the standards for invoking an "imperfect" self-defense. Choice **C** is incorrect because an intentional killing cannot be involuntary manslaughter. Choice **D** is incorrect because Jenny did commit the crime of murder.

43. D Every person has the right to defend himself against unlawful force (i.e., force used in the commission of a crime or tort). Whether he may use deadly force depends on the nature of the force that threatens him. If the force he faces is either death or serious bodily harm, then he may use deadly force in reply. His belief that he is facing deadly force must be reasonable. If it is reasonable, he may assert a claim of self-defense and will be acquitted. If it is unreasonable, the claim of self-defense will not be available. The cases turn on the facts leading to the homicide. Here, Jeremy had received a series of death threats and would be reasonably apprehensive of any threat-ened aggression. He was reasonable to believe that, under the cir-cumstances, his life was at risk. He saw someone running toward him with what appeared to be a loaded gun, shouting what could reasonably be interpreted as a threat. He had no reasonable way of knowing that the teenager was engaged in an initiation or even that the boy was only 12 years old. Given these facts, Jeremy can suc-cessfully assert a claim of self-defense to the homicide charge. The correct answer is choice **D**. Choice **A** is incorrect because Jeremy's self-defense is considered a perfect, rather than an "imperfect," defense. (Note: The claim of self-defense becomes "imperfect" when the accused kills in a mistaken belief about the need for deadly force or when he is the original aggressor. In these cases, as suggested above in the answer to Question 44, some states would allow reduction to manslaughter.) Choice **B** is incorrect because, although Jeremy committed an intentional homicide (voluntary manslaughter is an intentional homicide committed under extenuating circumstances), he has a perfect defense. Finally, choice **C** is incorrect because the crime of involuntary manslaughter depends on a homicide caused by criminal negligence, not specific intent. Jeremy intended to kill because he pointed and shot the gun at the boy's chest. In any event, he can assert the claim of perfect self-defense.

44. **B** The crime of involuntary manslaughter occurs when the grossly negligent or reckless conduct of the accused results in the death of another human being. The jury must consider and decide two criti-cal questions: (1) How far did the accused deviate from standards of reasonable care? (2) Was the accused aware of the risk of death or bodily harm? The Model Penal Code, §210.3(1)(b), requires that the accused act recklessly, with awareness of the risk. On these facts, the jury would almost certainly find Biff guilty. Biff acted with complete disregard of the danger when he ordered Morton to run through the "wall" of fire. There was always the risk that a pledge would be burned seriously and might die. Biff was aware of the danger, and his conduct was grossly negligent and, indeed, reckless. The fact that Morton died from a contaminated blood transfusion will not relieve Biff of liability. Although the prosecution must show a causal link between the defendant's acts and the death, intervening medical treatment is not a superseding intervening cause if it results directly from the injuries sustained by the victim. Obviously, when medi-cal treatment is made necessary, there is always the possibility that

the treatment will involve some negligence. That should not oper-
ate to benefit the person who caused the injuries in the first place.
Accordingly, ordinary negligence in the medical treatment is not
considered so "abnormal" as to constitute a superseding event. *State
v. Clark*, 248 A.2d 559 (N.J.2d 1968). The correct answer is choice **B**.
Choice **A** incorrectly states the degree of negligence that is required
for involuntary manslaughter. Most jurisdictions require more than
a showing of ordinary tort negligence; they require a showing of
criminal negligence (i.e., gross negligence or recklessness). Choice **C**
is incorrect because the waiver is ineffective. A consent that pur-
ports to waive a risk of death or serious bodily harm is effective
only in very limited circumstances (i.e., organized sporting events).
Finally, choice **D** is incorrect under the analysis of negligence in
supervening medical treatment, as discussed above.

45. **A** In recent years, the courts have broadened the liability for ***attempt
crimes***. Traditionally, the prosecution was required to show that the
accused had committed acts that brought him close to commission
of the crime itself. The modern view is that any overt act that shows
a substantial step toward commission of the crime will be adequate.
The Model Penal Code imposes attempt liability if (1) the accused
intends to commit the substantive crime itself, and (2) the accused
has taken a substantial step toward completion of the crime. MPC
§5.01(1). Under the MPC, "lying in wait" constitutes a substantial
step toward accomplishment of the target crime. MPC §5.01(2)(a).
The correct answer is choice **A**. Because Barney was waiting in the
abandoned office building to assassinate Jordan, rifle in hand, his
actions come within the MPC standard. Choices **B** and **C** are incorrect because Barney had already committed overt acts that were a
substantial step toward commission of the crime—he had positioned himself at the right spot in the building, he was carrying a
high-powered rifle, and he was "lying in wait." Choice **D** is incorrect.
When a defendant argues that it was impossible for him to commit
the crime because of some intervening fact, he will almost always
lose. This is because we are dealing with the crime of *attempt*, which
should be punished if the accused intends to commit the crime even
if the crime itself was never factually possible.

46. **B** The courts have imposed a number of limits on the application of
the felony murder rule. One of the most difficult to comprehend is
the merger doctrine, or the requirement that the felony that forms
the basis of a felony murder conviction be independent of the killing.

Another way to state the rule is that the felony cannot merely be the means by which the defendant killed. Because that is exactly what happened here, Choice **B** is the correct answer. Choice **A** is incorrect because it identifies a different judicial limit on the felony murder rule, namely the requirement that the underlying felony be inherently dangerous. Knowingly giving another poison certainly seems to satisfy this requirement. Answer Choice **C** is very incorrect. The MPC has rejected the felony murder rule entirely; thus if this jurisdiction follows the MPC, a felony murder prosecution will necessarily fail. Finally, Choice **D** is incorrect because the felony murder doctrine obviates the need to prove the intent to kill; one of the central features of the doctrine — one that is widely criticized — is that it substitutes intent to commit a felony for any *mens rea* with regard to the death of another person. Thus, the only correct answer is Choice **B**.

47. **B** The idea to kill the drug dealer originated with Larry and was communicated by him to Francine. Larry also suggested that they hide behind the trashcan to fire at the dealer. Clearly, Larry aided, abetted, encouraged, and assisted Francine and is, therefore, an accomplice to the homicide. The key issue, then, is whether Larry's decision to withdraw and his departure from the scene give him a defense to the accomplice to murder charge. The answer is "no." It's not enough that a defendant have a change of heart and leave the scene. That would be especially true under these circumstances in which Larry initiated the entire plan. Larry was obliged to tell Francine in no uncertain terms that he was withdrawing from the project. Although he was not required to stop Francine, he certainly had the duty of influencing her act by announcing his own withdrawal. Because Larry did not convey his withdrawal and disapproval to Francine, his withdrawal defense must fail. The correct answer is choice **B**. Choice **A** is incorrect because Larry is not required to stop Francine. He is only required to withdraw, as long as he advises Francine clearly that he is withdrawing. Choice **C** is incorrect because an accomplice can be culpable even if he didn't pull the trigger. Finally, choice **D** is incorrect because a conspirator need not be present at the scene when the crime is committed. (Note: The student should consider whether Larry is guilty of the crime of solicitation, as well as conspiracy.)

48. **A** The use of deadly force in self-defense is permissible only if the defendant is, or reasonably believes he is, being threatened with serious bodily injury or death. The evidence of their relative sizes

is relevant only if (1) a reasonable person would understand the words to threaten serious bodily harm or death, and (2) a reasonable person would fear that the threat might be carried out. *Even if* the words are viewed as a threat, had Herman been the threatener, no reasonable person of Hogan's size would actually fear serious bodily harm or death. Thus, the sizes of the two parties are relevant. For that reason, neither choice **C** nor choice **D** is correct. The problem is which remaining choice — **A** or **B** — is the "best." The question is close. Merely because Hogan *threatens* to hit Herman doesn't mean he actually will, and nothing *in his size* enhances a belief that he would. On the other hand, just because Herman might reasonably fear serious bodily harm or death *if* Hogan beats him, the *sizes do not* enhance the possibility that Hogan will actually hit him. Of these two choices, therefore, the best is choice **A**. A reasonable person of Herman's size, given Hogan's size, might reasonably fear that *any* hit would result in serious harm.

49. D This question requires an understanding of the elements that make up the different categories of homicide. The facts make it clear that Carl did not intend to kill Ethan. Because there was no intent to kill, neither murder in the first degree nor voluntary manslaughter is applicable (murder in the first degree requires a showing of pre-meditation and deliberation; voluntary manslaughter is essentially an intentional killing committed in the heat of reasonable passion). Because Carl's conduct cannot be said to exhibit an extreme indifference to human life — the test for murder in the second degree — he cannot be found guilty of that crime. Carl is guilty of the crime of involuntary manslaughter under the misdemeanor-manslaughter rule. This rule invokes the crime of involuntary manslaughter when a death occurs accidentally during the commission of a misdemeanor or other unlawful act, without inquiring into the mental state of the defendant with regard to the possibility of death. Carl committed a simple battery (and probably also the misdemeanor of criminal assault, by frightening Ethan into fearing immediate bodily harm), a misdemeanor, by throwing Ethan into the wall and poking him in the chest. Because Ethan's death occurred during the commission of the battery, Carl is guilty of involuntary manslaughter. The correct answer is choice **D**. Choice **A** is incorrect because Carl did not intend to cause death. Choice **B** is incorrect because Carl did not act with a reckless indifference to human life. Finally, choice **C** is incorrect because Carl did not intend the death of Ethan.

50. **D** The accused is guilty of the crime of attempt if he intends to commit a crime and commits some act or acts in furtherance of the crime that go beyond "mere preparation." The majority of courts look to see how close the accused came to committing the target crime. This is called the "proximity approach." Obviously, the closer the actual crime becomes, the clearer is the attempt. A number of tests have been developed in an effort to define "proximity." The facts show that Ilya stalked Jim with the intent to kill him and that he ran at Jim with knife at the ready. Clearly, his actions satisfy the proximity test for attempt. The Model Penal Code (and many courts), on the other hand, requires that the accused take a "substantial step" toward completion of the crime. MPC §5.01(1)(c). This is a significantly less stringent test than the proximity test, and it, too, was satisfied by Ilya's actions in following Jim and running at him with knife in hand. Ilya is guilty of attempted murder; the correct answer is choice **D**. Choice **C** is incorrect because mere intent is insufficient; some act is required that satisfies one of the tests for conduct beyond mere preparation. Choice **A** is incorrect because Ilya did take a substantial step as defined by the Model Penal Code and the courts. Finally, choice **B** is incorrect because the decision to abandon the attempt must be voluntary. In this case, Ilya's renunciation is not voluntary because he left out of fear that he would be caught by the police. The courts will not accept the withdrawal under these circumstances.

51. **A** The crime charged is conspiracy, not solicitation. (Angie is clearly guilty of the common law crime of solicitation for intending to kill her husband and offering Danny $20,000 to commit the homicide.) A conspiracy exists when two or more persons agree to commit an unlawful act or a lawful act by unlawful means, with culpable intent. The key issue is whether a conspiracy can exist when one party to a two-party agreement is an undercover police officer. The traditional rule was that a conspiracy occurs only when there is an actual agreement among two or more persons to commit a crime. Under this traditional view, a conspiracy cannot exist when one party, such as an undercover police officer, feigns agreement. The more modern view holds that a defendant can be convicted of conspiracy even if the other party lacks the subjective intent to commit the target crime. This means that a defendant can be convicted of conspiracy if she and a police officer agree to commit a crime even though the officer has no other intention than to secure an arrest. The Model Penal Code, §5.03(1)(a), also finds that the defendant

is guilty of conspiracy in cases where the other party feigns agreement. The Model Penal Code uses a unilateral approach in defining conspiracy, rather than the traditional bilateral approach. Under this approach, conspiracy is not defined as an agreement between two or more parties, but, rather, as a crime committed by any one party when he agrees with the other party to commit a crime. This means that if the defendant intended to reach an agreement, he is guilty of conspiracy, even if the other person is, in reality, not part of the plan. Because Angie agreed with Danny to have her husband murdered, she is guilty of conspiracy both under the modern view and under the Model Penal Code. The correct answer is choice **A**. Choice **B** is incorrect because Angie's mere intention to have her husband killed is an insufficient basis for conspiracy culpability. The crime requires agreement between two or more persons. Choice **C** is incorrect because, under the modern view and the Model Penal Code, the agreement of one of the parties can be feigned. Finally, choice **D** is incorrect on the law because no "substantial step" toward commission of the target crime is necessary for a conspiracy to occur. On the facts, it may be said that Angie had taken a substantial step by offering Danny the money. The "substantial step" requirement is a necessary element for attempt crimes; only an "overt act" is required for conspiracy liability, and then only if a statute, or case law in the jurisdiction, requires it.

52. **B** The defense of duress can be asserted when the accused commits a crime because he receives a threat that produces a reasonable fear that he is in imminent danger of suffering death or serious bodily harm. A common rationale for the duress defense is that the defendant should not be forced to suffer a greater harm than the crime itself. Therefore, some courts will not permit the defense if the crime the accused commits is more serious than the harm or injury with which he is threatened. The Model Penal Code, however, does not require that the harm threatened be greater than the crime committed. Instead, the MPC's test is whether the threat was sufficiently great that "a person of *reasonable firmness* in [the defendant's] situation would have been unable to resist." MPC §2.09(1). In addition, the MPC requires only that the defendant face a threat of bodily harm, not serious bodily harm. MPC §2.09(1). Even under the more stringent test in jurisdictions that do not follow the MPC, choice **B** is probably the best choice. Given Frederick's reputation for violence, Bruce was reasonably entitled to believe that he was in imminent

danger of serious bodily injury that could be prevented by the lesser evil of mailing the letter. However, the defense of duress is not generally available against a charge of intentional homicide. The facts raise the interesting question (choice **C**) whether Bruce can assert a defense based on the risk of injury to himself if he believed that Frederick would carry out the threat to harm the president. It may be reasonable to argue that choice **C** is the better answer on the theory that Bruce should not be permitted to prefer his own safety to that of the president in the face of a threat on the president's life. Choice **A** is incorrect because it does not recognize the defense of duress. Finally, choice **D** is incorrect because the defense of duress does not require a threat of death; it may be asserted when the threat involves serious bodily injury. The MPC does not even require serious bodily injury; all it requires is a threat of bodily harm.

53. **B** If Bruce is acquitted on the theory of duress, that defense is obviously not available to Frederick. When a crime is committed by the instrumentality of an innocent or nonresponsible agent, the agent is regarded as a tool of the sponsor of the crime. In these cases, the sponsor is considered the principal and the person who commits the act, his agent. The principal is as responsible as if he had committed the act himself. Because Bruce was a mere instrument of Frederick, Frederick is deemed to have sent the letter himself. The correct answer is choice **B**. Frederick had the necessary *mens rea*, and the *actus reus* is imputed to him. Choice **A** is incorrect because the doctrine of transferred intent applies when a defendant intends to harm one victim, but actually harms another. The intent to harm is transferred from the intended victim to the actual victim. The doctrine does not apply to this case. Frederick did not, in fact, transfer his intent to Bruce. Bruce would not have acted except for the duress. Choice **C** is incorrect because the fact that Frederick did not actually write or mail the letter is immaterial to his guilt. Frederick is guilty because he forced Bruce to write and mail the letter. Choice **D** is incorrect under the general law of agency, which provides that a principal may be vicariously liable for the torts of his agent.

54. **B** Under common law principles, a conspiracy occurs when there is an agreement between two or more persons to commit a crime. Some jurisdictions also require an overt act by one of the conspirators in furtherance of the conspiracy. The Model Penal Code uses a unilateral approach in defining conspiracy, rather than the traditional bilateral approach. Under this approach, conspiracy does

not require an agreement between two or more parties; the crime is satisfied as to any one party as long as he has committed to join others in the commission of the crime. MPC §5.03(1)(a). In addition to the agreement, the crime of conspiracy also requires that the conspirators have the *mens rea* to commit the target crime. In this case, there was no agreement because Bruce was an unwilling agent of Frederick, and Bruce lacked the *mens rea* required for the crime. Choice **B**, therefore, is the correct answer. Choice **A** is incorrect because the crime of conspiracy is an independent crime that is not normally merged into the completed target crime. Choice **C** is incorrect because Bruce's participation was not done as a consequence of any "agreement" with Frederick, and Bruce did not have the required *mens rea*. Finally, choice **D** is incorrect because compliance under duress cannot be considered to exhibit either an agreement to commit the target crime or the necessary *mens rea*.

55. **A** Sharp was a private citizen employed by the bank to thwart robberies. A private citizen may use a reasonable degree of nondeadly force to prevent the commission of a felony or of a misdemeanor amounting to a breach of the peace. He may use ***deadly force*** only to prevent a ***dangerous felony***. If the robber is armed and it is likely that serious bodily harm could occur to anyone, then the use of deadly force is permissible. However, the Model Penal Code takes a more restrictive view of the use of deadly force even in situations involving dangerous felonies. MPC §3.07(2)(b)(ii). The rationale behind the MPC view to discourage rash action by untrained private citizens may not be applicable here, however, because Sharp was a trained former police officer. Choice **A** is correct because robbery is a dangerous felony, the robber was armed, and he pointed his gun directly at a cashier (the security officer doesn't have to wait until the robber actually pulls the trigger). (Note: There is one troubling aspect about these facts. It could be argued that the bank and Sharp contributed to the dangerous situation by hiding Sharp in the ceiling outside of Rob's sight, because if Sharp had been stationed on the floor in uniform, Rob might have refrained from attempting the robbery.) Choice **B** is incorrect because Sharp was not only protecting property but also preventing serious bodily harm to the teller and the bank's customers. (Note: Deadly force may ***not*** generally be used in the protection of property.) Choice **C** is incorrect because, if the killing was justified, it was justified precisely because a warning would not necessarily have prevented Rob's use of his gun. Finally, choice **D** is incorrect

because Sharp was justified in using deadly force deliberately to prevent the commission of a dangerous felony.

56. B The crime of larceny requires that the accused take and carry away, in a trespassory manner, personal property of another, with the intent to steal (i.e., permanently deprive the owner of the property). The taking is trespassory if the accused is not in lawful possession of the property at the time he appropriates it. If Leo's delivery of the clock to Mike conveyed lawful possession to Mike, then he cannot be convicted of larceny. However, the rule is that, when a lower-level employee receives property from his employer, he is deemed to have only custody of the property (possession remains with the employer). His appropriation of the property is, therefore, a trespass that satisfies the requirements for larceny. Choice **B** is correct because Mike was merely a salesperson and had only custody of the clock (not lawful possession) when he appropriated it. Choice **A** is factually incorrect (Mike saw his opportunity to keep the clock at the moment Leo handed it to him). Choice **C** is incorrect. The fact that Leo voluntarily gave the clock to Mike does not change Mike's status as a mere employee who is being given temporary custody of property with specific instructions to use it only as dictated by the employer. Finally, choice **D** is incorrect because a trick or inducement by Mike would be relevant only if the crime charged was larceny by trick, not simple larceny, which does not require the element of fraud or deceit.

57. D If the accused had the intent (*mens rea*) to commit a criminal act against A, but succeeds, instead, in committing the same or a similar crime against B, he is said to have ***transferred his intent*** from A to B, and he is guilty of an intended crime against B. This is called the "doctrine of transferred intent." However, the doctrine does ***not*** apply to attempt crimes, because of the difficulty of relating the attempt to the result. Because the question asks whether Deft is guilty of ***attempted murder***, his intent with respect to Vic cannot be transferred to Cal. The correct answer is choice **D**. Choice **A** is incorrect because, as noted above, the doctrine of transferred intent does not apply to attempt crimes. Deft is not guilty of attempted murder of Cal, but he is guilty of attempted murder of Vic and of criminal battery on Cal. Choice **B** is incorrect because, although Deft acted with premeditation and malice toward Vic, two elements of murder that prove that he intended to kill Vic, his intent does not transfer to Cal. Choice **C** is incorrect because the extent of injury to Cal is not material to the issue of Deft's *mens rea* (his intent to kill Vic) or to the crime of attempted murder as it relates to Cal.

58. **A** The law surrounding the right of an individual to use deadly force against a fleeing suspect has many ramifications. If he is a police officer, he is allowed to use deadly force to stop a fleeing suspect *in cases of dangerous felonies*, if that is the only way to effect an arrest. In cases involving misdemeanors, or nondangerous felonies, even a police officer may not be free to use deadly force. *Tennessee v. Garner*, 471 U.S. 1 (1985). The law for persons who are not police officers is even stricter. The Model Penal Code specifically prohibits private citizens from using deadly force to stop a fleeing felon, even in those cases where the suspect has committed a dangerous felony. MPC §3.07(2)(b)(ii). Under the MPC, because Cal was no longer facing a threat to himself, he was not justified in shooting Deft. *People v. Crouch*, 439 N.W.2d 354 (Mich. App. 1989). However, Cal is probably guilty of voluntary manslaughter instead of murder. An individual is guilty of voluntary manslaughter if he kills another intentionally *and* (1) he acts in response to a provocation that is sufficient to cause a reasonable man to lose self-control, (2) he, in fact, acts in the heat of passion, (3) the period of time between the provocation and the killing is not enough to cause a reasonable man to cool off, and (4) the defendant has not, in fact, cooled off. A gunshot fired at you by a fleeing gunman is almost certainly enough provocation to cause a reasonable man to lose his self-control and act in response. Similarly, under the MPC, a defendant who commits what would otherwise be murder is guilty of manslaughter if he is acting in an "extreme emotional or mental disturbance." Cal would seem to fit this language. Thus, choice **A** is the correct answer. Choice **B** is incorrect because Cal is likely suffering from extreme emotional disturbance for which there is a reasonable explanation or excuse. Choice **C** is incorrect because Cal intended to kill Deft, negligent homicide does not apply to intentional homicide. Choice **D** is incorrect because, as noted above, Cal's actions satisfy the elements of manslaughter.

59. **A** The crime of embezzlement involves a *fraudulent conversion* of the *property* of *another* by one who is in *lawful possession* of the property. Because Ace was authorized by Lender to collect Borrower's debt and received the money initially as Lender's agent, Ace came into possession of the money lawfully. However, Ace's possession was solely as agent for Lender. When Washington fraudulently paid

the money to Lender not for the account of Borrower but for the joint account of Ace and himself, he converted the money (i.e., he claimed and applied it for his own benefit and not Borrower's). (Washington's obligation was to deliver the money collected to Lender for application against Borrower's debt.) Because all the elements of embezzlement are satisfied, choice **A** is the correct answer. Choice **B** is incorrect because the facts do not tell us that the $5,000 was obtained through fraud or other deceptive circumstances (presumably, Little represented to Borrower that he was acting for Ace as collection agent for Lender). Thus, the $5,000 was not obtained by Ace fraudulently, a necessary element of the crime of false pretenses. Choice **C** is incorrect because a necessary element of larceny is a trespassory taking, and Ace came into possession of the money lawfully. Finally, choice **D** is incorrect because Ace caused Lender to misapply the funds to the account of Ace and Washington instead of to the account of Borrower, thereby creating an unlawful conversion of the funds.

60. **A** A corporation can act only through its officers, employees, and agents. The liability of the corporation for crimes committed by these individuals is a matter of debate and flux. Increasingly, the courts are attributing guilt to corporations, especially in strict liability cases and in cases of serious crime. A corporation may be held criminally culpable if a high-level managerial agent, acting for the corporation and within the scope of his employment, has a direct connection with the crime by authorizing, requesting, commanding, performing, or recklessly tolerating its commission. MPC §2.07(1)(c). Washington was president of Ace. As president, he had the authority to hire Little, contract with Lender, collect the funds from Borrower, and remit them to Lender. Because Washington embezzled the money in order to satisfy Ace's (as well as his own) obligation, Ace can be convicted of the same offense. ***Commonwealth v. Beneficial Finance Co.***, 275 N.E.2d 33 (Mass. 1979). The correct answer is choice **A**. However, because a corporation cannot be imprisoned, the only penalty that could be assessed against Ace itself would be a fine. Choice **B** is incorrect because the prosecution would not be required to proceed against Washington before trying Ace. It could charge and convict Ace before proceeding against Washington. Note, however, that it might be impossible to convict Ace if Washington is tried first and acquitted, because a corporation is generally only vicariously liable for the torts and crimes of its employees. Choice **C** is incorrect

because, even though a corporation cannot be imprisoned, it may be convicted and fined. Finally, choice **D** is incorrect because there is no rule that limits a corporation's culpability to specific-intent crimes.

61. **C** The claim of entrapment can be asserted by the accused as a defense to all but the most violent crimes. MPC §2.13(3). The courts use one of two tests to determine whether entrapment exists. A majority of courts, including the Supreme Court, use the predisposition test. Under this test, the defense of entrapment is available when (1) a government agent induces the defendant to commit the crime, and (2) the defendant is not predisposed to commit the crime. In this case, Deft responded immediately to the agent's offer to buy drugs "at the going rate" and also immediately acknowledged the correct code word. This exchange, combined with Deft's prior record, shows a predisposition to sell drugs. Choice **C** is correct. A minority of courts prefer the police conduct test. Under this test, the government's agent must originate the crime, and his inducement must be sufficiently strong to lead even unpredisposed individuals to commit the crime, whether or not the defendant himself is predisposed. Deft's entrapment defense would fail under the police conduct test because the ordinary, unpredisposed person would not have responded to the agent's offer to buy by agreeing to make the sale, acknowledging the code word, and accepting the cash. Choice **A** is incorrect because it doesn't help Deft that he was willing to sell only when he thought it was safe. His use of the code word only proves his predisposition to sell. Choice **B** is incorrect because it is too narrow a definition of entrapment. The government agent must not only offer to buy but also induce the sale. In any event, the defense is not available to a defendant who is predisposed to commit the crime. Finally, choice **D** is incorrect because a defendant's entrapment defense can succeed even if the defendant commits the crime. But he must prove, at least, that he was induced to commit it and that he was not predisposed to do so.

62. **A** The law relating to finders of lost or mislaid property revolves essentially around the intent of the finder at the moment he takes possession of the property. If he intends at that moment to keep the property for himself, he has satisfied the intent necessary for larceny and will be guilty of larceny *if* he knows who the true owner is or has reason to believe that he can learn the name and address of the true owner. If neither of these conditions exists, he is not guilty of larceny even if he intends to keep the property. The Model Penal Code

rejects this traditional view by imposing an obligation on the finder to take **reasonable measures to restore the property** to the rightful owner. MPC §223.5. Because Roger never intended to return the wallet though he had the owner's address, Roger is guilty of larceny under both views. The correct answer is choice **A**. Choice **B** is incorrect because Roger did not have lawful possession. Because Roger intended immediately to keep the wallet though he knew the identity of the true owner, his possession was larcenous and unlawful. Choice **C** is incorrect because Roger's taking was trespassory (i.e., he converted the wallet and its contents though he knew the identity of the rightful owner). Finally, choice **D** is incorrect because Roger was wrong on the law—the finder of a lost item is not entitled to retain it (or any part of it) if he knows the identity of the owner.

63. **D** A conspiracy is an agreement by two or more persons with culpable intent, either to commit an unlawful act or to commit a lawful act by unlawful means. Although there must be an agreement, it is not necessary that each conspirator participate equally in the commission of the crime. Here, Mike knew that he was supplying guns and ammo that would be used to commit a robbery. The normal rule is that merely knowing that two (or more) are going to commit a crime does not make one either an accomplice or a co-conspirator. To impose criminal liability, the State must show that the defendant had a "stake in the action." Moreover, merely supplying persons with materials the defendant knows will be used for a crime does not create such a "stake" as to make him a co-conspirator. *U.S. v. Blankenship*, 970 F.2d 283 (1992); *People v. Lauria*, 59 Cal. Rptr. 628 (1967). Generally, unless the defendant is taking a share of the proceeds or has charged more than the market price, the supplying itself does not make him a co-conspirator. In the problem, Mike has expressly **not** taken a share of the proceeds and has not charged more than the market price. The difficulty is created by the first sentence of the problem, which says that Mike "planned to rob" the store. This appears to establish Mike's liability without regard to any of the other facts. Because of this language, and not because of the later facts, Mike can also be held as an accessory before the fact. Because Mike agreed to supply the guns for the robbery, he is a co-conspirator and he is guilty of conspiracy. Mike is also guilty as an accessory before the fact. Anyone who provides pre-crime assistance to the perpetrator of the crime but who is not present at the commission of the crime is an accessory before the fact. He may be the

brains behind the crime or even a small contributor. Because Mike supplied the guns and ammunition with the intent that these items be used for the robbery, he was an accessory before the fact, even though he insisted on not being present at the time of the robbery. An accessory before the fact is liable for the target crime. Choice **D** is the only correct answer because Mike can be held liable for the robbery as a co-conspirator and as an accessory before the fact. The other choices are wrong because they do not include both I and II.

64. **D** An accused who is prosecuted for attempt *must intend* to commit the target crime and must undertake some act toward the completion of the crime. There are essentially two different views on what kind of act is required to establish intent. The more modern view is exemplified by the Model Penal Code. The code (and many courts) requires only that the accused take a "substantial step" toward completion of the target crime. MPC §5.01(1)(c). The more traditional view uses the "proximity test," which requires that the accused come reasonably close to completion of the crime. Under either of these approaches, Art has satisfied the *actus reus* part of the crime. The critical questions, therefore, focus on whether Art intended the crime of robbery—the target crime. The crime of robbery occurs when the accused, by force (or the threat thereof), takes and carries away from a person (or from his presence) his personal property with the intent to permanently deprive him of the property. Because Art acted under duress, it cannot be said that he had the intent necessary for the crime of robbery. If he does not have the *mens rea* necessary for the target crime, he cannot be guilty of attempting that crime. Duress is a defense when the accused can show that he committed a crime under a threat that put him in reasonable fear of immediate or imminent bodily harm. The defense of duress on these facts negates not only the target crime of robbery but also the attempt. The correct answer is choice **D**. Choices **A** and **B** are incorrect because Art committed the acts described under duress and not because he intended them. Choice **C** is incorrect because Art never had the intent to commit robbery. Although he did carry out some of the steps necessary for robbery, he did so under duress, which occurred before any of the steps. His surrender is only one element in proving his lack of intent.

65. **C** The facts tell us that Dave did not intend to injure Abel, but only to scare him. However, he did fire a gun at a relatively distant target. We are not told that he was an expert marksman, so it must

be said that his conduct was probably so reckless as to constitute criminal negligence. By causing the cup in Abel's hand to shatter, Dave committed a battery on Abel, under the elemental principles that battery consists of either bodily injury or an offensive touching and that an offensive touching extends to the personal effects of the victim (clothing, jewelry being worn, coffee cup being held, etc.). Because the battery was committed with a deadly weapon, in many jurisdictions, Dave's crime will constitute a felony rather than a misdemeanor. MPC §211.1(2)(b). Further, Dave committed the felony of assault with a deadly weapon. The crime of assault requires that the defendant's actions instill the fear of imminent injury in the victim. If he uses a deadly weapon in instilling fear, he is guilty of the felony of assault with a deadly weapon. The correct answer is choice **C**. Dave is guilty of aggravated battery and of assault with a deadly weapon. Choice **A** is incorrect because it identifies only the crime of battery, and Dave is guilty of both crimes. Choice **B** is incorrect because it also depends on only one of the two crimes. Choice **D** presents some difficult issues. If Dave had killed Abel, he would be guilty of murder, even though he did not intend to kill him. This conclusion is based either on the felony-murder rule, which defines any homicide that results during the commission of a felony as murder, or on the theory that Dave acted with reckless indifference to the value of human life by shooting into the kitchen. Generally speaking, however, the accused cannot be convicted of an ***attempted crime*** if he does not intend to commit the crime itself. Under this view, Dave would not be guilty of attempted murder because he did not intend to kill Abel. Many courts, however, would apply a much more stringent test and convert the recklessness exhibited by Dave into an intent to commit homicide and, therefore, culpability for the attempt. However, choice **C** is a less controversial answer than choice **D**.

66. B First-degree murder, a crime now recognized by most states, generally requires premeditation and deliberation by the defendant. These concepts are difficult to define and are usually established at trial by circumstantial evidence as to the accused's motives and degree of planning. Because the facts tell us that Dave did not intend to kill Abel but only to scare him, it may be hard to prove a first-degree murder charge. However, some states do classify some felony murders as first-degree murders, if the statute specifically articulates the felony as a predicate for first-degree murder. Because Dave committed two intentional felonies—aggravated battery and assault with a deadly weapon—he may be guilty of first-degree murder in those states. Second-degree murder is a catchall for all murders that are not murders in the first degree. It includes the following: murders in which the defendant does not intend to kill, but has acted "recklessly under circumstances manifesting an extreme indifference to human life" (MPC §210.2(1)(b)); murders in which the accused does not intend to kill, but does intend to inflict serious bodily injury; and felony murders. In this case, even though Dave did not intend to kill Abel, he did fire a pistol in his direction, displaying an extreme indifference to the value of human life and committing the two felonies of aggravated battery and assault with a deadly weapon. In most jurisdictions, choice **B** is the most serious crime for which Dave can be convicted. Choice **A** is incorrect because, as noted above, Dave would be guilty of murder in the first degree only in those states that included felony murder among murders in the first degree. Choice **C** is incorrect because Dave is guilty of murder, which is a more serious crime than voluntary manslaughter. Choice **D** is incorrect for the same reason.

67. **C** Choices **A** and **B** contain *parts* of the *McNaghten* test of insanity. To qualify for that plea, however, the defendant must show both that she has a mental disease and that the disease caused her not to know the nature and quality of her act. Separately, the claims are irrelevant. Moreover, choice **A** is incorrect for another reason—one bout of intoxication does not constitute a "mental disease," even if Georgia were an alcoholic. Choice **D** is incorrect because most crimes of mistake of fact, even in extraordinary situations, must be reasonable to "negate" *mens rea*. Because we do not judge a reasonable person by the "reasonable drunk person" standard, the mistake is irrelevant. On the other hand, first-degree murder is a specific-intent crime (premeditation is the same as a specific intent). And in most jurisdictions in this country, intoxication may negate a specific-intent offense. Thus, the correct answer is choice **C** (at least in 40 states).

68. **D** This question goes to a critical distinction between criminal law and tort. In tort, one usually applies an "objective" standard in assessing the defendant's liability: If a reasonable person would have acted otherwise, the defendant is liable. Not so in criminal law, at least in most instances. Criminal liability, particularly recklessness, requires that the defendant *know* that there is a particular risk (here of death) and consciously ignore it. Choices **A** and **B** are incorrect because

they incorporate a tort standard, rather than asking about the defendant's individual, subjective mental state. Choice **C** is true, but asks the prosecution to prove too much. "Purposely" requires not only that the defendant see a risk (of death) and ignore it but also that he *want* the risk to eventuate (i.e., he wants Daisy to die). That is not the case here. Choice **D** is the correct answer. The criminal law requirement of "recklessness" is met only if Ferdinand thought Daisy might die, but laced her drink anyway.

69. B The common law crime of conspiracy occurs when there is an agreement between two or more persons to commit either an unlawful act or a lawful act by unlawful means. The agreement need not be the kind of item-by-item recital of promises and obligations that defines the usual "agreement" in the law of contracts. All that is required is any communication between the parties proving a common criminal purpose. Here, Bob did not need to say a word. His agreement to aid in the burglary was confirmed when he gave the money to Art. The correct answer is choice **B**. Choice **A** is incorrect because Art's *request* for the money would constitute only the crime of solicitation by Art; until Bob actually gave the money to Art, no conspiracy existed. Choice **C** is incorrect because the accused need not participate in the commission of the target crime; he is guilty if he supplies goods or services to the perpetrator or if he has a stake in the proceeds, both of which are true here. Finally, choice **D** is incorrect because a conspiracy exists once there is an agreement to commit the target crime. It is not necessary under common law that any overt act be committed in furtherance of the target crime. Today, some jurisdictions do require an overt act in furtherance of the agreement. The Model Penal Code restricts this requirement to nonserious crimes, of which burglary is certainly not one. MPC §5.03(5). Furthermore, if Art argues that he withdrew from the conspiracy because he never bought the gun and gave the money away, he will be met with the fact that the common law does not generally permit the defense of withdrawal because the crime of conspiracy is complete when the agreement is made. Even under the more liberal Model Penal Code, he must at least inform the police to avoid culpability. MPC §5.03(6).

70. C It's important to note that the question asks, "Did Art commit a crime in using the money for another purpose?" not "Can Bob sue Art for the money?" In taking Bob's money without returning it, Art is certainly guilty of one or another of the larceny crimes. He is not guilty of the crime of simple larceny (choice **B**) because he did not take the money by trespass; he was given the money voluntarily by Bob himself for a common purpose. Nor is he guilty of the crime of false pretenses (choice **D**), which requires as an essential element that the accused obtain the money as the result of the false representation of a material fact. Here, Art did not misrepresent his purpose or his motive. Moreover, the crime of false pretenses generally requires that the defendant obtain title to the goods; it is not clear that Bob intended nonconditionally to hand over title to the money. The crime of embezzlement occurs when the defendant fraudulently converts the tangible personal property of another, at a time when the item is rightfully in the defendant's possession. Because Bob had voluntarily delivered the $200 to Art (even though the money was to be used for an unlawful purpose), the money was lawfully in Art's possession because Bob intended to put it there. Choice **C** is the best answer. Choice **A** is not the right answer only because it is not responsive to the question asked. If the question had instead asked whether Bob could recover the money from Art, then choice **A** would be the correct answer because of the doctrine of *in pari delicto*. This doctrine prevents a court from enforcing a claim based on an illegal contract by one participant against the other. Some courts construe the doctrine to require weighing the guilt of one party against the guilt of the other. On these facts, it's hard to believe that any court would allow either party to recover anything.

71. **C** Most crimes are defined so as to require both *actus reus* and *mens rea*. *Actus reus* requires that the accused have committed the act that constitutes the crime. *Mens rea* requires that, in committing the act, the accused have the state of mind that evidences either specific intent or recklessness. As defined in this statute, the crime required the sale of Xtol. Because defendant Druggist sold Customer Ytol, not Xtol, an essential element of the crime is missing. The correct answer is choice **C**. Defendant did, however, manifest the *mens rea* necessary for the crime as defined, because he meant to sell the prohibited drug, Xtol. Because he did not intend to make the mistake of substituting Ytol, his mistake does not negate his intent. Choice **A** is, therefore, incorrect. Choice **B** is incorrect because it addresses only the *mens rea* element of the crime; whether or not *mens rea* exists, the *actus reus* element of the crime (the sale of Xtol) is absent. Finally, choice **D** is incorrect because, even in a jurisdiction that holds that legal impossibility is no defense to the crime of attempt, we are not

dealing here with the crime of attempt, but with the defined crime of selling the proscribed drug Xtol.

72. **D** Attempt requires an intention to complete the object offense coupled with steps taken toward the commission of that offense. Here, it is posited that Druggist intended to sell Xtol to his patient. Furthermore, he sold to her what he believed was Xtol. Had things been as he believed them to be, he would have completed the crime of selling a controlled substance. The modern trend is toward the MPC position that if the circumstances were as D believed them to be he would have committed a crime, then he may be convicted of an attempt to commit that crime. MPC Sec. 5.01(1)(a). This result is best captured by answer **D**. Choice **A** is incorrect because the defendant clearly had the intention to sell a prohibited substance. It would be a fallacy to say that his intent was to sell Ytol; he both believed the drug that he was selling was Xtol and hoped that it was. Choice **B** is also incorrect. It's true that it was impossible for Druggist to sell Xtol to the customer because the product that he was selling her was in fact Ytol. But that is merely an explanation of why he is guilty of an attempt rather than a completed offense. For the same reason Choice **C** is also incorrect; while it correctly states that the thing D sold to Customer was Ytol and not Xtol—a legal substance and not a prohibited one—this simply explains why the most Druggist can be convicted of is an attempt.

73. **C** The best answer is offered by choice **C**, but even that answer may be subject to question itself. In general, conduct that violates a rule or law is not excused because the accused was ignorant of the law. The modern view has eased this principle somewhat. Many states now permit the defense of ignorance of the law when there is reasonable reliance by the accused on a judicial decision that the conduct involved was not illegal. If the defendant's belief was based on his attorney's reasonable interpretation of an outstanding court decision, most jurisdictions would absolve the defendant of culpability. This principle makes **C** the best choice. However, it is certainly arguable that the defendant on these facts probably should not have relied on the decisions of the lower courts, but waited instead until the issue was resolved by the jurisdiction's highest court. The answer is made even more difficult because most states do not allow reliance on an attorney's advice. Because the reliance here was on the court's opinion, however, the claim is stronger. Moreover, the Model Penal Code, §2.04(3), allows reasonable reliance on the opinion of

any court, at whatever level. Defendant's interest in selling a drug prohibited by statute would not seem to outweigh the public interest of enjoining sales of Xtol. Choice **A** is incorrect because it is too broad. An attorney's opinion may not always be relied on, but it is not necessarily irrelevant on the issue of *mens rea*. Furthermore, as we have seen, misunderstanding of the law is sometimes a defense. Choice **B** is incorrect because a defendant's mistake or ignorance of law, alone, will not negate *mens rea* in most instances. Finally, choice **D** is incorrect because the defendant relied on his misinterpretation of the law, not on a mistake in fact.

74. **B** The question carefully calls for the ***best*** defense, not necessarily the one that will actually result in acquittal. This is an important distinction because Jimmy is probably guilty under all the possible answers. The crime of involuntary manslaughter requires (1) that the defendant's gross negligence result in the accidental death of another (or, under the Model Penal Code, that the defendant act recklessly) or (2) that the death occur unintentionally during the commission of a misdemeanor or other unlawful act. Under both tests, it's necessary for the prosecution to show that the defendant's actions were the proximate cause of the victim's death. The defendant here will try to show that his conduct was not the proximate cause of Mrs. Jones's death because the drug was not an ordinarily dangerous drug and because the offense was *malum prohibitum* (i.e., prohibited by a public-welfare statute) and not *malum in se* (i.e., inherently dangerous or reckless). This makes choice **B** the ***best*** defense. (However, it is unlikely that Jimmy will prevail on this defense because, as a druggist, he was held to a higher standard than the ordinary citizen. When Doctor X told him that the drug was misprescribed, he had an affirmative duty to notify the authorities and to find Mrs. Jones to keep her from taking the drug. His conduct displayed criminal negligence.) In the absence of the misdemeanor statute, however, his failure to notify the authorities would have no necessary causal relation to Mrs. Jones's death, unless the State can show that the authorities would have attempted to reach Mrs. Jones. Choice **A** is not as good an answer as choice **B** because Jimmy did commit a misdemeanor by violating the statute. Choice **C** is incorrect because Dr. X was not exclusively culpable for Mrs. Jones's death. She notified Jimmy that the prescription was wrong, and Jimmy had the opportunity to avoid the death. In addition, Jimmy arguably contributed to the death by violating the statute. Finally, choice **D** is incorrect

because the statute required notice to the authorities, not only a search for the patient; if Defendant had reported the violation to the authorities, they would have had the opportunity to locate Mrs. Jones in time to prevent her death.

75. **D** The law recognizes several defenses that either negate the *mens rea* necessary for a guilty intent or excuse the act that constitutes the crime. Among these defenses are insanity, duress, and reasonable defense of others. All three are often said to be ***affirmative defenses***; that is, the defendant is required not only to produce the evidence supporting them but also to carry the burden of persuasion (usually, as here, by a preponderance of the evidence). In the jurisdiction described in this question, all three must be proved by a preponderance of the evidence, or they will not be submitted to the jury. It is not necessary that the prosecution ***disprove*** these defenses because the burden is on the defendant. These moves are themselves hotly debated and involve, as well, distinctions between "justifications" and "excuses," which need not concern us in this question, but which would be relevant in an argument in court on these matters. The English have totally abolished the distinction and require the prosecution to carry the burden on every "defensive claim" once it is properly raised. Moreover, the recent Supreme Court decisions in ***Apprendi v. New Jersey***, ***Blakely v. Washington***, and ***Booker v. United States***, although on their face dealing with sentencing, might be interpreted as requiring the prosecution to disprove, beyond a reasonable doubt, any affirmative defense that would, mandatorily, reduce the defendant's sentence. These decisions themselves are highly controversial, and there would certainly be debate as to whether they apply to affirmative defenses at all. But a good defense counsel would certainly raise the question. In this instance, however, the accused would raise the claim that his actions were ***reflexive*** and, therefore, ***involuntary***. This claim goes to the element of *actus reus*, which requires that the criminal act be voluntary. On this issue, many courts merely require that the defendant produce some evidence of the involuntary nature of his actions and then shift (or activate) to the prosecution the burden of showing beyond a reasonable doubt that the defendant was acting voluntarily. Choice **D** is the correct answer because it is the only one that identifies a defense that the prosecution must disprove. Choices **A**, **B**, and **C** are all incorrect because insanity, duress, and the defense-of-others privilege

are affirmative defenses that must be proved by a preponderance of evidence by the defendant.

76. **A** The crime of involuntary manslaughter requires either (1) that the defendant's gross negligence (or, under the Model Penal Code, his recklessness) result in the accidental death of another or (2) that the death occur unintentionally during the commission of a misdemeanor or other unlawful act. Under the misdemeanor-manslaughter rule, the defendant is guilty if his actions are the proximate cause of death. They will be deemed the probable cause if his actions are *malum in se* (i.e., they are inherently wrong, even if he did not intend or desire the victim's death). Simple battery, a misdemeanor, occurs when the accused intentionally causes either (1) bodily injury or (2) offensive touching of a person or of property held by or near the person. Because Dan committed a battery (a *malum in se* misdemeanor) when he pushed Arthur, he is guilty of involuntary manslaughter. The correct answer is choice **A**. Choice **B** is incorrect because a person may be guilty of involuntary manslaughter under the misdemeanor-manslaughter rule even though he did *not* intend the victim's death. Choice **C** is incorrect because, as discussed above, Dan is criminally responsible for Arthur's death under the misdemeanor-manslaughter rule. Finally, choice **D** is incorrect because voluntary manslaughter requires the same *mens rea* as murder. It involves an intentional homicide that is reduced from murder only by virtue of a provocation that would cause a reasonable man to lose his self-control or to act in the heat of passion. Dan's insult was not the kind of provocation (e.g., battery, assault, combat, adultery by spouse) that the law requires.

77. **D** The common law crime of conspiracy occurs when there is an agreement between two or more persons to commit either an unlawful act or a lawful act by unlawful means. John and Dick formed a conspiracy to rob the bank. A conspirator is liable for the criminal acts that occur in the course of the conspiracy and that are in furtherance of the conspiracy and are a reasonably foreseeable outgrowth of it. The objective of the conspiracy was robbery, and the murder occurred during the commission of the robbery. While John and Dick agreed to use toy guns, it was reasonably foreseeable that a guard would mistake the toy for a real gun and respond by shooting at Dick. Indeed, fear of someone's being injured was one of the reasons John did not wish to use a real weapon. Thus, the death of an innocent bystander was a reasonably foreseeable outgrowth of the conspiracy.

The felony-murder rule holds a defendant guilty of murder when a homicide is committed during the felony, even if the defendant lacks the intent to kill. Because this murder occurred during the commission of a dangerous felony, it was not necessary that John or Dick have an intent to kill. Therefore, choice **D** is the correct answer. John can be convicted of murder under the felony-murder rule because he was a co-conspirator involved in a dangerous felony. Choice **A** is incorrect because a conspirator does not have to participate in the target crime in order to be found culpable; he doesn't even have to be present when the homicide is committed. Choice **B** is incorrect because John did not effectively withdraw from the conspiracy. Most jurisdictions require that the party attempting to withdraw communicate the fact of his withdrawal to the other conspirators or to the police. Choice **C** is incorrect because John should have realized that robbery is a dangerous felony and that it was reasonably foreseeable that a guard might mistake the toy gun for a real gun and respond by shooting at Dick.

78. **A** The question asks for the distinction between **motive** and **intent**. Under both the common law and the Model Penal Code, the law is concerned only with the latter; the former is irrelevant in determining guilt (though it may, on some occasion, play a part in sentencing). Here, Forrest clearly intended his mother's death. This makes him guilty of at least second-degree murder. Therefore, choice **B** is correct. But not enough. Most first-degree murder statutes require the prosecution to show that the killing was "premeditated, deliberate, and willful," which will be easy here. Thus, choice **A** is even "more correct." Forrest's killing was not common law manslaughter, which required either (1) a killing as a result of adequately legal provocation (which does not characterize Ena) or (2) "recklessness." But Forrest's mental state is **higher** than recklessness—he intended to kill Ena. Therefore, choice **C** is inadequate. Forrest could argue, under §210.2 of the Model Penal Code, that he is guilty only of manslaughter because he was acting under "extreme mental or emotional disturbance," but unless he can adduce psychiatric evidence to support that argument, he will be unsuccessful. Choice **D** is incorrect as a matter of law. Even under the MPC's "extreme emotional disturbance" language, the defendant has committed manslaughter. In practice, however, the law may be different; many juries confronted with "mercy killings" of this type actually do acquit the defendant.

But having a good motive does not, under current law, negate criminal intent (ask Robin Hood).

79. **A** There has been a continuing conflict in the cases over the misappropriation of funds by a lower-level employee who receives the funds from a third person rather than from his employer. Misappropriation by a bank teller, as in this question, furnishes a perfect example of this dilemma. Some cases hold that the teller receives funds from the bank's customers as custodian for the bank, which is said to have *constructive possession*. In these cases, the teller is found guilty of larceny rather than embezzlement because he comes into *possession* of the money only when he converts it for his own use. (In other words, when he takes it, we first have the elements of larceny—a trespassory taking and carrying away.) The more widely accepted view is that, because the teller is taking the money from a third person (the customer) rather than from his employer (the bank), he has lawful possession, not custody, immediately and is, therefore, guilty of embezzlement when he keeps the money. The broad embezzlement statutes of many states make it embezzlement rather than larceny when an employee steals property that comes into his possession or "under his care." Under these statutes, even a lower-level employee would be guilty of embezzlement rather than larceny if he kept property that came into his possession. Note that if Bill had put the money in the bank's till and later removed it, this would clearly be larceny. The best answer is choice **A**. Choice **B** is incorrect for the reasons we have stated. Choice **D** is incorrect because the crime of larceny by trick requires that the accused acquire possession of the property by fraud or deceit. Choice **C** is incorrect because Bill's actions do not satisfy the elements of the crime of false pretenses. These require the passage of title to property as a result of a false representation of a material fact by a person who knows that the fact is false. Even if Bill obtained title, he made no false representation.

80. **D** The common law crime of conspiracy requires an *agreement* between two or more persons to commit a crime. The components of the crime are the agreement, a criminal objective, and a culpable intent (*mens rea*). Knowledge is not agreement. The mere fact that Maud was informed by Mick of his intent to rob Jim does not amount to an agreement by her to join in the crime. On the contrary, Maud specifically stated she could not participate because her license had been revoked. The correct answer is choice **D**. Choice

A is incorrect. In the absence of a statute making it a crime not to inform the police when a person acquires knowledge that a crime is about to be committed, there is no requirement that the police be informed. A co-conspirator may have an obligation to inform the police if she wishes to withdraw from the conspiracy, but Maud was not a conspirator. Choice **B** is incorrect because the receipt of stolen property does not make the recipient guilty of conspiracy in the crime that produced the property. Maud would, however, be guilty of the crime of receiving stolen property. The elements of this crime are the ***receipt of stolen property*** with ***knowledge*** that the ***property is stolen*** and with ***the intent to deprive*** the owner of his property. All these elements are satisfied by Maud's actions in taking some of the stolen funds. Finally, choice **C** is incorrect because the crime of conspiracy is complete when the agreement is made. It does not require that the accused participate in the commission of the target crime or that she even be present.

81. D Anyone who aids or abets in the commission of a crime becomes an ***accomplice*** to the crime and is guilty of the commission of that crime. The facts of each case will determine whether the accused has actually aided and abetted in the commission of the crime. Even words of encouragement may be enough. The failure to intervene when the accused is told of the ensuing crime, or to speak out against the crime, is generally not enough. The question before us presents a close call. Sue was not only told by Mick that he was about to rob Jim but also actively encouraged him by disparaging Jim and announcing that she would gladly participate in the crime if she could. Except that she was not present at the crime, she is not very different from the mother who is judged guilty of aiding and abetting her husband when she stands by and watches him abuse their child. Nevertheless, she is probably not guilty because she did not evidence the intent ***to bring about the robbery*** (i.e., to associate herself with the robbery, to help bring it about, or to make it succeed). ***U.S. v. Peoni***, 100 F.2d 401 (2d Cir. 1938). On this analysis, choice **D** is the correct answer. Choice **A** is incorrect because an accused does not become an accomplice simply because he has knowledge that a crime is to be committed or because he fails to notify the intended victim. Choice **B** is incorrect because a person does not become an accomplice simply because he fails to inform the police of an impending crime that he has not aided or abetted. Finally, choice **C** is incorrect for the reasons stated in our analysis of the knowledge and intent required for accomplice liability.

82. **C** The crime of conspiracy requires an agreement between two or more persons to commit either an unlawful act or a lawful act by unlawful means. Because the essence of a conspiracy is an agreement between two or more parties, the acquittal of one defendant in a conspiracy involving only two people would appear to mandate acquittal of the other defendant. The courts do, therefore, grant automatic acquittal when the two are tried together and one is found innocent. The rationale is that the jury cannot legally find "agreement" if one of the two is found not to have agreed. This rationale does not apply when the conspirators are tried separately, which happens often. If they are tried separately, one accused may be convicted of conspiracy even if the other is acquitted. In separate trials, there are different juries who have heard different evidence and are entitled to reach different conclusions. Under the unilateral view of the Model Penal Code, which makes each conspirator separately culpable for his own agreement, it is an open question whether one conspirator might be acquitted and the other convicted even in the same trial. MPC §5.03, Comment 2(b). Mick can be convicted of conspiracy even after Bill's acquittal. With respect to the crime of robbery, because the crime can be committed by one person acting alone and we do not know the facts and circumstances that the jury considered in acquitting Bill, the acquittal would not preclude Mick's trial or conviction. The correct answer is choice **C** because it includes both crimes. Choices **A**, **B**, and **D** are incorrect because they do not rely on both crimes.

83. **C** The crime of common law burglary requires the ***breaking and entering*** of the ***dwelling house*** of ***another*** at ***night*** with the ***intent*** to ***commit a felony***. For purposes of this question, the key elements are ***breaking*** and ***felony***. A breaking occurs when the accused creates the opening that permits entry. If the owner leaves his door wide open, as in this case, there can be no breaking and no burglary. The correct answer is, therefore, choice **C**. (Note, however, that many states have eliminated the ***breaking*** requirement for burglary.) At first impression, it may appear that Choice **D** is the correct answer because John did not intend a larceny. However, it is not necessary for the crime of burglary that ***larceny*** be the intended crime; any ***felony*** will do. Because John intended to strike Michael with a hammer, a dangerous instrument, he certainly intended a criminal battery. Choices **A** and **B** are incorrect because, even though the facts stated are true

and both choices identify elements of burglary, it is also true that another element essential to common law burglary—the ***breaking*** element—is still missing.

84. **C** The question tests the various elements that divide homicides into different crimes. The homicide characterized as murder occurs when it is the ***killing*** of one human being ***caused*** by another with the ***intent*** (*mens rea*) to ***kill*** or ***cause*** the victim ***serious bodily harm***. The facts clearly establish that John intended to use the hammer on Michael; did, in fact, hit Michael repeatedly with the hammer; and did, in fact, cause his death. Because all the elements of murder are satisfied, choice **C** is the correct answer. Choice **A** is incorrect. Although voluntary manslaughter requires all the elements of murder, it is a homicide that is reduced from murder to manslaughter upon proof by the accused that he acted in the heat of passion or was otherwise reasonably provoked. Here, John did not even know for certain that Michael had indeed taken the tools and power saw. And a reasonable person would not be likely to kill with a hammer in response to a theft of tools. Under the Model Penal Code, which does not require a provocation, much less a provocation stemming from the victim, John might argue that he acted under "extreme emotional or mental disturbance." But that disturbance must be "reasonable" from the viewpoint of a person in the defendant's "situation." While this leaves the ultimate question for the jury, it is unlikely that the jury would find John's actions reasonable, even if he were deeply attached to his tools. Choice **B** is incorrect because an intentional killing (one committed with intent to kill or to inflict serious bodily harm) cannot be ***involuntary*** manslaughter, which is based instead on a homicide resulting from criminal negligence or recklessness. Finally, choice **D** is incorrect because there was no legally sufficient excuse for John to kill Michael.

85. **A** The common law crime of arson consists of the malicious (i.e., intentional or reckless) burning of the dwelling of another. A person acts recklessly if he consciously disregards a substantial and unjustifiable risk of harm or injury. The burning of any part of the house is sufficient for arson. "Charring" constitutes "burning." It was reasonable to assume that setting fire to the sofa would result in the spread of fire to other parts of the contents and structure, especially because John intended that the fire consume both the sofa and the bodies of Anne and Michael. John is guilty of a fire maliciously set with reckless disregard for the dwelling. The correct answer is choice **A**. Choice

B is incorrect because the crime of arson is an independent crime, which does not have to be supported or accompanied by another felony; besides, John was not involved in the commission of a burglary because there was no breaking. Choice **C** is incorrect because it's not necessary that "substantial" damage result to the dwelling for an arson to occur; charring is usually sufficient to satisfy the burning requirement. Finally, choice **D** is incorrect because the requisite malicious intent (*mens rea*) is supplied by John's reckless and unreasonable indifference to the reasonably foreseeable consequences of setting fire to the sofa.

86. **C** The crime of murder can result from the commission of a felony when the felony results in a killing, even if the killing is accidental. Here, John had just committed three felonies—criminal battery upon Michael, the murder of Michael, and the arson of the home. The homicide that results during the commission of another felony is called "felony murder." Because Anne was present during the attack on Michael and saw him fall, her death constitutes felony murder. This is true especially because John's actions were ***inherently dangerous***. The correct answer is choice **C**. Choice **A** is incorrect because voluntary manslaughter is appropriate only in situations in which a crime that has all the elements of murder is deemed justified by some external factor (e.g., adequate provocation). Because there was no reasonable provocation on these facts for John's attack on Michael, voluntary manslaughter is inapplicable. Choice **B** is incorrect because a charge of involuntary manslaughter is appropriate in the case of a homicide resulting from the commission of a misdemeanor, not a felony. This is called "misdemeanor manslaughter." Choice **D** is wrong because, even if the victim's death is accidental or fortuitous, if it results during the commission of an inherently dangerous felony, it is felony murder.

87. **B** See the answer to Question XX above for a discussion of the elements constituting felony murder. Because the felony of arson is an inherently dangerous felony, any death resulting from its commission would be classified as felony murder. John is guilty of the felony murder of Ellwood, the first firefighter to arrive on the scene. An accused who commits arson can expect that injury or death will occur to any resident of the building as well as to firefighters who arrive to fight the fire. This is because these deaths are the natural and probable consequences of the act of setting fire to an occupied building. Deaths involving firefighters have been deemed to satisfy

the elements of probable cause in setting a fire. ***State v. Glover***, 50 S.W.2d 1049 (Mo. 1932). Choice **B** is the correct answer. Choice **A** is incorrect because John's suspicions that Michael had stolen his tools are irrelevant to the crimes committed by John. His suspicions were not sufficient justification for the crimes of murder and arson. Choice **C** is incorrect because, under the felony-murder rule, the intent (*mens rea*) necessary to commit the felony is ***deemed sufficient to meet the mens rea requirement for murder***. Finally, choice **D** is incorrect because the missing power saw could not be construed by any reasonable person as sufficient provocation for a severe beating resulting in death.

88. **C** Agnes married Clyde while she was still legally married to Fred. Unless she comes within one of the exceptions listed in Section II of the law, she is guilty of bigamy. Because Fred left only four years prior to Agnes's marriage to Clyde, the five-year period required by Section II(b) of the statute is not satisfied. Because Clyde was an unmarried individual, he can escape liability under Section III of the statute if he did not have actual knowledge of the circumstances constituting the departure of Fred and the length of his absence. Clyde was entitled to rely on Agnes's assurances to him, and he was not required to conduct his own independent investigation into Fred's departure. Choice **C** is the correct answer because Agnes is guilty of bigamy and Clyde is innocent. Choices **A**, **B**, and **D** are incorrect because they are inconsistent with the facts.

89. **C** The question deals with the effect of intoxication on the mental state required for the commission of a criminal act such as bigamy. If the intoxication is involuntary, a strong argument can be made that the accused cannot possibly have the required intent. The issue is more difficult when the intoxication is voluntary. However, increasingly, courts are holding that intoxication, voluntary or involuntary—although clearly not an excuse for crime—is a valid defense when it negates the intent necessary for the crime. Section III of the statute states that an unmarried person can be convicted only if she-***knowingly*** marries another under circumstances that would make the other individual guilty of bigamy. Peggy believed that Susan had died. Her intoxication prevented her from knowing that she might be alive. Therefore, she did not have the knowledge required by the statute. The excuse of intoxication—even voluntary intoxication—has been recognized even in crimes of violence (rape, murder) and should be recognized on these facts which show only that

Peggy had no recollection of being told of Susan's letter. Choice **C** is correct because Peggy did not have the knowledge necessary under the statute. Choice **A** is incorrect because Peggy would have an even better excuse if her intoxication were involuntary. Choice **B** is incorrect because even her voluntary intoxication nullifies knowledge. Choice **D** is wrong because Peggy's intoxication negates the required element of knowledge.

90. B The common law provided various tests to determine whether a defendant had "attempted" a crime. Each of these tests—the last proximate act, whether the defendant would "probably desist" if there were no intervention, dangerous proximity to the target crime, the *res ipsa loquitur* test—focused on what remained to be done. Under these and other similar tests, Namath is not "close enough" to constitute an attempt. Therefore, both choices **A** and **C** are incorrect. The Model Penal Code, §5.01, has significantly changed this approach. It asks, instead, whether the defendant has taken a "substantial step" toward the target offense and whether that step is "strongly corroborative" of his intent. Under the common law, the trial court often decided, as a matter of law, that a step was not "close enough" to constitute attempt. The MPC, however, makes these questions ones for the jury, as a matter of fact. The buying of the paint, therefore, is likely to be a "substantial enough" step. The question is whether it "corroborates" Joe's intent. Someone watching Joe at the store would not have a clue as to what he was planning. But *if* they knew of his intent (i.e., if there is evidence of that intent), then the step would demonstrate that Joe is no longer "dreaming," but actually "on his way." The correct answer, therefore, is choice **B**. Choice **D** is incorrect because choice **B** is correct.

91. A It appears that Namath would qualify as an attempt or under the tests of the common law set out in the preceding answer. He's *very* close to actually carrying out the target crime. That should be enough. Therefore, choice **A** appears correct. But, under the Model Penal Code, Namath may have a claim of "renunciation." If he voluntarily stopped before the target crime, the code will allow him to avoid liability for the attempt (which he committed; see the answer to Question 99 above). Therefore, choice **B** is not correct. The common law did not recognize renunciation—once the defendant had attempted, he was guilty of that crime even if he voluntarily gave up trying to complete the crime. Thus, neither choice **C** nor choice **D** is correct. The issue is whether he has "renounced" his attempt. Only under the MPC may Namath raise the claim of renunciation to the jury and avoid liability for attempt. Choice **A** is the correct answer.

92. **C** Under the common law, attempt "merged" with the target crime if it was completed. Thus, choices **A** and **B** are incorrect. Because the Jets all agreed to commit a crime, and committed an overt act in furtherance of that conspiracy, they have committed conspiracy to vandalize. But beware; under the common law, conspiracy was seen not only as a "different" crime from the target crime but also as a "separate," "nonmerging" one. Thus, they can be guilty of both the target offense and the conspiracy. Thus, choice **C**, not choice **D**, is the correct answer.

93. **D** Under the MPC, a conspiracy to commit a crime—like an attempt to commit it—merges with the completed offense. See MPC, §5.05(3). A defendant therefore may be convicted of committing an offense, or of attempting to commit it or of conspiring to commit it, but he cannot be convicted of more than one. Hence **D** is the best answer. Answers **B** and **C** are incorrect because they permit the defendant to be convicted of two crimes that merge into one. For this reason, Choice **A** is extra wrong. It permits triple punishment for the same crime.

94. **C** Choice **A** is clearly incorrect. Maddon was a "but for" cause of the deaths. Choice **B** is more likely, but most courts have rejected the idea that merely being a proximate cause of a death would make one liable for murder, even felony murder, although this is somewhat inconsistent with the entire thrust of the felony-murder doctrine (that one is strictly liable for a death that occurs during a felony). Choice **D** is absolutely incorrect because the so-called "merger" (or "independent felony") limitation on the felony-murder doctrine applies only where the underlying, predicate felony is "person endangering" (such as aggravated assault). The prosecutor, not the defense, would find comfort in the nonmerger doctrine in this case. This would mean that choice **C** is the correct answer, by default. But, beyond that, it is the correct answer. Many courts have held that only "inherently dangerous" felonies may act as the basis for a felony-murder doctrine. While these courts are divided over whether to consider the felony "in the abstract" (the majority) or "as perpetrated" (the minority), in this instance, fraud is simply not dangerous in the abstract.

95. **D** Let's take the easy one first. Choice **C** is incorrect. The common law did not recognize a claim of "abandonment (renunciation)" once a

defendant had passed the point of an attempt. The question, then, is between the tests that the common law courts did lay down to determine when someone had crossed the line of "preparation" and become an "attemptor." Choice **B**'s language is taken from §5.01 of the Model Penal Code (see the next question) and does not reflect the common law's view that the attemptor must be "very close" to consummating the target crime. That leaves choices **A** and **D**. It is clear that Matilda *did* desist. But had someone stopped her ten feet earlier and known of her purpose, a jury could easily conclude that she had passed the point of "probable" nondesistance. Thus, choice **A** is incorrect. Choice **D** was the most extreme test of the common law, requiring that the actor be "very very very close" to the actual target offense (think of putting one's finger on the trigger). Indeed, this is the reason many courts have rejected the "last possible act" test of attempt. While it is still debatable, this is Matilda's best claim under the common law.

96. **C** This question reflects the change that the MPC made in attempt doctrine. Under the MPC, a person who has taken a "substantial step strongly corroborative" of his purpose is guilty of an attempt. Under that language, Matilda is clearly guilty of an attempt. Thus, a jury under the MPC need not reach the tests laid out by choices **A** and **D**. Matilda has committed an attempt. *However*, the MPC, in contrast to the common law, also creates a defense of abandonment. If the jury believes that Matilda's abandonment was fully voluntary, it may find Matilda not guilty, *not* because she never committed an attempt (she did under choice **B**), but because she finally saw the light and has decided to forego crime. The correct answer is choice **C**.

97. **C** Nancy's age is irrelevant to whether rape has been committed (although if Nancy were a minor, Gary would be guilty of statutory rape). Thus, choice **D** is incorrect. Choice **B** is also incorrect because the mere relationship between the aggressor and the attacked woman was not, in and of itself, sufficient to constitute rape. Thus, the choice is between choices **A** and **C**. The common law required that the aggressor use "force" to obtain the victim's consent. In the modern view, Nancy might seem "forced" to choose Gary's advances, because it is the only way to obtain her goal of getting Harry into the school. But the common law did not recognize nonphysical coercion as sufficient force to constitute rape. Had Gary offered Nancy sufficient cash to allow her to pay for Harry's tuition, Nancy's consent, however grudging, would have been "voluntary" under the common law.

Thus, the correct answer is choice **C**. Under modern sexual assault law, some courts would see the intimidation here as sufficient force and convict Gary of that crime. But Gary would not be convicted under the common law.

98. B Choice **D** is incorrect because fortuity merely describes the means of death, not the defendants' *mens rea* with regard to death. While they might not have anticipated that the victim would die in this way, that by no means excuses their felonious conduct. Choice **C** is incorrect because malice aforethought, the essence of common law murder, does not require that a defendant intend death. It is enough that he personally recognize, and then ignore, a significant possibility that a death could occur. That sounds like what Alex and Pat did. Surely a jury could find that, during a five-minute chase through traffic, each of them had recognized the possibility of death—to themselves or to Gregory. Therefore, choice **B** seems correct. We ***should*** be able to readily eliminate choice **A**. Whatever Alex and Pat did, they did not "premeditate" Gregory's death, at least as that term is usually defined. However, in many jurisdictions, courts have determined that premeditation "can occur in a second." This would be a jury question. But the likelihood is that the jury will find no purpose—and, thus, no premeditation—behind Gregory's death. Choice **B** is the best answer.

99. C Here, we come to the difference between a consummated crime and one that is the goal of a conspiracy. While the former (such as murder) may be committed recklessly, conspiracy requires an agreement to carry out the actual result obtained (often referred to as "specific intent"). At best, particularly given the discussion in the answer to Question 98 above, Alex and Pat agreed only to stop, and possibly hurt, Gregory (and turn him in to the police). They did not intend his death and, hence, did not agree to that result. Choice **A**, therefore, is not correct because intent to harm is insufficient; they must intend to kill Gregory. Choice **D** is incorrect because conspiracy cannot be committed recklessly. Similarly, even if they did not agree that Gregory should die, the jury could find that they intended some crime. Therefore, choice **B** is incorrect. That leaves choice **C**. They could not be guilty of ***conspiracy*** to kill, even though, if Gregory dies, they might be guilty of murder.

100. B Abdullah's best chance of avoiding homicide liability is to claim provocation. However, the common law rule regarding provocation was that mere words were never sufficient provocation. Therefore answer **C**, though attractive, is incorrect. Similarly, it should be clear that choice **D** is incorrect. If the intentional killing of the taunters cannot be mitigated from murder to manslaughter, there is no justification for excusing it altogether. Finally, choice **A** is also incorrect. Although premeditation can occur in an instant in some jurisdictions, this appears to be a paradigmatic case of an unpremeditated killing—the category of second degree murder seems best to capture this kind of rash, but intentional killing. Therefore choice **B** is the best one among these choices.

Table of References to the Model Penal Code

References are to the number of the question raising the issue. "E" indicates an Essay Question; "M" indicates a Multiple-Choice Question.

Index

References are to the number of the question raising the issue. "E" indicates an Essay Question; "M" indicates a Multiple-Choice Question.